Praise for *My Enemy, My Brother*

"The author of this magnificent book has focused upon the men involved rather than those impersonal matters so dear to the military historian." —*Los Angeles Examiner*

"This dramatic reconstruction of the Battle of Gettysburg ought to swell the ranks of Civil War buffs." —*Publishers Weekly*

"[The book] has an earthiness and immediacy that are compelling." —*Saturday Review*

"The heroism and horror of those three days of bloody struggle in July 1863 are perhaps best captured in the words of those who fought there; *My Enemy, My Brother* presents the story of Gettysburg in memorable and gripping accounts."
—**Brooks D. Simpson,** author of *Let Us Have Peace: U.S. Grant and the Politics of War and Reconstruction*

"This is an exciting book about Gettysburg for both the Civil War buff and the novice. Persico's lively writing style makes it read like a novel." —*Cleveland Press*

"A gripping, entirely believable account that explains why ordinary men were willing to die in the Civil War." —*The Washingtonian*

"This is a book to read, absorb, and treasure."
—*Chattanooga Times*

Joseph E. Persico

MY ENEMY, MY BROTHER
Men and Days of Gettysburg

DA CAPO PRESS

Library of Congress Cataloging in Publication Data

Persico, Joseph E.
  My enemy, my brother: men and days of Gettysburg / Joseph E.
Persico.—1st Da Capo Press ed.
    p.   cm.
  Originally published: New York: Collier Books, 1988.
  Includes bibliographical references.
  ISBN 0-306-80692-4 (pbk.: alk. paper)
  1. Gettysburg Campaign, 1863. I. Title.
[E475.51.P45   1996]   95-45864
973.7'349—dc20   CIP

First Da Capo Press edition 1996

This Da Capo Press paperback edition of *My Enemy, My Brother*
is an unabridged republication of the edition published in
New York in 1988. It is reprinted by arrangement with the author.

  4 5 6 7 8 9 10   0201

Published by Da Capo Press, Inc.
A Member of the Perseus Books Group

Manufactured in the United States of America

To Sylvia
. . . there, indispensably, from the start

CONTENTS

ILLUSTRATIONS

PREFACE TO THE SECOND EDITION

Of the rewards of writing, perhaps the most satisfying is the letter from the pleased reader. After *My Enemy, My Brother* was first published, I received so many letters from readers who told me that of the oft-told tale of Gettysburg, my book had brought the battle to life for them in a new way. It had helped them to experience the battle through the eyes of the ordinary foot soldier, the GI of another age. And of these letters, the most gratifying were from teachers, both in high schools and universities, who wrote to tell me that they were using the book in their courses to get beyond tactics and politics to reveal the authentic face of the Civil War.

And then, in time, the book went out of print. I was, consequently, delighted when Da Capo Press chose to publish a new edition. I hope that the book's reappearance will make this pivotal battle of America's most painful conflict a more vivid part of their heritage for a new generation of readers.

JOSEPH E. PERSICO

ACKNOWLEDGMENTS

Many people helped this book come into being by providing me either with invaluable information or with equally invaluable encouragement. An incomplete list of those to whom I am indebted must include: John Earnst, Superintendent of the Gettysburg National Military Park, and his colleagues Thomas Harrison, Frederick Tilberg, Kathryn George, Mark Nesbitt, and Robert Fidler; Mildred Ledden, Audrey Smith, and Adele Jackel, librarians with the State Education Department of the New York Public Library; Marvin Kranz of the Library of Congress; Elaine Everly of the National Archives; Oliver Jensen of *American Heritage* magazine; my colleague, Hugh Morrow; and Deborah McPherson and Nancy Malagold for indispensable assistance in preparing the manuscript.

MY ENEMY, MY BROTHER

INTRODUCTION

THIS BOOK was written in quest of an answer. What was it that led Americans—dairy farmers from Wisconsin and dirt farmers from Georgia, New York urchins and Richmond patricians, shopkeepers and shoemakers—to gather at a small town in Pennsylvania in the summer of 1863 and slaughter each other in fearful numbers?

Do the historic roots of the Civil War provide a satisfying answer as to what motivated the ordinary soldier at Gettysburg, or on the other battlefields of that conflict? Was it slavery? Abolition? States' rights? The Union? These reasons may have sufficed for politicians and the power classes, both North and South. Perhaps for the professional soldier, once he determined his loyalty to state or nation, no further motive was necessary. Battle was his craft.

But what of more than three million citizen-soldiers, the overwhelming number of whom voluntarily answered the call to arms? What would induce young men today, from, say, New Jersey and California, to battle each other to such bloody effect? There is a lingering unbelievability about this American fratricide, which may explain more than any other single reason the Civil War's enduring fascination for us.

Of 169,821 Confederates who died in the four years of war, fewer than twenty percent came from slave-holding families. The soldiers of the South were largely poor men. Did they offer their lives so that the privileged few might live on as slave owners? Was the abstraction of states' rights cause enough to heat the blood of Alabamans and set them against Vermonters?

The War cost the North 364,511 men. Did they risk their lives to expunge the stain of slavery, to prove, indeed, that "all men are created equal"? If so, the Emancipation Proclamation fell far short of that worthy objective. It did not take effect until the War had been under way for almost two years. And then, ironically—perhaps hypocritically—the Proclamation freed only those slaves in the Confederate states—beyond the Union's reach. Slaves in states loyal to the Union—Delaware, Maryland, Kentucky, West Virginia, and Missouri, even in Union-occupied parts of the Confederacy—remained in bondage. Abolition was not a mass movement, it was the crusade of a zealous, largely intellectual elite, akin to our antiwar activism of the 1960s. In the uniformed ranks, the word "nigger" flowed with the same casual ease from the lips of soldiers wearing either blue or gray.

If, then, the historic causes of the War fail to explain satisfyingly the motivations of the ordinary men who spent their lives so extravagantly in that conflict, what does? In search of that answer, I went, in the only way possible, to the men themselves—to their diaries, their letters home, their journals and notebooks, to the torrent of personal reminiscences published after the Civil War. All the persons who appear in the book and the incidents described are based on these historical sources. My methodology in using this material is described in the Bibliography at the end of the book. From these sources, usually written with the moment, rather than posterity, in mind, the sentiments of the ordinary Civil War soldier emerge. And it is this mood from the ranks that I hope will rise from these pages.

The search for their motivating impulses was paralleled by an equal passion to march alongside these men, to hear their speech, to overhear their conversations, to know the mechanics of their daily lives. How was Johnny Reb or Billy Yank recruited, trained, paid, fed? How did he live, die? What did they feel about each other, about their officers, about blacks, about the ostensible causes for which they went to war?

What of the arms they carried? How did they load, fire, sound? What was their accuracy? How did they wound, maim, kill? What was the feel of army wool on sweltering summer marches, the texture and taste of hardtack, the sound of the Southern battle cry? What was battlefield medical treatment like in the era before the germ theory of disease? What was life like back home in the towns and villages that sent their sons to Gettysburg? How did the battle raging around them affect the ordinary people of Gettysburg? How did they behave, first toward their Union defenders, later toward their Confederate occupiers?

My Enemy, My Brother is not primarily a story of generals and competing military strategies, though the ebb and flow of the battle is faithfully traced. I have tried to keep the military chess, with "Jones wheeling his left against Smith's right, rolling up the enemy flank," to a useful minimum. Essentially, this is the story of the G.I., circa 1863, men for the most part unremembered, and unmemorable except that they were caught up in an epic drama which, for thousands, became their last role on earth.

The book will have served if this struggle of American against American becomes somehow more comprehensible, if no more sensible. It should be an unhappy story, as any honest portrayal of battle will be, for, surely, war remains the ultimate in human madness.

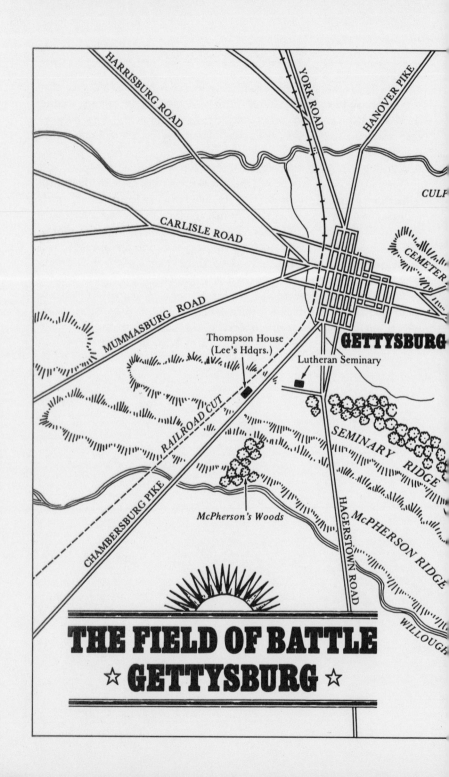

THE FIELD OF BATTLE
☆ GETTYSBURG ☆

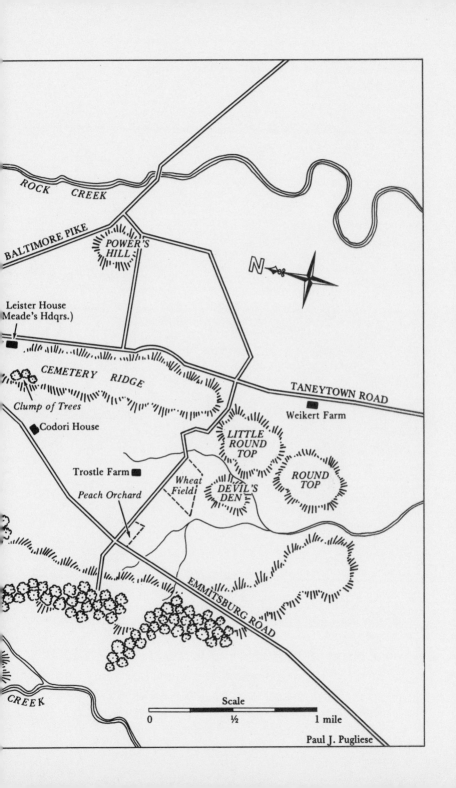

ROCK CREEK

BALTIMORE PIKE

POWER'S HILL

N

Leister House
Meade's Hdqrs.)

CEMETERY RIDGE

TANEYTOWN ROAD

Clump of Trees

Weikert Farm

Codori House

LITTLE ROUND TOP

Trostle Farm

ROUND TOP

Peach Orchard

Wheat Field

DEVIL'S DEN

EMMITSBURG ROAD

CREEK

Scale

0   ½   1 mile

Paul J. Pugliese

GETTYSBURG *is my native place as is doubtless known to many of my readers. It is most pleasantly located in a healthful region of country, near the southern border of Pennsylvania. Fondly do I cherish the scenes of my childhood. Often do I think of the lovely groves on and around Culp's Hill; of the mighty bowlders which there abound, upon which we often spread the picnic feast; of . . . Spangler's Spring, where we drank the cooling draught on those peaceful summer days. There too, our merry peals of laughter mingled with the sweet warbling of the birds. What pleasant times were ours as we went berrying along the sodded lane that leads from the town to that now memorable hill.*

From my mind can never be effaced those far off mountains to the west, whose distant horizon gave a gorgeousness to sunsets, which when once seen, can never be forgotten. . . . As I often stood in the quiet Evergreen Cemetery, when we knew naught but the smiles of Peace, gazing to the distant South Mountains, or the nearer Round Tops, or Culp's Hill, little did I dream that from those summits the engines of war would, in a few years, belch forth their missiles of destruction. . . .

With pleasant recollections I bring to mind the Young Ladies' Seminary on the corner of High and Washington Streets. Here I received instruction; here in the bright and happy flush of young womanhood, I was graduated and given my diploma. . . .

We had often heard that the Rebels were about to make a raid, but had always found it a false alarm. . . .

7

Rumors were again rife of the coming of the Rebel horde into our fair and prosperous State. This caused the greatest alarm; and our hearts often throbbed with fear and trembling. To many of us, such a visit meant destruction of home, property and perhaps life.

Tillie Pierce Alleman
1889

1 | THE ROAD DIVIDES

IT WAS A SAD, strange party. Conversations snagged at awkward pauses and faltered. Labored banter met with tolerant smiles and heavy, hanging silences. Nothing cut the gloom clinging to the evening. The men at the party had long ago marched the same frost-stiffened plain on gray November afternoons at West Point. They had pored over the same texts—Mahan on field fortifications, Casey on tactics, Lallemand on artillery. They had shared the months of barracks tedium and the moments of battle terror common to their calling. They loved the Army and each other in the way of men who spurn bourgeois lives and choose instead the priesthood of arms. Here, in the spring of 1861, in a far western army outpost, a tiny, roughneck California town called Los Angeles, events unfolding across the continent were driving a wedge between them.

The host at the party was a tall, faultlessly dressed, iron-erect figure of stern gaze and automatic authority. One could imagine him approaching soldiers as a total stranger, in or out of uniform, and commanding instant obedience. He was Captain Winfield Scott Hancock, thirty-seven years old.

Hancock's wife, Almira, a beautiful woman, was talking to an older officer, General Albert Sidney Johnston, a native Kentuckian, once a soldier in the brief-lived Republic of Texas and until recently her husband's commanding officer.

"I'm truly sorry you felt you had to resign, General."

9

"Yes, my missus felt so too. She dearly hates my giving up certainty for uncertainty. But my sympathies are well known. I had no real choice.

"Well, no matter." The general dismissed his fate with a wave of the hand and turned to his wife. "Come, my dear, sing me one of the old songs. Let's hear 'Kathleen Mavourneen.' "

Hesitantly, the general's wife sat at the piano. "I'm afraid our days for singing are past," she said. But she began. Soon her soft, bittersweet melody was the only sound in the room.

At midnight the party drew to a close. Balding and bearded, Major Lewis Armistead, twelve years in the Army of the United States, held his hand out to his host. They were old friends.

"Hancock, this is good-bye." Armistead's voice was unsteady. Tears clouded his eyes. "Goddammit, man. You can't know what this has cost me."

Hancock sighed deeply, but said nothing.

The major's voice rose. "I hope God strikes me dead if I ever have to leave this soil, if worst comes to worst." Armistead went to a chair and picked up a bundle. "Here's something I want you to have. I won't need it any more." Armistead handed Hancock a blue dress uniform, the gold leaves of a major's rank woven into the shoulder straps.

The departing men gripped the hands of their comrades tightly. They kissed the tear-streaked cheeks of the women and were quickly gone. Early next morning they would head east to join the army of a new nation, the Confederate States of America.

Warren Goss of Brewster, Massachusetts, had a fine sense of irony for a man just twenty. He was vastly amused by the soaring phrases of the speakers at patriotic rallies in those months just before the war. The fellow especially fascinated him who had leaned into the audience and, with wagging finger and a hoarse stage whisper, warned, "Human life must be cheapened, if necessary, to save the Union." Warren listened to the audience cheer and wondered if the speaker had yet lowered the price of his own life.

Once, Warren almost weakened. That night, the band stirred the crowd with powerful renditions of "The Red, White, and Blue" and "Rally 'Round the Flag." The oratory was inspired. When the last speaker finished, Warren's neighbors stumbled over each other in their haste to sign the enlistment papers. As soon as a man put his name down, he was hoisted onto the shoulders of admiring friends and swept to the platform to frenzied cheers.

How can I hold my head up if I don't go? Warren wondered. Will they think me a coward? But he caught himself and judged it best to let time clear his confused emotions.

When the rally was over, one of the speakers stood by the doorway vigorously pumping the hands of new enlistees. "Did you join, young man?" The smile was warm and eager.

"No, I didn't. Did you?"

"Well, no." The man sighed his disappointment. "They won't take me. I've got a lame leg and a widowed mother to look after."

In the end, it was not oratory but ice that decided it for Warren Goss. He could not drive the image from his mind. The vision of dead young men laid out on ice haunted his sleep. They had been soldiers of the 6th Massachusetts, marching through Baltimore headed south. The taunts had grown louder, more angry. "Yankee sons of bitches! Go on home! We don't need nigger lovers down here!" The mob had rushed forward. Bricks and rocks thudded against human skulls.

Warren read in the newspaper the telegram the Governor of Massachusetts had sent asking that the men killed "be preserved on ice" and sent home. Tears stung his eyes. Rage pounded in his chest. Warren Goss had made his decision.

Gettysburg in the 1860s was a town of 2400 population located in the heart of fertile Pennsylvania farmland, seven miles north of the Maryland border. Directly to the east of Gettysburg, 110 miles off, was Philadelphia; Baltimore was to the southeast, 45 miles distant; and almost directly south lay Washington, 62 miles away. The town had some significance at this time as the junction of eleven roads and a railway line.

Gettysburg's neat, mostly wooden buildings formed a white patch in a rich quilt of wheat fields and pastures, corn fields and orchards. The surrounding landscape was dotted with the plain houses and ample barns of frugal, no-nonsense farmers. Indeed, it had often been remarked that the barns of these farm families were more handsome than their homes. The farmers' names testified to preponderant German and Dutch roots: Hummelbaugh, Benner, Weikert, Trostle, Leister.

Prominent to the southeast of town was Culp's Hill, named for the family which had owned the hill and adjacent farmland since 1787. Among the numerous Gettysburg Culps was young Wesley, a dark-haired, engaging youth barely over five feet tall.

Wesley Culp worked for William Hoffman, a Gettysburg carriage maker. When Hoffman decided to move his shop to Shepardstown, Virginia, Wes Culp and some of the other Gettysburg workmen went with him.

His departure upset Culp's adoring mother and two sisters to whom he was deeply attached, Annie, older than Wes and married, and his kid sister, Julia. His brother, Will, shared Wesley's sense of adventure in the move. Wes confided to Will that if he liked the South enough, he just might leave Hoffman and the carriage business and go on to something bigger, maybe run a plantation.

There was in Shepardstown a local militia called the Hamtramck Guards, named for a veteran of the Mexican War, Colonel J. F. Hamtramck. To Wes Culp, lonely and homesick, though Shepards-town was only forty-two miles from home, the Guards offered a place to replenish friendships he had left behind. He enlisted, quickly made friends, and, in the course of part-time soldiering, discovered a pleasure in and an aptitude for the rituals of military life. The uniform, carrying a weapon, even the discipline gave Wesley Culp a feeling of equality that his short stature had habitually denied him. He could drill, load, aim, and shoot as well as the next man, which eventually quieted the wits in the company: "Hey, Culp. You get out of that trench, y'hear. Come up and march with us!"

Occasionally, the Virginia boys talked a little politics too, about the South taking no guff from Yankees. Wes Culp paid scant attention and skirted controversy. He became fond of Shepardstown, liked his new friends; most of all he enjoyed the Hamtramck Guards.

The editorial in Mississippi's *Oxford Mercury* of November 21, 1860, was, if anything, more temperate than most at that time. "The Union was founded for the common safety and protection of all the states. Now it is on the eve of passing into the hands of Abraham Lincoln, a coarse, illiterate, low-born scoundrel, and Hannibal Hamlin, a man whose blood is one-half Negro, who intended to pervert it for the oppression and annihilation of the South."

These were the words, not Dr. Holmes' lectures in Mental and Moral Philosophy or Professor Millington's discourses on Natural Science, that inflamed the imaginations of the students at the University of Mississippi on the eve of secession. The fussy, old-womanly admonishments of the faculty could not cool their passions. In December of 1860, the students formed a military company on their own and elected handsome, courtly Billy Lowry their captain. They called themselves the University Greys.

William B. Lowry had arrived at the verdant, rolling acres of the Mississippi campus with a slave, two horses, his guns and bird dogs. From the beginning, Lowry had displayed a monumental indifference to the academic aims of the college. When he became commander of the student company, his small desire for book learning vanished completely. By the time he was expelled early in 1861, he had cut fifty classes. Lowry ignored the orders of school officials to leave the campus immediately. A commander's place was with his men. And so the student soldiers, with their ex-student commander, both amused and excited the citizens of Oxford, as they drilled and marched about town on those lovely evenings in the spring of '61.

The schoolboy soldiering ended abruptly. Soon after Fort Sumter fell, Confederate President Jefferson Davis put out a call for active duty troops. Mississippi's quota was 8000. The University Greys furnished 79 men, 37 of them college students, the rest farmboys, mechanics, and clerks from the Oxford area who were allowed to fill out the ranks.

At five a.m. on May 1, 1861, the dawn's quiet was broken by unaccustomed festivity as families and friends thronged the Oxford railroad station to bid the University Greys good-bye. All was amiable confusion as fathers strutted about pumping the hands of the new warriors. "Take care of my boy, y'hear, Junius." "Absalom, what wouldn't I give to trade places . . ." ". . . done a masterful job, Captain . . . made my Henry a man in . . ." Mothers swept lint from uniforms, brushed aside tears, and said foolish, embarrassing things about warm clothing, eating well, and sleeping enough. Girl friends felt faint with the excitement and communicated newfound depths of feeling with lingering handclasps, adoring eyes, and, for those engaged, quick, warm kisses.

They looked magnificent, these men of Mississippi. Every unwanted wrinkle had been banished from well-cut gray frock coats and matching trousers trimmed in bright red. They wore their black felt hats at a rakish angle low over the eyes, cocked their heads back, and thrust their chins forward. They had been trained by habit and instinct to ride, to shoot, and to tell the truth. They were the cream of the South and knew it.

Few heeded Professor Lamar's farewell message. "Young men," he said, "you are not going on a holiday excursion; for I believe you will see hard service and serious work." As the professor spoke, Dr. Ballard, Chancellor of the University, found his attention wandering to the college's new buildings and the latest equipment they had purchased for the laboratories. The first call-up had riddled the student ranks. In months to come, enrollment would dwindle to nothing. "My college," he mused, "appears to be the first casualty of the war."

One soldier did listen attentively to Professor Lamar. He was a tall, strongly built youth with yellow hair and an intense, earnest expression. He had graduated from the University's school of literature the year before. He had then entered the law department but left to join the University Greys. His name was Jeremiah Gage.

Captain Lowry shouted his commands over the babble of goodbyes, the handshaking, the farewell kisses. The University Greys disentangled themselves from this loving throng and boarded the waiting train bound north.

Representative Daniel Sickles of New York City had left Washington and the Congress in 1861 under a double cloud. He had murdered his wife's lover, Philip Barton Key, a forgivable enough crime. But he had compounded the offense, unforgivably, by taking back his dishonored wife.

This breach of both law and custom had destroyed a once shining political career. Dan Sickles was a graduate of Tammany wigwams and barroom scrapes, but no clubhouse hack. He had fused a piercing intelligence, supple morals, raw ambition, generosity toward friends, ruthlessness toward foes, and a scent for the main chance into a rocketing political career: state legislator, Counsel to New York City, Secretary to the American Minister to England, James Buchanan. His election to Congress at the age of thirty-seven had been another easily won handhold in his agile climb up the political pole.

Though small and hardly handsome, Daniel Sickles was an arresting figure. Great, sweeping mustaches, hard, intent eyes, and parade-ground bearing projected a powerful presence that magnified his stature. Barely contained energy pulsed just beneath his surface composure. He was attractive to women and a practiced rake. His style churned a wake of worshiping friends, detesting enemies, and roiling controversy. He won his electoral victories in spite of indictments and charges, which included misappropriation of funds, theft of a mortgage, and mail tampering. On his first trip to Albany as a state legislator, Sickles had brought along a New York City whore, whom he grandly escorted into the august State Assembly Chamber.

Congressman Daniel Sickles cut a more decorous figure in Washington. He arrived with his young wife, Teresa, a striking beauty of Italianate features whom Sickles had married five years before when the girl was sixteen. But Sickles' political ambitions had left the lovely Teresa too much alone and too often in the company of the aristocratic Barton Key, the son of Francis Scott Key and a man judged by many the handsomest in all Washington.

Sickles had dispatched his wife's paramour by pistol shot on a sunny Sunday morning in Lafayette Park opposite the White House. He was tried and acquitted. His lawyer, the shrewd Edwin Stanton, had argued "temporary insanity."

But if life went on for Sickles, his political career had died. He attended the House, voted, made speeches, and was cut dead socially and professionally. He had not bothered to run for reelection in 1860, and by April of 1861 was back in New York City practicing law.

Before leaving the House, Dan Sickles underwent a sharp turnabout on secession. As a Democrat who had routinely voted with the Southern bloc, as one who had cultivated friendships with Washington's Southern elite, Sickles had not opposed secession. He questioned the wisdom of withdrawal from the Union, but not the right.

As late as December 10, 1860, just ten days before South Carolina seceded, Sickles spoke in the House: "What is secession? . . . It is not nullification, nor invasion, nor is it the act of a mob. It is the act of Sovereignty."

Sickles had not reckoned with the violent Southern exit from the Union. The departing states seized federal forts, arsenals, navy yards, and customhouses within their borders. South Carolinians fired on an unarmed transport, the *Star of the West,* when the ship tried to provision beleaguered Fort Sumter. Whatever other damage these shots inflicted, they killed Dan Sickles' secessionist sympathies outright.

Just before Sickles had left the House of Representatives, the chamber received a caller. The gangling President-elect arrived and, with innate country courtesy, went first to meet the opposition side of the aisle. Not a Democrat stirred to greet him.

"I can't stand this damned nonsense," Sickles muttered. He rose, strode over to the towering visitor, and had himself introduced to Abraham Lincoln. Lincoln smiled in recognition: "Why, Mr. Sickles, I expected you to be a giant of a man, big and broad-shouldered, as tall as I am. But I would take you to be a more scholarly kind of fellow, eh?" Sickles laughed. He studied the craggy face, the deep-set eyes. Under the countrified exterior he sensed an unfathomable depth in this man. The eyes seemed to peer clear through a man to the buttons on the back of his coat.

As Sickles chatted with Lincoln, other Democratic Congressmen began to follow his lead and now crowded around the President-elect. Sickles' cocksure independence had not gone unnoticed; an unusual man, Lincoln thought. Sickles, sizing up the nation's new leader, returned the judgment.

Josiah Favill, a young man of good family from New York City, began a diary when the war began.

> Monday, April 15, 1861. *I have actually joined the army and am going to the war as a high private in Company C of the Seventy-first New York Regiment. . . . The regiment has been accepted for three months' service by the general government. . . . I left the armory rejoiced to find myself a real soldier, and could hardly realize that in less than a week's time I should be leaving home and marching to the front. I have always dreamed of a soldier's life as an ideal one, and have been enthusiastic on all things military since I was old enough to read. . . . The Seventy-first is a swell city regiment, called the American Guard, none but native Americans ordinarily being enlisted, and in its ranks are many very rich men, several of them taking private servants along. . . . These hotheaded Rebels will surely find themselves more than accommodated in the matter of fighting and will before long bitterly repent their foolish actions. . . .*
>
> Tuesday, April 16th. *Tomorrow we are to meet at the armory, fall in and march in a body to Develin's clothing store, lower Broadway, there to be measured, each and all of us, for a uniform suit, to consist of*

dark blue jacket and sky-blue trousers. The jacket will have light blue shoulderstraps and cuffs, and will be made as quickly as possible, and forwarded to us wherever we may be. It is a thousand pities we cannot have them by Sunday, there will be such an enormous crowd to see us off. . . .

Saturday night, April 20th. *Tomorrow we start for the war. Since Wednesday I have been receiving the utmost attention from everybody. It is so strange to see this wonderful enthusiasm and loyalty. It is impossible for a man in uniform to pay for anything he wants. . . . I went home, turned into my comfortable bed, wondering what sort of bed we should probably have in the army.*

The men who had come from Gettysburg to Shepardstown, Virginia, to work in William Hoffman's new carriage shop had a choice to make, not a particularly hard one. The North and South were at war. Shepardstown was the South. They were Pennsylvanians. They would go home. Wesley Culp, for motives best known to himself, decided to stay. Culp had scant interest in politics, but placed great store in personal friendship, which he had amply generated in Shepardstown, mostly through membership in the Hamtramck Guards.

These local militia units provided the Confederate States of America with a ready-made core for the newly organizing Confederate Army. The Hamtramck Guards were quickly absorbed as Company B, Second Virginia Infantry, into what would become the Army of Northern Virginia.

Virginians in the regiment from other companies who did not know Wesley Culp found him an irresistible target. He was taunted for his accent and his size, particularly when the quartermaster issued him a cutdown musket fitted to his height. "A God damn Yankee and a God damn midget in the Second Virginia?" a gruff sergeant had bellowed. "If that don't beat all!" But his Shepardstown comrades sprang to Culp's defense, and he won grudging acceptance in the regiment as he had won friends in the Hamtramck Guards.

Wes Culp had repeated opportunities to prove courage and loyalty. Company B and the rest of the Second Virginia were quickly bloodied in battle. They became part of General Jackson's vaunted "Stonewall Brigade." "The little Yankee bastard" eventually was, simply, "the little Yank."

Back in Gettysburg, Wes's brother, Will Culp, burst into the kitchen of his married sister, Annie Myers. Since their mother had died, Annie had become the maternal anchor of the Culp family. "We'll all be in the same company," Will said, beaming. "Me, Nick Codori, Billy Weikert, we've all joined up and we'll all be together. Jack Skelly, too." Skelly was a youth of twenty who lived across the street from Annie.

She stood, forcing a small smile for her grinning brother Will, thinking of her brother Wes, and wondering what this war was doing to the Culp family.

Robert Stiles was a Union man. He had been raised in New York City and New Haven, Connecticut, where his minister father had served Presbyterian congregations. Robert had graduated from Yale. His friends, his associations, his life were all in the North. True, years before, the family had come from Georgia, and for an unremembered time in his childhood, Robert had lived in Richmond, Virginia, where his father had a church.

He began to change his views with a visit he made, early in 1860, to Washington and Richmond. All that he saw, all those he met in Richmond charmed and delighted Robert Stiles. He felt, inexplicably, more at ease in Virginia than Connecticut. Only the war fever that he encountered in the South puzzled and somehow amused him. All the young men of good family in the Virginia capital seemed to belong to the Richmond Howitzers, a local artillery company. The Howitzers, they told Robert gravely, were the advance guard of an army to defend the South.

Talk of imminent war had a ridiculous ring to Robert Stiles. These Southern gallants did not understand the North or else Stiles could have explained the groundlessness of their fears. War against the South held no attraction to New England merchants and bankers, he assured them. And when Robert Stiles returned home to Connecticut he confirmed this judgment. All was as before. Thoughts of war did not concern Yankee traders, only a dry passion for business and finance, for making money.

Stiles entered Columbia Law School in the fall of 1860. Since his father had once shepherded a prestigious New York City congregation, he enjoyed easy entry into the best homes. In these homes, men of affairs, men who understood what moves the world, indeed, the very men who moved the world, assured this serious young man that wise Virginia would scotch any foolish notions of secession among her Southern sisters.

But Lincoln's call of April 15, 1861, for 75,000 military men cast the die for Virginia. The Old Dominion seceded a few days after the call-up. New York City, swept by war hysteria and arrogant chauvinism, now made Robert Stiles exceedingly uncomfortable. His studies declined. He went home to New Haven. He needed desperately to talk to his family. Robert explained the mystic bond to the South that he had felt growing since his visit to Richmond. Surprised and relieved, he learned that his mother and father shared his sympathies. A family decision was made. The Stileses would all migrate to the South as soon as possible.

The infantry private was the basic molecule of both armies. From sixty-five to eighty privates, along with their commissioned and noncommissioned officers, formed a company. Ten companies formed a regiment. From four to six regiments comprised a brigade. From two to four brigades formed a division. Three divisions usually formed a corps. Various corps made up an army—the Army of Northern Virginia in the South, for example, or the Army of the Potomac in the North.

> Private Henry Raison
> Company B
> 7th Tennessee Regiment
> Archer's Brigade
> Heth's Division
> Third Corps
> Army of Northern Virginia

The death, rather the cowardly murder, of Colonel E. Elmer Ellsworth was the North's first great shock of the war. This peerless soldier from upstate New York, this favorite of President Lincoln, had organized one of the most colorful units in the Federal army, the First New York Zouaves.

Early in the war, Colonel Ellsworth had been ordered to take his Zouaves to Alexandria, Virginia. There he spotted a Rebel flag flapping insolently from a housetop. Ellsworth entered the house, ran upstairs, and personally tore down the offending banner. On his way back down the stairs, he ran into the owner of the house, who shot Ellsworth through the heart. The entire North mourned the loss of this first Union officer to die in the war.

Upon his death, the Albany *Evening Journal* called for the formation of a special regiment, to be known as "Ellsworth's Avengers" and composed of one man from each town and ward in New York State. The idea caught fire. State officials quickly organized an elite corps, formally the 44th New York Volunteer Infantry. Each Avenger had to be at least five feet eight inches in height, unmarried, and in outstanding physical condition. The Avengers adopted a code appealing to high-principled men. Many of the original regiment took the unsoldierly pledge not to "use intoxicating liquors, tobacco in any form nor profane language" for as long as they wore the Avenger uniform.

Among the endless, indistinguishable regiments then streaming through the Port of New York for the South, Ellsworth's Avengers still drew a crowd. "Look at the size of them apple-knockers, would you," a city native observed as they marched down Broadway. "Damned if they don't all look like a bunch of foreigners!" a woman snorted. The Avengers wore a Zouave uniform of startling novelty. Months before, these upstate farmboys, blacksmiths, printers, and small-town lawyers could scarcely have imagined such style. Their headgear was a red fez, their jackets were short, heavily embroidered, with large brass buttons. They wore blue trousers bloused above the ankles with a bold red stripe down the side, and brilliant yellow leggings that caught the sun as they swung down Broadway.

By near unanimous consent, the finest-looking Avenger was twenty-five-year-old Lucius Larrabee from the upstate New York village of Ticonderoga. Larrabee's silken black beard framed a resolute chin and a sensitive mouth. His gaze had a searching intensity, and, in response, the eyes of women invariably lingered over this striking Union soldier.

The University Greys of the University of Mississippi first tasted battle at Bull Run in Virginia, on June 21, 1861, under handsome Billy Lowry. For one hour, 2800 Rebels dammed the advance of 15,000 Yankees. The superiority of enemy numbers, however, proved too much. The outflanked men fell back. Then, on a ridge above them General Thomas Jackson appeared, oblivious of a hail of gunfire.

Pointing to the ridge, General Bernard Bee shouted, "There is Jackson, standing like a stone wall." The audacity of this officer, silhouetted against the skyline, revived the Confederates' spirit. They held fast. Moments later Bee was shot dead. In one vivid simile, he had rechristened Jackson and made his greatest contribution to the Southern cause.

The University Greys paid their first blood dues this day. Three former students and three town boys died at Bull Run. When the guns were stilled, Jeremiah Gage of the Greys walked slowly over the field. He traced scattered bodies to a point where the Union dead lay thick upon the ground. The broken, lifeless forms were clothed in a bizarre, alien uniform. Jeremiah picked up an odd-shaped red hat. Inside the band it read, "Revenge Ellsworth's Death."

George Pickett was born a thousand years too late. He belonged in Arthur's Court. He was Tristan, should have worn chain mail, not army wool, was more knight than soldier, more chivalrous than wise. Pickett graduated from West Point at the bottom of his class. Yet, his first year out, it was Pickett, predictably, who was the first man up the parapets at Chapultepec, flamboyantly unfurling the American flag over the castle in the war with Mexico.

Pickett in war was glorious. Pickett in love was star-crossed. His first wife, the lovely Sallie Minge of Richmond, died in their first year of marriage. As a young officer posted in the remote Northwest, George Pickett later married the daughter of an Indian chief. His Indian princess died, too.

When war broke out, Pickett gave his allegiance to his native South. He resigned from the U.S. Army and took a Confederate commission. At thirty-six he was an aging Tristan, with his flaxen hair, delicately perfumed, worn in long ringlets down to his shoulders. His Isolde now was La Salle Corbell of Virginia, a beautiful girl half his age, whom he loved wildly. Pickett was a frequent and ardent correspondent of his beloved Sallie.

> *My Dearest Sallie,*
> *. . . No, my child, I had no conception of the intensity of feeling, the bitterness and hatred toward those who were so lately our friends and are now our enemies. I, of course, have always strenuously opposed*

*disunion, not as doubting the right of secession, which was taught in
our text-book at West Point, but as gravely questioning its expediency. I
believe that the revolutionary spirit which infected both North and South
were but a passing phase of fanaticism which would perish under the
rebuke of all good citizens, who would surely unite in upholding the
Constitution; but when that great assembly, composed of ministers,
lawyers, judges, chancellors, statesmen, mostly white-haired men of
thought, met in South Carolina and when their districts were called,
crept noiselessly to the table in the center of the room and affixed their
signatures to the parchment on which the ordinance of secession was
inscribed, and when in deathly silence, in spite of the gathered multi-
tude, General Jamison arose and without preamble read: "The ordinance of secession has been signed and ratified; I proclaim the state of
South Carolina an independent sovereignty," and lastly, when my old
boyhood's friend called for an invasion, it was evident that both the
advocates and opponents of secession had read the portents aright.*

*You know, my little lady, some of those cross-stitched mottoes on the
cardboard samplers which used to hang on my nursery wall, such as
"He who provides not for his own household is worse than an infidel"
and "Charity begins at home," made a lasting impression upon me; and
while I love my neighbor, i.e., my country, I love my household, i.e.,
my state, more, and I could not be an infidel and lift my sword
against my own kith and kin, even though I do believe, my most wise
little counselor and confidante, that the measure of American greatness
can be achieved only under one flag, and I fear, alas, there can never
again reign for either of us the true spirit of national unity, whether
divided and under two flags, or united under one.*

*. . . We did not tarry even for a day in 'Frisco, but under assumed
names my friend, Sam Barron, and I sailed for New York, where we
arrived on the very day that Sam's father, Commodore Barron, was
brought there, a prisoner, which fact was proclaimed aloud by the pilot
amid cheers of the passengers and, upon our landing, heralded by the
newsboys with more cheers. Poor Sam had a hard fight to hide his
feelings and to avoid arrest. We separated, as mere ship acquaintances,
and went by different routes to meet again, as arranged, at the house of
Doctor Paxton, a Southern sympathizer and our friend.*

*As I was walking up from the dock a stranger rather roughly jostled
against me, saying "I beg your pardon, sir, but you've dropped your
pocketbook." I was about to resent this intrusion and disown the purse*

when a telegraphic expression on the stranger's face made me suddenly change my mind, and, carelessly putting the purse into my pocket, I thanked him and made for the bus. Opening the purse to pay my fare I found a roll of bank notes, some silver, several clippings and a very much soiled card of a New York hostelry, and across this worn and greasy card, in the well-known hand of an old friend and comrade, were some very pertinent lines written in Chinook jargon and labeled in English: "This is a part of a copy of a letter written to me by my Indian sweetheart." Now, Bright Eyes, that you may not be jealous, and that you may know how loyal and unselfish and generous a brother officer can be, even though he may differ from you in principles, and is fighting against you and your flag, I will copy this alleged "love-letter," in its literal translation:

"Ah you've come. I too have just arrived. You look out. The bald eagle cries out. No you go friend's house. Understand? Rattle snakes everywhere. Steal away at once. Make haste. Everybody watches. Get out. That is best. I no idle talk. Escape or you a prisoner. This money is a present for you. I love you. Send away fear. From you all evil.

Yours very well"

Now, Chula, Carrisima, was not that a "for-truly" love-letter? It was well that we obeyed to the letter its injunctions, "Kah-kwah spose," for the "friend's house" and his friends' homes were searched during the night while we were concealed in a neighbor's stable.

On the next day we left for Canada by the earliest train. Thence we made our perilous way through Kentucky to Tennessee, barely escaping arrest several times, and finally arrived in dear old Richmond, September 13, just four days ago. I at once enlisted in the army and the following day was commissioned Captain. But so bitter is the feeling here that my being unavoidably delayed so long in avowing my allegiance to my state has been most cruelly and severly criticized by friends, yes, and even relatives—near relatives, too.

Now, little one, if you had the very faintest idea how happy a certain Captain in the C.S.A. would be to look into your beautiful, soul-speaking eyes and hear your wonderfully musical voice, I think you would let him know by wire where he could find you. I shall almost listen for the electricity which says, "I am at _____. Come." I know that you will have mercy on your devoted . . .

Your own

Richmond, September 17, 1861   *Soldier*

They called it "sheet iron crackers," "teeth dullers," "hard bread," hard crackers," but most often "hardtack," a flour and water biscuit of granite consistency, and the staple issue of both the Union and Confederate armies.

The men ground hardtack into a powder, soaked it in coffee, fried it in bacon grease, toasted it over coals, and boiled it in water. With it they produced meals called "Burnside stew," "Washington pie," "Potomac chowder," "hell fire stew."

Soldiers might occasionally be issued fresh bread, meat, and coffee, but always could count on hardtack. At the orderly sergeant's call, "Come and get your crackers," men fell in for the day's ration, usually from nine to twelve crackers, as few as three or four in scarce times. They fished the hardtack out of barrels and wooden boxes in packages marked "B. C.," which may have stood for "Brigade Commissary." The soldiers said it meant "Before Christ."

Soldiers told of beating hardtack with musket butts to make it edible. They claimed that hardtack worn over the heart would stop a bullet. In one popular story a sergeant says, "Boys, I was eating a piece of hardtack this morning and I bit into something soft."

"What was it, Sarge?"

"A nail."

Another soldier drove his lieutenant to distraction by endlessly eating hardtack. The ceaseless grinding of the man's teeth against the flinty substance finally unnerved the lieutenant. "Keegan," he screamed, "why are you always crunching hardtack?"

"The juice, sir, I am very fond of the juice."

Warren Goss of Massachusetts had not regretted his decision to enlist, though what he saw of the army did nothing to blunt his ironic outlook. In April of 1862, Warren's regiment boarded steamers, headed down the Potomac, and debarked at Old Point Comfort on the Virginia Peninsula. They marched through April days, either drenched in sun and sprouting greenery, or soaked with rain and awash with mud.

Behind them forever was the toy-soldiering on Washington camp grounds, the parade formations, the bullying drill sergeants, the endless burnishing of buttons and mindless buffing of leather, the officers, often drunk and coarse, who still commanded a private's salute and who seemed to carpet the capital's streets. If there were half as many officers in battle as in Washington, Warren thought, the Union Army must be marvelously well led.

Warren felt the Virginia mud oozing through his boots. His legs were numb beyond fatigue as he plunged them into the muck. Hunger stabbed at his stomach. Yet he felt an inner contentment, watching his mud-caked comrades and listening to the fresh curses inspired by their first contact with war-ravaged Virginia.

Old Joe from Beverly, Massachusetts, plodded alongside Warren. "Christ!" Joe groaned. "This country's like walkin' through a hundred miles of pig shit."

A skinny eighteen-year-old redhead named Wad Rider nodded. "Amen, reverend, this Virginia's poor'n skimmed piss."

Big Bethel, where the exhausted Massachusetts troops rested, was little more than a dozen houses recently abandoned by the Confederates. Warren watched while Old Joe and Wad Rider crouched over a fire, frying hardtack and salt pork. "Want a piece of the pan, Warren?" Old Joe asked.

"What are you making?"

"Sowbelly with the tits on."

"No, never mind." Warren grimaced and walked off. With a little enterprise, he thought, he might improve on the usual field menu. Warren approached one of Big Bethel's small, neat houses. His rapping was answered by a woman who cracked the door open to expose a face hard with suspicion.

"Can you sell me something to eat, ma'am?" He rustled some greenbacks in her face.

Her gaze softened slightly. She opened the door. "Reckon I can sell you something. C'mon in."

Warren entered a plainly furnished room where two little girls, one black and one white, stood baking a cornmeal johnnycake over an open fireplace. The black child tended the cake. The white girl directed her. From time to time the mother offered suggestions to her daughter. The mother's suggestions were snapped into testy commands by the white girl. "Move that pan, you stupid thing." The girl stamped her foot. "You sure gonna burn my cake." The black child cowered at each fresh outburst, and struggled to keep pace with a flood of erratic orders.

"Suppose you Yanks are gonna interfere with our servants now?" The woman glared at Warren.

The young soldier had been absorbed in the small drama before the fireplace. "Your servants, uh? Oh, I don't know. I suppose you'll get compensated for any liberated Negroes." Warren watched the black child hovering over the baking pan. "What's your black girl worth?" he asked.

"That 'un?" The woman cast a practiced eye over the child. "I reckon it's worth about five hundred dollars."

"It . . . is?"

He shifted the conversation to the recent skirmish at Big Bethel. "Did you see it, ma,am?"

"Why, your Major Winthrop died right in there." She pointed to a small adjoining bedroom.

"How did he die?" Warren asked.

"Oh, he was shot by a colored boy belonging to one of our officers."

"By a colored boy?" Warren's eyes narrowed.

"Yep. During the fighting this colored boy was astandin' by his master. The boy saw your Major Winthrop up ahead of his men, and he says, 'See that officer? Can I take your rifle and shoot him?' The master handed him the rifle, and the boy shot Major Winthrop."

"How old was this boy?"

"Oh, about forty."

Former Congressman Dan Sickles, back living in New York City with his dishonored wife, Teresa, passed his time with friends at the bar at Delmonico's. This day his companion was the wealthy William Wiley, and they talked of the War.

"Dan, you've had military experience," Wiley was saying. "You were with the city militia. I'll tell you what." Wiley raised his glass. "If you'll raise a regiment and command it, I'll arm it and equip it."

Sickles' long-sidetracked energies leaped to the challenge. Within weeks, he raised, not a regiment, but a full brigade of over three thousand men. Rank was awarded to a volunteer officer in proportion to the number of men he brought to the colors. Since he had raised a brigade, former Congressman, briefly city militiaman Daniel Sickles was now entitled to the star of a brigadier general. And Sickles was not indifferent to rank.

New York Republican politicians, displeased by the military resurrection of Democrat Dan Sickles, sought to have his command chopped back to a regiment, which would have reduced Sickles to a colonel. Sickles sped to Washington to seek the aid of President Lincoln. Lincoln was again struck by the New Yorker's combativeness. The President was unwilling to see an obvious scrapper lost because of the petty rivalries of state politicians. Sickles had an idea for circumventing the control of state officials. He proposed that his brigade be taken in, not as state troops, but as U.S. volunteers.

Sickles returned to New York, and months later his brigade was sworn in, but not before the brigade had endured experiences unexpected in soldiering. They were housed in P. T. Barnum's circus tents, underwent payless paydays, and watched creditors hound their commander, who ran up bills for rations, fuel, horses, and rent of $283,000. As soon as the troops were sworn into Federal service, Sickles left it to his rich friend William Wiley to face the creditors, while he led the proud new "Excelsior Brigade" off to war.

Daniel Sickles had a friend in the new Republican President, but he had paved his past with so many enemies that the U.S. Senate, on March 17, 1862, disapproved his appointment as brigadier general. Sickles, now technically reduced to a colonel, again headed for Washington to mobilize a campaign to recapture his general's star. He wheedled and lobbied key Senators, found his cause taken up by influential newspapers, such as Horace Greeley's New York *Tribune* and James Gordon Bennett's New York *Herald*. Most helpful, his old friend and defense counsel in the Barton Key murder trial, Edwin Stanton, was now Secretary of War. Lincoln continued to admire the feisty Sickles and was persuaded to resubmit his name to the Senate, where he was confirmed a brigadier general by an unflattering nineteen-to-eighteen vote.

While Sickles was away fighting for his star, his Excelsior Brigade met the enemy for the first time in the Peninsula campaign in the spring of 1862. Of 4500 men in the Excelsior Brigade, 772 were killed or wounded in one day in the assault on Williamsburg. "The slain, unburied, lay in heaps," wrote Joseph Twichell, a young brigade chaplain. "I shall remember it long."

From the letters of General Pickett:

My Dearest Sallie,

  *My heart beat with joy this morning, my darling, when Captain
Peacock returned to camp, bringing me your beautiful letter—beautiful
because is was the echo of a pure spirit and a radiant soul. I am humbly
grateful, my little sweetheart, for this loyal devotion which you give
me—your soldier. Let us pray to our dear Heavenly Father to spare us
to each other and give us strength to bear cheerfully this enforced
separation. I know that it cannot be long, and that sooner or later our
flag will float over the seas of the world, for our cause is right and just.*

  *Why, my Sallie, all that we ask is a separation from people of
contending interests, who love us as a nation as little as we love them,
the dissolution of a Union which has lost its holiness, to be let alone and
permitted to sit under our own vine and fig tree and eat our figs peeled
or dried or fresh or pickled, just as we choose. The enemy is our enemy
because he neither knows nor understands us, and yet, hating us, will
not let us part in peace and be neighbors, but insists on fighting us to
make us one with him, forgetting that both slavery and secession were
his own institutions. The North is fighting for the Union, and we—for
home and fireside. All the men I know and love in the world—comrades
and friends, both North and South—are exposed to hardships and
dangers, and are fighting on one side or the other, and each for that
which he knows to be right. . . .*

                                                    Your own
                                                    Soldier

Headquarters, May 1862

The custom was punctually observed in Waterville, Maine. Twice a
day, at eleven in the morning and four in the afternoon, the men of
the town gathered in the taverns to break the day's labor with a toddy
of rum or brandy.

In the summer of 1862, the citizens of Waterville felt a glowing
pride in their town. Fast disappearing was the sluggish rural village
of twenty years before. Waterville now throbbed with industry. The
banks of the Kennebec were lined with tanners, clothiers, tool makers, boot makers, and furniture manufacturers. Substantial brick
business buildings rose along Elm and Main streets. Along the
residential streets, handsome and generously proportioned white frame
houses rested behind tall shade trees.

Waterville was making its mark culturally as well. Waterville College was fast growing in academic stature. And even those who labored a long day flocked to evening classes at the local night school.

Waterville had made a proud contribution to the Union. The year before, the town elders had opened a recruiting office just twenty-four hours after Lincoln's call for troops. Enlistments were taken in the office of Josh Nye, the treasurer of the railroad. No sooner was the office opened than Charley Hendrickson, a student at Waterville College, became the first to sign up. Over seventy more men quickly followed suit.

Now, a year later, conversation in the taverns had again turned to enlistments as state officials sought to raise new Maine regiments. The year before, the talk had been of saving the Union and giving the "Secesh" a quick hiding. Now the townsfolk speculated about enlistment bounties.

"Do you realize," old Fred said, jabbing his finger into the oaken bar, "do you realize, take the state bounty, take the federal bounty, take what the town is putting up, why, a young man can get himself three hundred dollars cold cash just for joining up!"

"Too bad you ain't a young man, Fred."

"Not even a man of middlin' years." Old Fred laughed. "But I tell you, that's a peck of money just for puttin' down your name. Yup. And those fellers went last year didn't get a red cent."

Maybe it was the money. Partly it was still patriotism. Mostly, if a man was young, single, and healthy and his friends were going, what else was he to do? Whatever the motive, this Maine town of 4852 citizens gave another 102 of its sons to the Union cause in the summer of 1862. Most joined a new regiment, the 20th Maine, including a handsome fellow named Charles W. Billings who lived just up the road from Waterville, in Benton.

Robert Stiles, the New Haven minister's son, had not fled the North merely to add another mouth for the South to feed. Soon after his family had made their way from Connecticut to Virginia, Robert enlisted in the Richmond Howitzers, which, as he knew from his earlier visit, boasted the flower of Richmond's young manhood.

During the year in which he trained in the science of artillery, Stiles often retraced the intersections of his life which had made him a Confederate soldier. He could never find any cool logic to

equal the deep emotional sense of rightness he felt about his new
allegiance.

He wondered what had motivated the men around him. Slavery?
Few Richmond Howitzers had ever owned a slave. Most had little use
for the institution. Was it the principle of secession—that all-consuming
controversy in the years before the war? Stiles himself had vigorously
disputed the right to secede in heated student debates at Yale.
Certainly Virginia was not fighting for the right of secession. Virginia had steadfastly counseled against this rash course, had indeed
refused to secede right up to the moment of Lincoln's call for troops.
Secession was not the answer, Robert Stiles concluded.

Not the desire to hold black men slaves? Not an abstract cause, the
solubility or insolubility of the Union? What, then, was it that was
worth dying for? Robert Stiles understood it all so suddenly, so
clearly. Here was the reason he fought. Here was why they all fought.
It was the primal, God-sown instinct to defend one's lair against an
aggressor. Was not Lincoln invading the South? Then Southerners
must repel the invader, and this was cause enough to fight and, if
need be, to die.

"No man shall be accepted who cannot, at two hundred yards, put
ten consecutive shots in a target, the average distance not to exceed
five inches from the center of the bulls-eye."

Hiram Berdan of New York had first made the proposal. His idea
was to gather the finest marksmen in all the Union into one unit and
to arm them with the best weapon available.

The best weapon, Berdan knew, was the newly patented Spencer
breech-loading, repeating rifle which fired a .52-calibre conical bullet. The gun took a seven-round tube inserted into the stock. A man
could get off over twenty rounds a minute with the Spencer. The
Union Army's Chief of Staff, General Winfield Scott, and his Chief of
Ordnance, General James Ripley, however, favored the old reliable
musket-loading Springfield. Ripley, in fact, abominated the Spencer
repeating rifle. Any gun that could be loaded and fired so rapidly, he
knew, would waste precious ammunition.

The newspapers carried both sides of the raging debate for weeks.
For the moment, Berdan prevailed. His sharpshooters, armed with
the Spencer breech-loading rifle, moved to a training camp outside
Washington, where they continued to draw the fire of critics.

Thomas Scott, Assistant Secretary of War, seized the opportunity of a visit by President Lincoln to the camp where the sharpshooters were training for some close-up sniping. On the drive out, Scott asked peevishly, "What's the wisdom of having a privileged unit with fancy, special weapons?"

"We shall see, Mr. Scott, we shall see," Lincoln answered absently.

General George McClellan met the President's party on arrival and took them on a tour of the camp and then to observe Berdan's riflemen on the firing range.

The targets were two life-sized soldiers painted on canvas, set up six hundred yards distant. One hundred Berdan sharpshooters each fired a single round. One hundred rounds struck the two painted figures.

"Mr. President," Berdan said, "we'd be honored to have you shoot." He handed Lincoln a loaded Spencer repeating rifle. The President handled the weapon with easy assurance. He raised it to his shoulder, aimed, and got off three rounds. A soldier at the target shouted back, "One of three!" A great cheer went up.

The President smiled and handed the rifle back to Berdan. "Colonel, I like it."

"Colonel Berdan," Assistant Secretary Scott spoke up, "I imagine your own interest in marksmanship surpasses the theoretical?"

Berdan instantly accepted the oblique challenge. He loaded the rifle and walked up to the line. "Set a fresh target," he ordered. He raised the rifle to his shoulder and looked to the Assistant Secretary. "Any particular part, Mr. Scott?"

"The right eye." Scott smiled.

Berdan squeezed the trigger. A long silence followed the report of the gun. A private ran back with the target. Berdan laughed inwardly at his colossal luck. The painted figure was punctured through the right eye.

The soldier's musket usually fired a round called a "minié ball," a cone-shaped missile made of soft lead. The minié ball tore a large hole in a man. On entering the body, the ball would mushroom, shattering bone, chewing out flesh over a wide area, leaving a horrendous site of destruction. The shape and relative slowness of the minié ball allowed it to pick up bits of cloth and surface skin as it penetrated, and carry this foreign matter into the wound, a virtual guarantee of infection. A wound in a limb usually required amputation. A wound in the abdomen or chest usually meant death.

Richmond was a disappointment to Private Napier Bartlett. The Confederate capital had hardly responded with the hospitality due one of the South's elite corps. Every member of the Washington Artillery was a gentleman of standing and property back in New Orleans. The commander, Colonel Walton, a man of wealth, had sacrificed all to fight Yankee tyranny. When the Washington Artillery left New Orleans, Edouard of Victor's Restaurant, perhaps the finest chef in a city famed for its cuisine, came along as the cook.

So exclusive was this unit that Nap Bartlett, a graduate of the University of Louisiana, a man who had been a journalist and a lawyer, could manage no better than a private's rank. The commissions went to natives of New Orleans—quite understandably, Nap Bartlett reflected—and he was a transplanted Georgian.

The day they left New Orleans, the company had mustered in front of City Hall, and from its steps Nap Bartlett heard the Reverend Dr. Palmer deliver a powerful oration. "And should the frequent fate of the soldier befall you in a soldier's death, you shall find your graves in thousands of hearts, and the pen of history shall write your martyrdom. Soldiers, farewell, and may the Lord of Hosts be round about you as a wall of fire and shield your heads in the day of battle." An eloquent silence had followed the minister's words, then a deafening ovation exploded. Ladies of the highest fashion and respectability rushed heedlessly from their carriages, through ankle-deep dirt and dust, and dodged among the mules and horses to embrace the departing heroes.

But that had been New Orleans. Richmond was a rude jolt. They had arrived eager to know the capital of their new nation. Instead, they were locked into a tobacco warehouse with a guard placed over them to dissuade deserters. Deserters, indeed! When they finally earned the freedom of the streets, no admiring crowds gathered. The New Orleans elite artillery received the same anonymous reception accorded hundreds of thousands of other uniformed strangers who had overrun this city of 38,000.

Respectable people kept their daughters from these passion-starved strangers. The fresh-faced belles who had fed the artillerymen's vanity and fueled their courage in New Orleans were replaced in Richmond by painted tarts who exacted cash for their affections.

As he stood at the crowded bar of the Hotel Spotswood, Nap Bartlett observed that, instead of a cause demanding common sacrifice, the war had become a mint to the merchants of Richmond, the hotel owners, saloon keepers, the madams.

Nap did a rapid calculation as he carefully nursed his fifteen-cent whiskey. At that price, still well below the quarter this profiteer was charging for mint juleps and cherry cobblers, Nap figured he was earning less than three drinks a day. His now empty glass threatened his place at the bar. A large, bearded man in a boldly checked suit, reeking of the military contractor, noticed his plight. The man smiled through stained teeth, snapped his fingers at the bartender, and pointed disapprovingly at Nap's empty glass, then turned back to his companions.

Nap raised his whiskey in a silent toast to his benefactor. Ah yes, the true wartime aristocrat, he thought, the one who can command money, and willingly spends it.

Of the thirteen Taylor children, Isaac and Patrick Henry were closest. They were different enough to fill in the chinks of each other's character. Isaac was quiet, introspective. His love was botany. P.H., as they called Patrick Henry, was fun-loving and spirited. He had gladly dropped his teaching job to join the First Minnesota. The scholarly Isaac, to no one's surprse, took over P.H.'s teaching position when his brother left.

Isaac thought he was happy, at first. He found new orders of flora to explore in the region of Minnesota where P.H. had taught. But he soon felt uncomfortable. No one ever asked right out why the younger brother had gone off to war while the older brother had taken the schoolteacher's job. But the students and the faculty did love to reminisce about what a spunky fellow that P.H. was, fooling those recruiting physicians into passing him. They never caught on that he had been blind in one eye since childhood. It seemed that almost every day someone was asking Isaac what he had heard from P.H. lately.

One day, Isaac Taylor packed his beloved botany books, expressed his regrets to the principal, who complained bitterly about finding a replacement in the middle of the year, and enlisted in P.H.'s outfit.

When the brothers were reunited, P.H. took Isaac to the sutler's store, where P.H. bought some pies and Isaac bought a small leather-bound diary. "Just like you, Isaac." P.H. laughed. "I suppose you'll write down every rock and weed between here and Richmond in that little book before this thing is over."

Actually, Isaac wrote in the fly leaf:

Mr. Secesh:

Please forward this diary to J. H. Taylor, Prairie City, McDonough Co., Illinois. By so doing you will exhibit your magnanimity, accommodativeness and divers other virtues, besides conferring no small favor on a defunct individual.

Yours truly,
I. L. Taylor
High Private of Co. E.
1st Reg. Minn. Vol.

Thomas Fondren McKie, age sixteen, found his every waking moment consumed by dreams of Mississippi's University Greys. He badgered his mother ceaselessly until the woman had no fight left. He won her hapless consent and enlisted in the Greys in 1862.

On arrival in Richmond, Tommy McKie and his comrades headed immediately to an artist's studio, where he posed proudly for a daguerreotype to send to his mother. He had wanted to look the hard-eyed fighter. Instead, the camera caught a Tommy McKie pale, sensitive, frightened-looking, a picture that made his mother cry.

By the end of the summer, Tommy McKie had survived three battles. He had seen death close up and knew that he was not immune. He had, in fact, skirted death, not heroically on the field of battle but from a wracking bout of diarrhea. The sickness, the "shits" the men called it, had scared him as much as battle. He had seen more men have the life sucked from them by tortured bowels than from bullet wounds.

In October of 1862, the University Greys burrowed deep into winter camp at Winchester, Virginia. The boy's badly weakened body craved rest. As soon as he felt well enough to muster his thoughts, McKie knew what must be done. Huddled in a corner of his tent, he braced a sheet of paper against his haversack and began scribbling furiously.

Mother, I want you to write to President Davis to get me off, say to him that I joined contrary to your will and that I am a minor and that you desire me at home and are compelled to have me. Do it immediately as soon as you recieve it. All the officers in our company advised me to do it. Do not hesitate to write because you half way consented, for every one in the county knows that up to the very moment that I started, you did not want me to do it. You recollect on the very evening that I mustered into service, that we walked out into the garden and you cried and asked me to go up to the depot and get off. But I fool-like did not want to do it. You had better write two letters for fear that one will be destroyed. My health is very good at present. My love to all my relatives and my acquaintances. My love to all at home.

Good-bye
your son

He folded the letter, took another sheet, and began to write again:

Dear Sister,
Get ma to write immediately. If she will not do it, write yourself. . . .

He was Gettysburg's village character, full of years and tales, a figure of exaggerated self-importance, a thick, gnarled old oak of a man, topped with a thatch of snow white hair. John Burns claimed descent from the Scottish poet. Whether true or not, he was a genuine veteran of the War of 1812. The ancient musket that he had carried as one of Miller's men at Lundy's Lane still hung over the mantel of his white frame house. In his middle years John Burns had left Gettysburg for a stint in the war with Mexico. He had tried to enlist in the Union Army, too, when the war against the Confederacy began. But the authorities sent this funny old fellow back home after brief service as a teamster.

John Burns returned to Gettysburg, where his fellow townspeople kept him alive in body with his work as a cobbler and kept him hale in spirit by electing him town constable.

The new draft of men from Waterville and other towns in Maine reported to the commander of the newly created 20th Maine Infantry Regiment, Colonel Adelbert Ames. What depressed Colonel Ames most that first day, what summed up the immensity of the task before him, was the Officer of the Day. The man wore a brown cutaway coat, striped pants, and a silk hat. For a sword he carried a ramrod. To Ames, a West Pointer, a man who had learned the harsh truth of battle at Bull Run, this amiable crowd bore no resemblance to a military regiment. The salute was an alien, subjugating rite to these independent down-Easters. They greeted their new commander with "Howdy, Colonel," spoken like as not while leaning against a tree chewing the end of a cattail. Adelbert Ames had to whip this implausible material into a fighting force.

Ames made little effort to conceal his contempt for what these men could contribute to the Union cause or to his military advancement. The sole bright patch on this first day was the man assigned as Ames' second in command. As far as the administration of Bowdoin College knew, Professor Joshua Lawrence Chamberlain had gone off on a two-year leave of absence to study in Europe. The college had rejected Chamberlain's earlier request for a leave to join the Union Army. A brilliant professor of rhetoric and language belonged in a classroom, not on a battlefield.

With his leave of absence in hand, Lawrence (which he preferred over Joshua) Chamberlain had gone directly to the state capital in Augusta, where he secured a commission as lieutenant colonel of volunteers. If this seemed a lofty beginning for a man of no military experience, Chamberlain at least looked the part. At thirty-five he was gracefully erect, not large, but radiated strength and presence. His high forehead and aquiline nose were in the classic mold, and sweeping mustaches gave him a definite military flair.

Colonel Ames felt a deep relief when Lieutenant Colonel Lawrence Chamberlain reported. Ames was grateful too for the arrival of Lawrence's younger brother, Thomas Chamberlain, who became a sergeant in the regiment. Though less commanding than his brother, Thomas too seemed to possess the instincts of a soldier.

The regiment arrived in Washington on September 7, 1862. The men from the plain, orderly towns of Maine were boggle-eyed at the coarse vitality of the nation's capital. In the fall of 1862, Washington was a rough, sprawling, unfinished boom town. Naked, arching girders suggested the future outlines of the Capitol dome. Around the half-erected Washington Monument, ten thousand cattle grazed.

The capital's prewar population of 60,000 had swollen overnight to 200,000. The city had become a lodestone attracting every kind of entrepreneur who could imagine the commercial potential of war:

saloon keepers, gamblers, pickpockets, freed blacks, blockade runners, contractors, embalmers, undertakers, makers of artificial limbs, and women—women from Ohio, New York City, New England, from farms, slums, and fine homes. They arrived innocent or jaded, naïve or knowing, clean-limbed or diseased. The best, the youngest, the freshest worked out of handsome brownstones and serviced officers, government officials, and profiteers. The concentration of over 450 whorehouses in Washington rivaled the alleyways of Naples or Port Said. Two years was the customary time span for a whore's descent from serving in the houses to working the street. Over seven thousand streetwalkers clogged the capital. The next step down from the street was to journey into nearby army camps, where whole companies were accommodated by a single woman in one night.

The men of the 20th Maine embarked from their train exhausted but wide-eyed at this unimagined Sodom that was their nation's heart. They were bivouacked and slept that night out of doors.

The next morning, the 20th Maine was issued muskets and ammunition from the arsenal and marched through the sweltering heat of a Washington autumn to Fort Craig on Arlington Heights. The regiment's drummers had difficulty coordinating the beat. The feat of marching in step was still beyond the 20th Maine. The regiment was a mobile pandemonium. Civilians and old soldiers en route watched with amusement, jeering and taunting the humiliated recruits.

On their arrival at Fort Craig, Colonel Ames, in cold anger, ran his eye over his ragged ranks. "If you cannot do any better than you have done today, you better all desert and go home." He turned and stalked off.

He was delicate, frail, weighed no more than 130 pounds, and cared little for vigorous activities. Some found him prissy. No one had ever seen a soldier in John Dooley.

At home, young Dooley was popular with the other young people in his circle. They found John's elaborate courtesies thoughtful and his lively conversation charming. They called him "Gentleman Jack." A family friend had described Dooley as "a nice boy trying to be a man."

His father, John Dooley, Sr., had emigrated from County Limerick and settled in Richmond in 1836. The elder Dooley made a quick fortune as a furrier and hatter. He fathered seven children, and the

Dooley home quickly became a popular center of Richmond social life.

When the War began, the elder Dooley briefly took command of a company in the First Virginia Infantry. Another son, James, entered the same regiment as a private, but was wounded and released.

Young John Dooley just before the War had been a nineteen-year-old student at Georgetown University in Washington. In April of 1861, he and the other Southern boys confronted Georgetown's President, Father John Early. They were unhappy in Washington, and found it impossible to fix their attention on Latin grammar and Greek translation amid the fever of secession. They wanted to go home. There was little the Jesuit schoolmaster could do but let them go. Within a year, they were all, including slight, sensitive John Dooley, Confederate soldiers.

Willie Mitchell was of Irish imigrant stock, too. His father, John Mitchell, was a political exile. The elder Mitchell's odyssey had taken young Willie from Ireland to France to Australia and finally to America.

John Dooley, Sr., had warmly embraced his expatriate countryman on John Mitchell's arrival in America. And it was natural enough that Mitchell's seventeen-year-old son should join the First Virginia, the regiment of Dooley Sr. and his two sons. Willie Mitchell caught up with the regiment near Winchester late in October of 1862. By then, of the Dooley family, only John Jr. still served with the First Virginia.

The two young Irishmen were inseparable. They marched together. They messed together. They hunted and hiked together in their free time. In the evenings, they huddled against the chill under the same blanket. Over the campfire, as they fried a piece of fatback and boiled their coffee, young Willie Mitchell held John Dooley spellbound with tales of his father's hairbreadth escapes from British officials. He would describe to John the gorgeously plumed birds and strange jumping beasts he had seen in Australia. This far-off land had quickened in young Mitchell a burning curiosity about nature. Willie had brought a microscope wih him to camp, to the amusement of the older men. He kept a small book in which he described in minute detail the rich natural life he discovered along the march of the First Virginia.

But in the chill night, as they pressed together under their blanket, it was John Dooley's turn to speak of things unknown to Willie. "What's it like, John?" Dooley surprised himself. Sentiments he

John E. Dooley.

never dared utter among the other men he poured out freely to his young comrade. "Why, the first time I saw dead men, I got sick. I ran off and vomited. I couldn't sleep for nights and when I did I had fearful dreams."

"Is it easier now?"

"No. It passes somewhat between battles, if enough time goes by. But it always comes back. When we're going into action, it's hard to explain, but I feel light and feathery as though I have no weight. I can't feel the weight of the musket in my hand. I don't feel my feet against the ground. My hands are damp. My heart pounds so hard that I fear the other men will hear it beating. And my voice, it seems I don't own it. And I'm always surprised to hear it sounding fairly firm and clear, as though it was coming from someone else. And the minié balls going past make this strange whirring sound, like they're saying 'Where are you? Where are you?' That bloody scream we make in charging, that helps some. But the worst of it is that it gets harder each time. Like the men say, I've seen the elephant. And I don't need another look."

Willie stared wide-eyed. "But you're no coward, John?"

"I don't know. How does one know?"

"No, John, you're no coward."

Both sides relied mainly on .58-calibre Springfield and .577-calibre Enfield rifled muskets—cumbersome, slow, sturdy, deadly weapons. The Springfields were named for the armory of the same name in Springfield, Massachusetts. The Springfield was the principal musket of the Union troops. The Enfields had been originally made in England and were copied by the South, where they became the staple weapon.

Both Springfields and Enfields had long, thin, grooved barrels, rather than the shorter, thicker barrels of actual rifles, which eventually replaced the rifled musket.

In 1860 the United States Army tested Springfields for accuracy, speed, and power. Of ten shots fired from 100 yards, all struck within a space 8½ inches by 12 inches. At 300 yards, all hit within an area 2½ feet square. At 500 yards, one shot in ten struck within an area four feet square.

In a speed test, one man got off ten shots in five minutes, six of the shots hitting a two-foot-square target from 100 yards.

In a test of power, a minié ball fired by a rifled musket at 100 yards penetrated 11 one-inch-thick pine boards placed one inch apart.

At 300 yards, the ball went through 6.4 boards. At 500 yards, it pierced 5.8 boards.

These guns were loaded in an involved set of motions known as "loading in nine":

1. Drop the gun butt to the ground between the feet. Hold the barrel with the left hand.

2. With the right hand, take a cartridge from the cartridge box on the belt. (The cartridge was composed of a solid lead slug and a powder charge, held together by a wrapping paper twisted at the bottom.)

3. Put the powder end of the cartridge between the teeth. Tear open the paper with the teeth.

4. Pour the powder down the barrel. Push the bullet into the barrel with the right thumb.

5. Remove the ramrod from under the gun barrel, and place the rammer head against the bullet in the barrel.

6. Drive the bullet down into the barrel with the ramrod as far as it will go.

7. Withdraw the rammer and put it back in its guides under the barrel (or stick it in the ground, ready for the next loading).

8. With the right thumb, bring the hammer back to the half-cocked position. Take a percussion cap from the pouch on the belt and place it over the nipple.

9. Aim, fire.

To the novice, the process seemed slow and cumbersome. But the soldier who had woven these steps into a smooth, unbroken motion, through a thousand repetitions, could easily get off two shots a minute. In the excitement of battle, soldiers commonly fired with the ramrod still in the barrel. The ramrod would go sailing through the air with a twang, leaving the man with no way to reload. More frequently, a man might forget to put on a percussion cap, or place a new cap over the old one. When he pulled the trigger, the gun would not discharge, though in the noise and excitement he might easily not notice the misfire and go on ramming unspent rounds down the barrel on top of each other. Or a man might ram the cartridge down the barrel without first biting off the paper at the end. The spark from the percussion cap would not strike bare powder, and the gun would not fire.

The men of the 20th Maine had learned to hate Colonel Adelbert Ames. Honest error he met with rage. Stupidity he crushed with ridicule. Performance he acknowledged with a bare nod. He drove men mercilessly. He marched them, ran them and drilled them beyond endurance, until their sole surviving energy was their common detestation of him.

Sergeant Tom Chamberlain and his comrades lay in their tent at the end of the day, too fatigued to sleep.

"God," the sergeant breathed heavily, "he's a hard man."

"You know where that kind belongs?" another piped up. "In state prison, not leading men! I bet he gets shot in the first battle we go into, and it won't be no Rebel bullet neither."

"Well, I only wish him the best," a third man said. Tom Chamberlain flung his cartridge box in the direction of the voice.

"Damn, Tom," the man chuckled, deflecting the box, "I'm only hoping Ames'll make brigadier and move out, so's a human being like your brother, Lawrence, can take over."

Their desultory conversation was interrupted by a soothing melody that the men had become fond of hearing. The refrain seemed to draw the fatigue from their aching bodies and invite slumber. As the bugler sounded the notes gently, the melody seemed to say ". . . go to sleep . . . go to sleep . . . all is well, all is well." The bugle call had been composed especially for their brigade, after the Peninsula campaign, by its commander, General Butterfield. The men called it "Taps."

Former journalist and lawyer and now Private Napier Bartlett of the elite New Orleans Washington Artillery had served the Confederacy nearly a year and a half. He now brought quick, cool insights to the trade of killing. He had found handy thumb rules for gauging the intensity of battle. Bodies spaced over thirty feet apart meant moderate fighting. Bodies spaced at less than thirty feet were evidence of heavy work. Bodies lying in piles indicated that breastworks had been stormed.

Still, Bartlett was unprepared for the events of September 21, 1862. The man wearing the uniform of a Confederate captain had ridden into their column, dismounted before General William Jones, and saluted casually. "General, I bring you the compliments of General Jackson. The general requests that you halt your advance in your present position."

Jones searched the courier's face for a long time. "Interesting, interesting," the general said, holding out his hand. "May I have your weapon, Captain?"

"I don't understand, General." The man's voice was outwardly calm. The eyes betrayed a fleeting terror.

The general's voice hardened. "Let me see your weapon!"

"Certainly." The man drew a revolver from his holster and surrendered it. General Jones turned to his two aides. "Seize that man. Search him." They jerked the courier rudely from his horse.

As the officers emptied the man's pockets, the general mused. "You bring me orders from General Jackson, do you? I'm to halt my advance here, am I? The commanding officer of this division happens to be General Longstreet."

With the search of the man completed, one of the aides reported, "General, we found some Union ciphers on him and what looks like some Yankee correspondence." The other aide added, "One of our men says he can identify this fellow. Says he looks like the man who shot down our courier from General Longstreet last night. We checked his revolver, and it's empty.

"Try him," the general ordered. "Do it quickly."

The man admitted to being Charles Mason of Terryville, Pennsylvania, a spy for the U.S. government. He made these admissions calmly, unapologetically. Mason's hands were tied behind his back. He was taken under a tree. He stood erect and motionless as they slipped a noose over his head and around his neck. Mason was lifted onto a mule, and the free end of the rope was thrown over and drawn up nearly taut to an overhanging limb of the tree.

"Mason, do you have anything more to say?" a Rebel major asked.

Mason cricked his neck uncomfortably, looked around at the semicircle of spectators. "I'm dying for the Union," he said with a clear voice. "I don't know what you're dying for."

The sergeant in charge of the execution party received a nod from the major. With a stout switch, he gave the mule a tremendous thwack across the hind quarters. The mule bolted forward. The rope yanked Mason off the animal's back and dangled him two feet from the ground.

Nap Bartlett turned his head aside to mask his nausea.

When the officers turned away, a ragged wagon driver sprang forward and pulled the elegant boots from the swaying body.

*   *   *

The President took long strides across the White House lawn to the War Department building. He mounted the steps quickly, tipping his hat and smiling briefly at government clerks, officials, and visitors along the way. He went directly to the library next to the office of the Secretary of War, Edwin Stanton. Actually, the room was no longer a library. At the start of the War, it had been converted into a telegraph office. Lincoln went to one of the cipher machines and leaned over the operator's shoulder as the man transcribed a message. These unannounced Presidential visits no longer flustered the operators. Lincoln made them two and three times daily. Today, as was his custom, he walked to a drawer, lifted out a stack of telegrams, settled his long frame into a chair, and flipped quickly through the pages.

"You boys aren't hiding any under the blotter, are you?"

The chief operator laughed. "No sir, Mr. President." It was a stock joke between them. Secretary Stanton suspected Lincoln of a loose tongue. He had placed the telegraph crew under strict orders not to reveal any messages disclosing troop movements to the President until he had seen them first. Lincoln knew of this prohibition, and it was a source of endless amusement to him.

Lincoln's conversation, an unending stream of anecdotes, narratives, and analogies, delighted the telegraph crew. Secretary Stanton, in the office next door, stood in stark contrast. The Secretary of War was stern-visaged, haughty, abrupt. He instilled fear where Lincoln generated warmth. Stanton was respected, Lincoln worshiped. Yet, the men in the telegraph office noted, the two got along well. Lincoln would address the Secretary, with a sly smile for the operators, as "Mars." Stanton endured the name stoically, but did not find it amusing.

On this visit, the President drew from his pocket a small, well-worn copy of *Macbeth* and began to declaim fervently, as though he had an entire audience before him. This was what Lincoln enjoyed most about the telegraph office, as much as its swift transmission of events—the opportunity to escape the strains of office, a chance to act as he pleased, the ease to chat idly with good, simple men as he would have done around a winter stove back in Illinois.

Lincoln often spent whole nights at the telegraph office when great events hung in the balance. It was here that he had learned of the death of the first Union officer, Colonel Ellsworth; of the defeat at Bull Run; of the clash of the *Monitor* and the *Merrimack;* and of the staggering Union debacle at Fredericksburg.

Death in battle. It was not the way Ted Gerrish had expected. Gerrish, along with the Chamberlain brothers, the other soldiers of the 20th Maine, and their accursed commander, Adelbert Ames, had just arrived on the battlefield at Antietam. Gerrish had received permission to climb a hill affording a sweeping panorama of the field. He was halfway up the hillside when a Union soldier came hopping over the crest, yelping, grabbing at branches and slim trees for support. The fellow sat down on a rock cursing loudly and trying to tug the boot off a blood-soaked foot. Gerrish started forward to help him when something dark and round came bounding over the hill and crashing through the brush and branches. The cannonball glanced off a rock, struck the wounded man on the back, and continued smashing its way downhill. Gerrish ran up to where the man had been sitting and found only a pulpy mass. Ted Gerrish became the first of the 20th Maine to see a man die in battle.

Just a few days later the full regiment would witness what Gerrish had seen. On September 20, 1862, they gathered at a shallow point on the Potomac waiting their turn to ford the river. They were part of an army pursuing the Confederate forces across the river to the Virginia side. But something had gone wrong. Instead of pressing forward, the Union cavalrymen came plunging and splashing back across the river to the Maryland side, glancing nervously over their shoulders.

The Maine men became edgily aware of howling and whistling overhead. A quiet terror gripped the recruits. Some lost control of their bowels and looked nervously at their neighbors to see if the smell had betrayed their fears. The officers talked too much, spoke too fast, repeated too often, "Steady men, steady men. Keep calm. Don't worry." The rest of the Union forces seemed to be pulling back across the river. Still, the 20th Maine received no change in its orders. Colonel Ames shouted to his company commanders to cross over. His hard-edged voice sounded through the crash of exploding shells, no different from on the parade ground, and now, as then, the men found themselves obeying mechanically. A shell exploding overhead hurled hot, jagged metal into their midst, and two men slid noiselessly into the water. Colonel Chamberlain's horse was shot from under him. Still they slogged ahead until they were almost across, when, belatedly, they were ordered back with the rest of the army.

Watching their disciplined, unhurried return amidst the bursting shells and falling comrades stood their exacting commander, Adelbert Ames. He showed no emotion. But a barely discernible smile crossed his face. He had produced soldiers.

He was now Major General Daniel Sickles, the highest rank in the Union Army. Since his confirmation as a brigadier, former Congressman Sickles had moved quickly on two fronts, the one he knew so well of making useful friends, then using them; the other, the newer science of war. He had handled himself well at both. Sickles displayed skill and daring after he had rejoined his men in the Peninsula campaign. He then gave himself two months' leave, which he spent in New York recruiting, speaking, being feted, and, most important, considering another bid for Congress. But war now coursed hotly through Sickles' veins. He returned from his leave to Alexandria, Virginia, and found that both his soldiering and politicking had paid off. He had been raised from command of a brigade to a division, which carried with it another star.

As the Army of the Potomac wintered during 1862–1863, General Sickles' headquarters became the bright spot on a bleak Virginia landscape. On New Year's Eve, hams, fowl, and delicacies were imported from Washington and washed down with a river of liquor to the accompaniment of violins, flutes, and an accordion. Colonel de Trobriand, a transplanted Frenchman serving with the Union, noted, "General Sickles did things in grand style. The champagne and whiskey ran in streams. I wish I could add that they were used in moderation."

The voluptuous Annie Jones, twenty years old, from Cambridge, Massachusetts, had been set up in a tent by the officers. This great favorite had followed the Union Army throughout Virginia for two years and was having her best season this winter.

Not all admired Sickles' style. A young cavalry captain, Charles Francis Adams, Jr., grandson of a President, a member of one of the nation's noblest tribes, described the Sickles winter encampment, too.

That was a period in its history when, so far as character was concerned, the Army of the Potomac sank to its lowest point. It was commanded by a trio, of each of whom the least said the better. It consisted of "Joe" Hooker, "Dan" Sickles and "Dan" Butterfield. All three were men of blemished character. During the winter when Hooker was in command, I can say from personal knowledge and experience that the headquarters of the Army of the Potomac was a place to which no self-respecting man liked to go, and no decent woman would go. It was a combination of barroom and brothel.

The Union Army maintained records from May 1, 1861, to June 30, 1866. Total cases of gonorrhea recorded were 102,893; syphilis, 79,589. The annual venereal-disease rate for one year was 82 per thousand men, or 8.2 percent of the Army. Reports of some Confederate units disclosed a gonorrhea rate of 17.8 percent and a syphilis rate of 3.8 percent. The standard treatment for these sicknesses was sulfate of zinc, nitrate of silver, cauterization, and a light diet.

One April morning in 1863, a ragged, unshaven band of Confederates squatting around a fire near the Rio Grande looked up to see an unlikely figure approaching. The man wore a Savile Row English hunting suit and black velvet tie. His boots were calf length, polished, and obviously expensive. His hat was high-crowned, with a curled brim, like none they had ever seen. He wore a fringed Indian serape over one shoulder. The man was aristocratically slender, and handsome, but to American eyes rather foppish. A long, drooping mustache semicircled his mouth. As he came closer his face broke into a toothsome half smile.

The sudden visitor was Lieutenant Colonel Arthur James Lyon Fremantle, Her Majesty's Coldstream Guards. Colonel Fremantle had chosen to spend a four-month leave with the Armies of the Confederacy. The twenty-eight-year-old Briton had entered Texas via Mexico and slipped across the Rio Grande into Texas at the point where he had encountered the stunned Confederates. He kept a diary throughout his stay in America.

2nd April: *I crossed the River from Bagdad (Mexico) with Mr. Ituria, at 11 o'clock; and, as I had no pass, I was taken before half a dozen Confederate officers, who were seated around a campfire contemplating a tin of potatoes. . . . Their dress consisted simply of flannel shirts, very ancient trousers, jack boots with enormous spurs, and black felt hats ornamented with the "lone star of Texas." They looked rough and dirty, but were extremely civil to me.*

25th April: *San Antonio is prettily situated on both banks of the river of the same name. It should contain about 10,000 inhabitants, and is the largest place in Texas, except Galveston. . . . All the male population under forty are in the military service, and necessary articles are at famine prices. Coffee costs $7 a pound. . . . None of the Southern people with whom I have spoken entertain any hopes of a speedy termination of the war. They say it must last all Lincoln's presidency, and perhaps a good deal longer.*

26th April: *(San Antonio) I dined with Colonel Bankhead, who gave an entertainment, which in these hard times must have cost a mint of money. . . . I spent a very agreeable evening, and heard many anecdotes of the war. One of the officers sang the abolition song, "John Brown," together with its parody, "I'm bound to be a Soldier in the Army of the South," a Confederate marching song, and another parody, which is a Yankee marching song, "We'll Hang Jeff Davis on a Sour Apple Tree." Whenever I have dined with Confederate officers, they have nearly always proposed the Queen's health, and never failed to pass the highest eulogiums upon her majesty.*

30th April: *Houston is a much better place than I expected. The main street can boast of many well built brick and iron houses. It was very full, as it now contained all the refugees from the deserted town of Galveston. . . .*

As a great favor, my British prejudices were respected, and I was allowed a bed to myself; but the four other beds in the room had two occupants each. A captain whose acquaintance I had made in the cars, slept in the next bed to me. Directly after we got into bed a Negro came in, who, squatting down between our beds began to clean our boots. The Southerner pointed at the slave, and thus held forth; "Well, Kernel, I reckon you've got servants in your country, but not of that color. Now, sir, this is a real genuine African. He's as happy as the day's long; and if he was on a sugar plantation he'd be dancing half the night; but if

*you was to collect a thousand of them together, and fire one bomb in
amongst them, they'd all run like hell." The Negro grinned and seemed
quite flattered.*

The President's face went ashen. His worst fears had been confirmed.
He handed the telegram to Noah Brooks, a Washington newspaper
reporter and a confidant of the President. Lincoln had hounded the
telegraph office for news of Chancellorsville. Early in the day he had
confessed his growing suspicions to Brooks. Now he wrung his hands
and paced nervously. "Hooker's been licked, I tell you."

Brooks read the telegram and, even in its careful circumlocutions,
saw that Lincoln was right. General Joseph Hooker, "Fighting Joe,"
commanding the Army of the Potomac, had gone into Chancellorsville
on May 2, 1863, with 76,000 men to Lee's 43,000. He held a
two-to-one edge in artillery. Hooker had nonetheless managed to
wrest a stunning defeat from these favorable odds. His army had been
cut to shreds with 17,000 dead, wounded, or missing.

"My God, my God, Noah. What will the country say now?" Lincoln's
voice trembled. Brooks began to answer, but the mournful, remote
eyes told him that Lincoln was already lost in a private melancholy.

A poem then sweeping the country expressed the frayed patience of
the people in the North.

> *Is there never one in all the land,*
> *One on whose might the Cause may lean?*
> *Are all the common ones so grand,*
> *And all the titled ones so mean?*
> *What if your failure may have been*
> *In trying to make good bread from bran,*
> *From worthless metal a weapon keen?*
> *Abraham Lincoln, find us a man!*

The Army of the Potomac, the North's chief sword in this conflict,
was already under its fourth commander in two years. For all the blood
spilled, the Army had given the Union only the meager victory of Antietam. The South could look to Lee's brilliant chain of triumphs—First
and Second Manassas, the Peninsula, Shenandoah, Fredericksburg, now
Chancellorsville. The latest Union commander, "Fighting Joe" Hooker,
was now crouched north of the Rappahannock, licking his wounds.

"Abraham Lincoln, find us a man." But who, Lincoln wondered.

2 | INVASION

THE MILITARY and political arguments for invasion were compelling. Confederate victories on home soil had been impressive but inconclusive. The Southerners enjoyed initial advantages, but time worked against them.

Southern men, accustomed to outdoor living, at home on horseback, skilled with firearms, and steeped in a code of manly deportment, had adapted easily to soldiering. Union men, so many out of factories, offices, and shops, so ethnically diverse, made brave but less natural warriors. Furthermore, the Yankee fighting spirit had been undermined by rampant draft dodging, antiwar dissension back home, a business-as-usual casualness about the war, and especially by inept generals, most flagrantly those leading the Army of the Potomac, first the ineffectual Irvin McDowell, then the overcautious George McClellan, then the rash Ambrose Burnside, and now "Fighting Joe" Hooker, bellicose in name only. Yet, if it became a war of attrition, pitting the rural South against the industrial North, the larger human and material reserves above the Mason-Dixon line must inevitably grind the Rebels down to defeat. Hence the Confederate decision to invade.

Confederate emissaries in London and Paris encouraged the idea. A smashing defeat of the North in the North could turn the tide, could persuade the British Prime Minister, Lord Palmerston, and France's Emperor Napoleon III that a Southern victory was to their advantage. When that happened, recognition could bring in its wake a breaking of the blockade, perhaps loans for the depleted Confederate treasury, maybe even military intervention on the side of the South.

Late in May, General Robert E. Lee, commander of the Army of Northern Virginia, stood looking over a map spread out on a table in his Fredericksburg headquarters. Lee had weighed carefully the strategic merits of invading the North. "Will it succeed, General?" Lee's secretary, Colonel A. L. Long, asked.

Lee was slow to answer. He stroked his beard and said, "We have already shattered two Federal armies in the vicinity of Washington. If we should defeat General Hooker in that same vicinity, his army would also find refuge in that city, just as the other two had done. And consequently, the fruits of our victory would again be lost.

"But if we draw him away from the defense of his capital, if we can defeat him on a field of his own choosing, his army would be irretrievably lost. Our victory would produce results of the utmost importance.

"I should think such a battle should be fought somewhere here." His finger traced a small circle on the map roughly encompassing two small cities, York and Gettysburg, in Pennsylvania, near the Maryland border.

In mid-June the decision was made, the orders issued. The invasion of the United States of America by the Confederate States of America began. The order went out from General Lee to his three corps commanders, Generals James Longstreet, Richard Ewell, and A. P. Hill. Within Hill's corps, the order was passed on to three division commanders, Anderson, Pender, and Heth. Within Heth's division the order was passed down to the four brigade commanders. One of these four brigade commanders, General Archer, passed the order down to his five regimental commanders. In the 7th Tennessee Regiment the order went down from the regimental commander to the company commanders. Captain John Allen passed the order to a sergeant, who passed it on to Private Henry Raison. "Come on, Raison," the sergeant growled, "get your finger out. We're moving!"

The fighting near Winchester, Virginia, had ended in Confederate triumph. The Rebels continued to push north. Among them marched Wesley Culp of the Stonewall Brigade, closer to his Gettysburg home than he had been in years.

"Culp! Is that you?" The faint voice was familiar. Private Culp searched the Yankee prisoners lining the side of the road. He had heard that boys from Gettysburg were among the Union enemy at Winchester.

The frail voice called again. Wesley Culp traced it to a soldier lying flat on his back with his head propped against a knapsack, his upper sleeve torn and stiffened with blood. "It's me, Skelly."

Culp walked over and studied the man. "Jee-sus! Jack Skelly!"

The wounded man smiled weakly. "I couldn't be sure it was you with that beard you got." Actually, it was Culp's height that confirmed his identity for Skelly.

Culp knelt down and peered into a garish parody of the boyhood face he remembered. Black gunpowder ringed the soldier's mouth where he had bitten off the ends of cartridges while loading his musket. His eyes stared out like dying lamps from a skin gone deathly white.

"Is it bad, Jack?" Wesley took the man's limp hand.

"I dunno. I feel so weak." With his good arm he pointed to the wound in the other arm. "Can't seem to get a sawbones to take a look."

Wes gazed around him, then headed toward one of the Southern soldiers guarding the prisoners.

"Where's the hospital?"

The guard waved a finger toward a house set a distance back from the road.

"Be back, Jack." Culp set off toward the temporary field station. He soon returned with two reluctant Rebel stretcher bearers. "I found a Yankee doctor, Jack. He'll be waiting for you." Culp smiled and let his hand rest on Skelly's shoulder. Skelly smiled back gratefully. Wes Culp felt uneasy. The surgeon he had found had obviously been drunk.

As the bearers lifted the wounded man onto the stretcher, Skelly called, "Wait up, fellows, just a minute. Wes. Do one thing for me before you go. Will you please? Do you think you Rebs'll be passing through home?"

The word sent a shiver through Culp. "We might, don't know."

"Do you remember Jennie Wade?"

"Jennie?" Culp strained to pick the face from his past. "Guess I do."

"She's my girl. Give her this." Skelly slowly drew himself up to a sitting position on one elbow. He reached into his breast pocket and pulled out a wrinkled envelope.

Culp took the letter, shoved it inside his jacket, and ran to catch up with his company.

"Hey, Wes!" Skelly called feebly after him. "Forgot to tell you. Your brother Will's a lieutenant in our outfit." He could not tell if Wesley Culp did not hear him or did not want to.

From Colonel Fremantle's diary:

21st May *(near Vicksburg, Mississippi): My friend "Major" very kindly took me to dine with a neighboring planter, named Harrold, at whose house I met General Gregg, a Texan, who, with his brigade, fought the Yankees at Raymond a few days ago.*

After dinner, I asked Mr. Harrold to take me over to the quarters of his slaves, which he did immediately. The huts were comfortable and very clean. The Negroes seemed fond of their master, but he told me they were suffering dreadfully from the effects of the war—he had so much difficulty providing them with clothes. . . . I have often told these planters that I thought the word "slave" was the most repulsive part of the institution, and I have always observed they invariably shirk from using it themselves. They speak of their servant, their boy, or their Negroes, but never of their slaves. They address a Negro as boy or girl, or uncle or aunty. . . .

4th June Thursday (near Shelbyville, Tennessee): I did not see or hear of anybody being killed today, although there were a few wounded and some horses killed. Colonel Richmond and Colonel Webb were much disappointed that the inactivity of the enemy prevented my seeing the skirmish assume large proportions, and General Cheatham said to me, "We should be very happy to see you, Colonel, when we are in our regular way of doing business."

After waiting in vain until 5 P.M., and seeing no signs of anything more taking place, Colonel Richmond and I cantered back to Shelbyville. We were accompanied by a detachment of General Polk's bodyguard, which was composed of young men of good position in New Orleans. Most of them spoke in the French language, and nearly all had slaves in the field with them, although they ranked only as private soldiers, and had to perform the onerous duties of orderlies (or couriers, as they

*are called). . . . I took leave of General Polk before I turned in. His
kindness and hospitality had exceeded anything I could have expected. . . .*

*His aides-de-camp, Colonels Richmond and Yeatman, are also excel-
lent types of the higher class of Southerner. Highly educated, wealthy,
and prosperous before the war, they have abandoned all for their
country. They, and all the Southern gentlemen of the same rank, are
proud of their descent from Englishmen. They glory in speaking English
as we do, and that their manners and feeling resemble those of the upper
classes in the old country.*

What upset Robert Stiles most that day was that he had always
imagined a certain nobility in the Southern soldier. One evening on
the march north the Richmond Howitzers had pulled their guns onto
a common. As they began to heat their rations and water their horses,
an ambulance train rolled up filled with wounded Union prisoners.
The litter bearers unloaded the injured men from the wagon and left
them on the grass until a hospital tent could be raised. One Union
soldier, shot through the bowels, rolled about on the ground screaming in agony. "Please, somebody, put me out of my misery!" The
man clapped his hands over the wound, drew himself into a tight
ball, and shrieked in unending short bursts.

A hulking man with a sweat-stained shirt open to the waist pushed
his way through the crowd and stood over the writhing figure. "Put
you out of your misery, eh? Why certainly, sir." The huge soldier
brought his rifle butt crashing into the wounded man's skull. The
soldier looked around at the other Yankee wounded. "Any other
gentlemen here'd like to be accommodated?"

Before the stunned Stiles could fully grasp what had happened and
carry out his determination to shoot the killer on the spot, the soldier
had melted into the crowd.

Wayland Dunaway and Charles Wesley were almost the same age.
They had grown up on the same farm. As boys, they had boxed and
wrestled, hunted and fished together. Had anybody thought to ask
his relationship to Charles Wesley, Wayland Dunaway's immediate
answer would have been "friend." Dunaway would have found the
term "slave" repugnant, though in fact that is what Wesley was.

When Wayland Dunaway went to war, his family sent Charles
Wesley along with him. Charley became a great favorite of Dunaway's

comrades. He had a special way of cooking the "cush" which the Confederate soldiers enjoyed. Charley would fry the bacon first to get the grease out of it, then cut up cold beef, put it in bacon grease, add water, and then stew it. He would crumble in some corn bread and stew it all again until the water was boiled off. Dunaway's friends agreed that Charley made the best cush in the Confederate Army.

This day Charley took advantage of a lull in the march to launder his master's clothes. He crouched beside a stream pounding the thinning, frayed fabric against the rocks, shaking his head, thinking how Mister Wayland's once fine uniform had become little more than a rag.

Soon, just as he did on the eve of every other battle, Dunaway would send Charley to the rear, repeating the instructions as to what the slave was to do with his body, with the horse, with the valuables, just in case. The conversation always made Charley Wesley uncomfortable.

"I know, I know what to do," he protested softly.

This time Dunaway added something else. "We've crossed into Pennsylvania. Do you know what that means?"

Charley said nothing.

"It means you could run away. You'd be a free man."

"Darkies all know that, Mister Wayland," Charley shrugged. "Don't mean nothing to me."

Dunaway squeezed the black man's shoulder and headed back to his company.

The day had been clear and sun-filled, almost dissolving the pall of war. The men had earned it. The Confederate push north had gone with breathtaking speed. Now generals needed time to consolidate, to fix their strategies, to refresh men and horses.

The trees provided cool, shaded places for the crap games and chuck-a-luck, for reading the Bible, or sleeping. A team from the Stonewall Brigade took on the Louisiana boys in a baseball game in a cow pasture. The bat was a piece of broken fence rail. The ball was a walnut wrapped in yarn. Men disappeared repeatedly into the woods. They had found the cherry trees in Pennsylvania at their ripe, red peak. They had gorged themselves. When they finished, nothing remained, not a leaf, not a branch, not a limb, only the trunks.

A soldier darning his socks turned to the man stretched out on the ground beside him. "Hey, how's Richmond?"

"Didn't go to Richmond. Went to Petersburg."

"Well, how's Petersburg?"

"Lotta grouse, my friend." The soldier scratched idly at his crotch.

"Well don't just lay there itching your graybacks. Tell me about it."

The soldier propped himself up and grinned with nostalgic contentment. "Spent every damned cent I had. I had me three whores the last night. Cost eleven dollars."

"That's a month's pay. You didn't spend no eleven dollars."

"Shit, I didn't!" The man lay down again shading his eyes with his arm. "But I tell you, it's more dangerous there than being out here. Nine times out of ten you're going to get wounded with those ladies, and I don't mean just the clap, neither."

"Oh, sure. But damn!" The man rammed his hand into his repaired sock. "I ain't had me nothing for so long."

Early in the evening, after supper, the men gathered around a flatbed farm wagon to watch a play. The wagon provided the stage. This evening's performance was entitled "The Medical Board." The cast included a supposedly wounded soldier laid out in the wagon, his head resting on a canteen. Around him, seated on kegs and boxes, were three men playing surgeons. The surgeons dipped into an imaginary whiskey supply, supposedly reserved for medical purposes. As they pretended to pass the bottle around, they garrulously diagnosed the patient's needs:

1st Surgeon: "Gen'lmen, I say what this here boy needs is we got to amputate his legs." (He whipped out a huge carpenter's saw and pretended to sever both legs.)

Patient: "Sir, does that mean I can get a furlough?"

1st Surgeon: "Nonsense, boy, your services are indispensable."

2nd Surgeon: "I don't think that was his trouble." (Takes a large swig from the bottle.) "I say we got to amputate his arms." (The saw was passed to him and he went to work.)

Patient: "Now can I have a furlough?"

2nd Surgeon: "Reee-diculous! Your services are indispensable."

3rd Surgeon (lurching about with the bottle to his lips): "All wrong, all wrong. We got to amputate his head."

Patient: "Then I know I can have a furlough!"

3rd Surgeon: "Malingerer! We are so short that we need to prop up your body in the breastworks to fool the enemy."

The audience cheered and hooted and whistled.

As darkness descended, the men gathered in knots of ten and twenty while they kindled campfires. A Virginia private rose and drew a flute from his knapsack. He blew a few notes across it, which summoned the members of a regimental glee club. They began with "Her Bright Eyes Haunt Me Still." As their voices floated on the soft night air, total silence reigned among ten thousand men.

Jacob Hoke, merchant of Chambersburg, Pennsylvania, sat peering out the window waiting for his city to be invaded. Hoke felt reasonably calm. He and his partners in the dry-goods store had shipped the bulk of their merchandise off to Philadelphia. Some of it they had secreted in the barns and storm cellars of trusted farmers. The rest they stowed in a beer vault under the tavern next door.

Hoke could hear faintly the Confederate melody "The Bonny Blue Flag" floating up over the brow of the hill outside town. It was odd how so spirited a song could prompt such foreboding, Hoke thought. His fellow townspeople peered out, at first cautiously, then openly from windows and doorways on the edge of town. The onlookers were puzzled by the paradox that marched past their homes. These gaunt, filthy, ragged creatures seemed a rabble, not an army. There was no consistency in dress that merited the word "uniform." To describe these Confederates as men in "gray" was more symbolic convenience than descriptive fact. The Northern blockade had denied the South clothing dyes. The Southerners had, therefore, relied on whatever color sources they could manage, including walnut hulls. And so, many of the men moving past presented a yellowish brown color, known as butternut.

Their clothes hung loosely on lean, sunburned frames. Most were hatless. Those with headgear wore a motley assemblage of torn, shapeless felt hats and gray caps. Their shirts, many obviously homemade, were worn through at the elbows, patched and re-patched, stained and faded. Many carried a rolled-up carpet with a hole cut in the center which they would put their heads through and wear against the rain or cold weather. The one consistency was an inevitable toothbrush riding in a buttonhole or breast pocket.

The people of Chambersburg could not help noting, uncomfortably, how many of the enemy wore faded blue trousers, stripped, probably, from the Union dead at Chancellorsville, Antietam, and Fredericksburg. Many marched in bare feet.

Their wagon train displayed the same catchall irregularity, farm wagons, delivery vans, converted private carriages, hay carts, and many vehicles with the letters "U.S." painted over but still detectable.

Yes, Jacob Hoke thought, watching them pass his window, they had the outward appearance of a mob, but Hoke knew he was watching an army. The bare feet, the stolen pants, the frayed shirts, the hatless heads marched with a finely machined discipline. There was little talking in the ranks, few stragglers. And these serious, hard-faced Southerners were all well armed.

A busty, red-haired girl leaned out a window and shouted, "You look like a bunch of tramps. You don't scare us."

A Virginia soldier looked up and said coolly, "Lady, we always put on our dirty clothes when we're going to a hog-killing."

From Colonel Fremantle's diary:

> 27th June. *I entered Chambersburg, Pennsylvania, at 6 p. m. This is a town of some size and importance. All its houses were shut up; but the natives were in the streets, or at the upper window, looking in a scowling and bewildered manner at the Confederate troops, who were marching gaily past to the tune of "Dixie's Land." The women (many of whom were pretty and well-dressed) were particularly sour and disagreeable in their remarks. I heard one of them say, "Look at Pharaoh's army going to the Red Sea."*
>
> *Others were pointing and laughing at Hood's ragged Jacks, who were passing at the time. This division, well known for its fighting qualities, is composed of Texans, Alabamians, and Arkansians, and they certainly are a queer lot to look at. . . .*
>
> *One female had seen fit to adorn her ample bosom with a huge Yankee flag, and she stood at the door of her house, her countenance expressing the greatest contempt for the barefooted Rebs; several companies passed her without taking any notice; but at length a Texan gravely remarked, "Take care, madam, for Hood's boys are great at storming breastworks when the Yankee colors is on them." After this speech the patriotic lady beat a precipitate retreat.*

29th June: *I went into Chambersburg again, and witnessed the singular good behavior of the troops towards the citizens. . . . To anyone who has seen as I have the ravages of the Northern troops in Southern towns, this forebearance seems most commendable and surprising. Yet these Pennsylvanian Dutch don't seem the least thankful, and really appear to be unaware that their own troops have been for two years treating Southern towns with ten times more harshness. They are the most unpatriotic people I ever saw, and openly state that they don't care which side wins, provided they are left alone. They abuse Lincoln tremendously.*

The conversation nearly four thousand miles away would have excited Richmond. The reporter from the London *Morning Advertiser* had brought his interview with the leader of Her Majesty's loyal opposition around to the Civil War in America.

"What about recognition now, Mr. Disraeli, with the Confederates having invaded the North?"

"Of course." The Tory leader smiled. "But it is of great importance that if the move is made, it should not assume a party character. It is equally important that the initiative should come from outside, that is, from the opposition. If the thing is to be done, I must do it myself. From all I know and hear, the resolution will be carried. Lord Palmerston should be quite disposed to accept the decision by Parliament, especially since it will favor a policy which he personally approves."

From the letters of General Pickett:

My Dearest Sallie,

I never could quite enjoy being a "Conquering Hero." No, my Sallie, there is something radically wrong about my Hurrahism. I can fight for a cause I know to be just, can risk my own life and the lives of those in my keeping without a thought of the consequences; but when we've conquered, when we've downed the enemy and won the victory, I don't want to hurrah. I want to go off all by myself and be sorry for them—want to lie down in the grass, away off in the woods somewhere or in some lone valley on the hillside far from all human sound, and rest my soul and put my heart to sleep and get back something—I don't know what—but something I had that is gone from me—something subtle and unexplainable—something I never knew I possessed till I had lost it—till it was gone—gone.

Yesterday my men were marching victoriously through the little town of Greencastle, the bands all playing our glorious, soul inspiring, Southern airs: "The Bonny Blue Flag," "My Maryland," and the soldiers all happy, hopeful, joyously keeping time to the music, many following it with their voices, and making up for the want of the welcome they were receiving in the enemy's country by cheering themselves and giving themselves a welcome. As Floweree's band, playing "Dixie," was passing a vine-bowered home, a young girl rushed out on the porch and waved a United States flag. Then, either fearing that it might be taken from her or finding it too large and unwieldy, she fastened it around her as an apron, and taking hold of it on each side, and waving it in defiance, called out with all the strength of her girlish voice and all the courage of her brave heart:

"Traitors-traitors-traitors, come and take this flag, the man of you who dares!"

Knowing that many of my men were from a section of the country which had been within the enemy's lines, and fearing lest some might forget their manhood, I took off my hat and bowed to her, saluted her flag and then turned, facing the men who felt and saw my unspoken order. And don't you know that they were all Virginians and didn't forget it, and that almost every man lifted his cap and cheered the little maiden who, though she kept on waving her flag, ceased calling us traitors, till, finally, letting it drop in front of her, she cried out:

"Oh, I wish—I wish I had a Rebel flag—I'd wave that, too!"

The picture of that little girl in the vine-covered porch, beneath the purple morning glories with their closed lips and bowed heads waiting and saving their prettiness and bloom for the coming morn—of course, I thought of you, my beautiful darling. For the time, that little Greencastle Yankee girl with her beloved flag was my own little promised-to-be-wife, my Sallie, receiving from her soldier and her soldier's soldiers the reverence and homage due her.

We left the little girl standing there with the flag gathered up in her arms, as if too sacred to be waved, now that even the enemy had done it reverence.

Forever your devoted
Soldier

Greencastle, Pa., June 24, 1863

Lee's invasion plan had wedded simplicity to boldness. While, as he hoped, Hooker's army would remain in Virginia, Lee had struck north. On June 3, the first of Lee's troops had begun to pull away from their position opposite Hooker on the Rappahannock. The invasion path that Lee had laid out ran northeasterly through the Shenandoah and Cumberland valleys to Chambersburg, Pennsylvania, thence eastward to threaten Harrisburg, Philadelphia, Baltimore, with luck even New York City. If it succeeded, this bold stroke would also sever Washington from the rest of the North. The attraction of the valley route which Lee had chosen was that it put an almost continuous wall of mountains, the Blue Ridge range and then South Mountain, between him and any pursuing Union army up to the point where he would turn right and propel his army eastward.

As his intelligence antennae, Lee had dispatched his cavalry under General J. E. B. Stuart. The brilliant, flamboyant, thirty-year-old Stuart, known as "Beauty," had a dual assignment. Primarily, he was to screen Lee's army against any sudden attack by the Federals. But, within this basic mission, Lee gave Stuart considerable leeway. "Your progress and direction, of course, will depend upon the development of circumstances. If Harrisburg comes within your means, capture it."

The plan went off stunningly. Lee's army, with General Richard Ewell's Second Corps as the point of the lance, had moved swiftly up the Shenandoah Valley. Ewell's 23,000 men advanced two hundred miles in three weeks, rolling up Federal troops before them. Ewell had left Virginia, crossed the Potomac River, and driven through Maryland across the Pennsylvania border and into Chambersburg by June 15. By June 28, forward elements of Ewell's corps had plunged eastward and were peering across the Susquehanna River at Harrisburg on the opposite bank, preparing to capture the Pennsylvania capital.

Behind Ewell, Lee's Third Corps under General A. P. Hill came pouring north through the Shenandoah Valley, followed by the First Corps under General James Longstreet. By the end of June, Lee had all his infantry and artillery into Pennsylvania, with Ewell's corps poised at Harrisburg, Longstreet already at Chambersburg, and Hill at a tiny place called Cashtown, eight miles west of Gettysburg.

Lee assumed that his adversary, the Army of the Potomac under

General Hooker, was still burrowed in its camps in Virginia. If not, his cavalry chief would certainly have informed him of any change. Stuart had always done so in the past.

The first phase of Lee's daring initiative had succeeded beyond expectation. Now the major sweep to the east could begin. Then Lee received an unusual visitor.

The richness of the enemy country baffled the Confederates. Where in Pennsylvania were the scars and pain of two years of war? Where were the shattered and deserted farms as in Virginia, the wrecked towns of Mississippi and Louisiana, the hungry children and old people? Chambersburg, Pennsylvania, floated serenely on a green sea of un-perturbed plenty.

The Southerners felt no qualms about taking whatever they needed from this milk-and-honey-laden Canaan which endured war without suffering. They gladly seized as many provisions as they could, making the Union, as usual, their quartermaster. General Ewell laid a heavy requisition on Chambersburg: 5000 suits of clothing, 5000 bushels of grain, 100,000 pounds of bread. But the Rebels could not get a fraction of the requisition. The wily Yankees had stripped the city of everything that could be moved. Here, empty shelves spoke not of what they lacked, but of what they had hidden.

General Jubal Early, one of Ewell's division commanders, had advanced east, stopped briefly at Gettysburg, and went on to capture York. He, too, had been frustrated. The obviously comfortable people of Gettysburg had pleaded poverty and had already placed most of their goods out of sight. He passed through the town virtually empty-handed. But when he took York, Early did extract a useful $28,000 in good Union money from the town's citizens.

When another of Ewell's subordinates, General Edward Johnson, came upon a group of paroled Yankee prisoners, he ordered them to give up their shoes to his barefoot men. Some of his own soldiers thought this cruel. "Nonsense," Johnson snorted. "These men will be home soon and from the looks of the North, it hardly seems they'll go barefoot long."

The evident prosperity of the enemy countryside was proving a cruel test of the loyalty of these hungry, ragged Southerners. Since the invasion of the North, desertions had multiplied swiftly. On June 25, General Ewell held a court-martial at his headquarters in a lovely grove outside Chambersburg. Two deserters were tried that day. They were convicted of the reduced charge of absence without leave, a common remedy these days with so many men abandoning the ranks. There was little point in shooting deserters. The officers well knew why a brave man might still abandon his comrades. At this day's trials, one shame-stricken corporal uttered not a word in his defense. He was barely able to articulate an answer to the colonel's simplest questions. Finally, prompted by his company commander, he handed the officer a letter. The soldier had received it the day he had run away.

The colonel read it:

My Dear Edward:

I have always been proud of you, and, since your connection with the Confederate Army, I have been prouder of you than ever before. I would not have you do anything wrong for the world; but before God, Edward, unless you come home, we must die! Last night I was aroused by little Eddie crying. I called and said what is the matter, Eddie? And he said, "Oh Mamma, I am so hungry." And Lucy, Edward, your darling Lucy, she never complains but she is growing thinner and thinner every day. And before God, Edward, unless you come home, we must all die.

Your Mary

In front of the Chambersburg courthouse, a young, bearded Virginia lieutenant argued the causes of the war with an old gentleman of the town.

"Well." The old man shook his head. "I really don't understand why you are up here. What exactly is it you're fighting for, my boy?"

"Why, our rights, sir, our rights!"

"Indeed, indeed." The old man looked bemused. "I wasn't aware we had taken them away."

"No matter, now." The Virginian smiled, as another regiment in gray marched past. "The war can't last much longer. In fact, I hear tell where old Abe has had to run off to Boston since we invaded."

"Has he?" The old man's eyes widened in mock horror.

"Why? Isn't it true?"

"Not a word." The old man shook his head.

The younger man looked sorely disappointed. "Maybe we don't have Abe. But, truly, how much longer do you believe it can last?"

"As long as you Southern people are able to fight." The old man gestured toward the passing Confederate legions. "If you can stand it twenty years, why then, twenty years.

"You gentlemen must have seen for yourselves since you came here. There are any number of able-bodied men yet to draw upon. People around here have scarcely awakened to the fact that there is a war on.

"Let me put it this way, young man, if you were to annihilate our entire army, it would only bring out a larger one to take you on some morning before breakfast."

The young bearded Rebel bade the old gentleman a disconsolate good-bye. "I do believe, sir, there may be more truth than fun in what you say."

The commander of the Army of the Potomac, General Hooker, was not playing according to Lee's rules. His men were not holding in Virginia. Instead, with Lincoln's sharp prodding, they were shadowing Lee's northward advance.

Hooker had not initially started out on this tack. Early in June, he had dispatched a reconnaissance in force to tangle with the Confederates on the other side of the Rappahannock in the area of Culpepper, Virginia. Thus he learned that Lee was indeed headed north. But this remarkable intelligence did not spur Hooker to attack the invaders. Fighting Joe had quite another strategy. In fact, he had moved the bulk of his force off in the opposite direction. Hooker informed Lincoln that, with Lee invading the North, he should pull closer to Washington to protect the capital. And, with Lee removed from the scene, he could mount his forces for a strike on Richmond, the capital of the Confederacy.

The poverty of Hooker's military imagination staggered Lincoln. Though he was unschooled in military science, Lincoln had grasped that wars were won by destroying the enemy, and not by seizing sentimental geography. He responded to Hooker's proposal by telegram: "I think Lee's army, and not Richmond, is your true objective point."

Four days later Lincoln again sought to shove Hooker toward the enemy. In this exchange of correspondence, Lincoln asked, "Where is the Rebel army?"

Hooker replied: "The advance is at the fords of the Potomac and the rear at Culpepper Court House" (a distance of approximately seventy miles).

Lincoln to Hooker: "If the head of the animal is at the fords of the Potomac and the tail at Culpepper Court House, it must be very thin somewhere. Why don't you strike it?"

Lincoln's pressures finally pointed Hooker in the direction of the enemy. Fighting Joe began paralleling Lee's northward movement, keeping his army between the Confederate army and Washington. By June 28, when Lee assumed that the Union army was far to the south, still holed up in Virginia, Hooker was actually concentrated near Frederick, Maryland, closer, in fact, to the strung-out ends of Lee's army than these units were to each other.

Lee had been left virtually blinded by the failure of Jeb Stuart's cavalry to keep him informed of Union movements. Lee had given Stuart enough latitude to choose between two alternate routes for fulfilling his intelligence-gathering mission, one prosaic, the other potent with possibilities. Stuart could, once he detected Hooker on the move, proceed up the east side of the Blue Ridge Mountains, getting between the Confederate and Union armies. Or else he could leave only part of his cavalry for this routine screening while the rest of his horsemen could make a grand sweep around Hooker's rear, wreaking havoc, destroying enemy stores, and cutting communications. Then he could join Lee in Pennsylvania.

Stuart's flamboyant character left little doubt as to which alternative he would choose. But from the outset he ran into trouble. Hooker's surprisingly quick movement north had sealed off most of the Potomac crossings Stuart would have used. Instead, he had to loop farther to the east than he had intended, and he finally crossed the Potomac only about thirty-five miles from Washington. While he had expected to rejoin Lee within thirty-six hours, he was actually out of touch for a full week, leaving Lee sightless and, unknown to the Confederate commander, with the Union army perilously near.

The Union march north on the trail of the Confederates took the Second Corps of the Army of the Potomac over the twice-bloodied field of Bull Run.

"God damn! Did you see that?" A man near the head of the column pointed into a pasture. Protruding from the earth were the washed-white bones of a skeleton with a Union cap perched on the skull. An unnatural silence stilled the usual banter among the men as they passed by the corpse. As they pressed on, the field revealed more of the unburied victims from the fighting the year before. Soon the rag-clad skeletons began to number in the hundreds.

A soldier strayed out of the column into the field and picked up a skull. He tossed it to another man.

"Hey, Peters, this one looks just like you. Must be your brother."

"Nah." The fellow laughed, tossing it to another man. "He's got the colonel's smile."

Soon the skull was bobbing from man to man down the length of the column.

One soldier near the end of the line held the skull high and said, "Ladies and gentlemen, I give you the hero of the Battle of Bull Run."

"Yep," another man said, "it was so great the first time that they had to bring it back by popular demand."

The man tossed the skull back into the field. "Rest in peace, friend."

The standard offensive tactic when the War began was based on the range of the smoothbore musket, which was inaccurate and ineffective much beyond one hundred yards. Troops were massed shoulder to shoulder and hurled against the enemy. Since the men would be under effective fire for only the last one hundred yards, the objective was to overwhelm the enemy before too many losses could be inflicted.

Then came development of the rifled gun barrel. This weapon was similar to the smoothbore musket except that the inside of the barrel was grooved, or "rifled." The rifling spun the bullet around as it exited the barrel. The spinning reduced air friction and gave the rifled musket far greater range and accuracy. An infantryman could now pour deadly fire on a charging enemy for up to half a mile.

The massed charge, dating from the Napoleonic era, was now out of date but, unfortunately for the foot soldier, not out of use. Troops were still lined up and flung against the enemy, with this difference:

they were now under killing fire, not for one hundred yards, but for half a mile. The men moving north were soon to stage another practical demonstration of the murderous potential when the old tactics confronted the new weapons.

Among the Union troops following Lee's invaders were the men of the 20th Maine. As they marched, the dust was omnipresent, all-consuming. It clogged their nostrils, dried them out, and made the men feverish. It caked their teeth, their throats, and coated their eyes to near blindness. Dust invaded their ears, their hair. It permeated their clothes, mixed with the sweat on their wrists and ankles to form a rough abrasive. Their shoulders were chafed red and raw under a fifty-pound pack of ammunition, blankets, tents, and rations. The sun beat down, scalding and unrelenting through the dust, and tortured the men with thirst.

A man died easily on this march, effortlessly, empty of drama. Knees would buckle and the man would crumple to the ground, not a scream, not a moan, not a sound but the thump of his musket and body against the dirt road. The man's tongue would be thick and swollen, his mouth parched and lips cracked. Had someone peered into his face before he fell, he would have seen an opaque curtain descending over the man's eyes. But the men were not looking into other men's faces. No words were spoken. They marched silently, sullenly, eyes fixed hypnotically on the waves of dust swirling beneath their blistered feet.

As the column snaked north along the burning Maryland countryside, a blanket seemed an inconceivably useless burden. Soon the roadside was littered, first with blankets, then knapsacks, spare clothes, Bibles, everything but weapons, food, and canteens of precious water.

In their pockets the officers carried scribbled slips for men who had to relieve themselves or tend to bloodied feet, or for those who fell sick. The slips read: "The bearer has my permission to fall out of ranks, being unable to proceed with the regiment." These slips, worn and smudged with sweat, were prized. The provost guard dealt harshly with stragglers who could not produce this evidence of permission to fall behind.

The 20th Maine stopped near a stream and seized the opportunity to wash weeks of sweat and grime out of their clothes. They flew dampened shirts as homely banners from their bayonet points as they resumed marching.

They grasped at any shield to break the burning rays of the sun. Some fixed leaves around their caps. Some cut boughs from trees and shoved the branch down their backs, while the leafy part shaded their heads in bobbing rhythm with their footsteps.

Still the sun took its toll. On June 17, regimental commanders reported to the division commander, General Barnes, the price of the day's march. Hundreds had collapsed of sunstroke that day. Four had died. The general gave the men a full day of rest.

Then the march resumed. The book of the 20th Maine's adjutant recorded the ground covered: June 26, 20 miles; June 27, 20 miles; June 29, 18 miles; June 30, 23 miles; July 1, 26 miles. On the next day the 20th Maine would fight a battle.

The man was an ideal barroom companion, the Union major thought. His intent gaze, his faintly bemused expression, his modest, sincere laugh assured the major that whatever he told this civilian fellow was clever, worthy of attention, even as the major's tongue grew thick and clumsy. The man said little himself, except to prod the conversation along with an occasional question. Best of all, the man was not afraid to spend a dollar. He paid as a gentleman, unobtrusively, not letting cash intrude on good fellowship. He was one of a handful of civilians in the blue-coated crowd of officers that night at Willard's Hotel in Washington. He wore a brown tweed suit, well cut, obviously expensive but subdued. He had a brown beard, was rather stoop-shouldered, his face sensitive to the point of delicacy, a small man. The major had not asked his name and did not care.

As he mentally sifted the ramblings of the drunken Union officer, the civilian thought, half annoyed, half relieved, how odd that he was never recognized. Few Union officers, evidently, were playgoers. The major's quiet companion was James Harrison, at twenty-eight already a seasoned Shakespearean, much admired as the "juvenile tragedian." Harrison was also a Confederate spy, in Washington on the orders of General Longstreet. Though a Baltimorean, James Harrison's sympathies were thoroughly Southern. He had been commissioned in the Confederate Army and became associated with James A. Seddon, the

Confederate Secretary of War, a man deeply enmeshed in espionage. Seddon had referred Harrison to General Longstreet in the spring of 1863, as the Confederate plan of invasion was being drawn. Harrison came to Longstreet with an astonishing reputation for ferreting out enemy movements. His information was invariably confirmed as correct. Skeptical officers wondered whether Harrison was too good to be true. The remarkable precision of his reports inevitably raised suspicions that he played both sides.

During that spring meeting, Longstreet had instructed Harrison to pass through the Union lines to Washington and remain there through the latter part of June—"Until you are in possession of information which will be of value to us."

Harrison remembered with lingering resentment Longstreet's curt answer when he had asked, "Where shall I find you, General, to make this report?" His command was large enough to be found without difficulty, Longstreet had replied. And he, naturally, was to be found with his command. In spite of fierce, demonstrated loyalty, grave risks run, and an unblemished record of performance, Harrison was, in the eyes of his fellow officers, after all, still a spy.

The Union major at the bar was bellowing now, attracting stares. Harrison became uneasy. No more was to be wrung from this injudicious braggart. Harrison had worked several of the capital's saloons that night, drank a bit too much perhaps in each, practically exhausted the $150 the Confederates paid him monthly in gold and Union greenbacks. But his practiced piecing together of a fact here, an innuendo there, a boast from one officer, the gripe of another had produced an astonishing, however incomplete, picture. Contrary to conventional speculation, Federal troops were not moving south against Richmond. Hooker was moving north against Lee. He had, in fact, already crossed the Potomac. It was time for Harrison to find Longstreet and deliver this startling intelligence. He slid some crumpled bills onto the bar, muttered, "Pleasure, Major, real pleasure," and moved on.

The Iron Brigade. They gloried in the name. If Hooker had done little else for the Army of the Potomac, he had fittingly knighted these troops. Before the battle at South Mountain in the fall of '62, they had been a loose band of undistinguished regiments from Wisconsin, Michigan, and Indiana linked into a brigade. They had advanced up the mountainside, taking heavy punishment, pushing forward inexorably. That night, the brigade's commander, General John Gibbon, swelled proudly as Hooker told him, "A fine peformance today, Gibbon. What I saw on that hillside was an iron brigade." Gibbon repeated the phrase to his staff. The staff spread the word to the regiments and the men passed it around the campfires that night. It stayed.

It was now nine months since their christening at South Mountain. The Iron Brigade formed part of the Union mass shadowing Lee's invading army northward. After days of forced marches, they finally rested at Guilford Station. The soldiers lolling along the roadside watched the Officer of the Day march a prisoner detail past them. Enclosed within its ranks, a young, fleshy soldier stumbled along miserably. The youth's uniform strained to cover rounded arms and legs. A belt of fat showed between his short jacket and sagging pants. The boy's hat perched precariously atop a head of curly hair. He seemed an outsize cherub stuffed into uniform. Only the dark, sleepless eyes detracted from a picture of pink innocence.

Lieutenant Colonel Rufus Dawes, commanding the 6th Wisconsin, came out of his tent at the request of the Officer of the Day. "Yes, Lieutenant, what is it?"

"This here man was caught sleeping on picket duty." The lieutenant paused and added menacingly, "In the presence of the enemy."

The offense carried a penalty of death. Colonel Dawes, his annoyance scarcely concealed, looked at the child before him. The boy, he knew, represented an exception to the substitute-buyers, bounty jumpers, deserters, and draft dodgers now living freely by the hundreds of thousands in the North. Yet he had fallen asleep on guard duty, with the enemy nearby. He should be shot.

"Very good, Lieutenant, you are dismissed. Leave the prisoner with me."

The lieutenant's brow rose in suspicion. He saluted with an insolent snap and marched the guard detail off.

"Son, this is terrible business." Colonel Dawes looked hard into the boy's eyes. The boy stared down at his feet. "You have placed me in a terrible position." Dawes spoke in a fatherly tone of the soldier's responsibility to his comrades, of the potential calamity of his offense. All that the boy sensed of it was that he was not going to die.

A great grin broke over his smooth, beardless face. "Thank you, thank you kindly, Colonel. You won't regret this kindness. No sir. You're going to see a real soldier now." He gave a fumbling salute and lumbered back toward his company.

General George Gordon Meade was in an ugly mood, a not uncommon state for this dyspeptic soldier. Saturday night, June 27, marked two weeks since Meade had last seen his superior, General Joe Hooker. His ignorance of his expected role in this northward march, or his relation to the other units, even the location of the rest of the army offended Meade's passion for order. He had driven his 5th Corps long and hard this day and bivouacked the men near a stream south of Frederick, Maryland. Exhausted though he was, Meade had spent the night searching the countryside for Hooker. To no avail. He stomped back to his tent, flung off his wrinkled, mud-spattered clothes, and fell into a fretful sleep.

It was shortly past midnight when Colonel James A. Hardie, in civilian clothes, descended wearily from the train at Frederick. He looked about with dismay. The station was draped in drunken soldiers, most of them too far gone to bait even such a tempting target as an elegantly attired civilian. Hardie had to locate General Meade and had not the slightest idea where to begin.

Hours before, Colonel Hardie had been summoned at the end of a conference at the War Department between President Lincoln and Secretary of War Stanton. It had been a morose, dispirited session. The Confederate Army, after an almost unbroken string of victories, had successfully invaded the North, and Lincoln had a dud commanding the Union forces. All of Lincoln's pleas for Hooker to attack had been countered by the general's requests for more troops, the same disease that Lincoln had dubbed "McClellanitis" in an earlier commander of the Army of the Potomac.

The President and the Union General-in-Chief, General Henry Halleck, had, therefore, deliberately maneuvered Hooker into a position from which Hooker's pride compelled him to ask to be relieved of his command. His request was granted instantly.

The discussion of a successor went aimlessly on. Stanton did the talking. Lincoln, gloomy, made only perfunctory remarks. General

John Reynolds and General Darius Couch had already turned down the proffered command. When all other possibilities had been considered, Stanton pursed his lips thoughtfully and said, with no great enthusiasm, "I can find no fault with George Meade. He's a Pennsylvanian, too."

Lincoln dwelled on the name, then nodded. "He will fight well on his own dunghill."

They called General Halleck into the room to execute the paper work. Halleck then summoned Colonel Hardie to deliver the orders to General Meade.

Now Hardie stood alone in the middle of the night somewhere in Maryland trying to find General George Meade to advise him he was the new Commander in Chief of the Army of the Potomac. Hardie bitterly regretted the decision that he travel in civilian clothes. The drunken troops ignored him or cursed him when he demanded their help. For a larcenous price, Hardie finally commissioned a surly buggy driver to aid him.

At three a.m. on June 28, Hardie located the tents of the 5th Corps. Meade's staff officers balked at letting Hardie into Meade's tent, since he refused to divulge his mission.

"Gentlemen," Hardie said, jaw set firmly, "I come direct from Washington to deliver President Lincoln's personal message to General Meade. If you will please stand aside." His tone carried an undeniable authority. They let him pass.

"General Meade, General Meade." Hardie shook the sleeping man's shoulder lightly. Meade's eyes popped open.

"I'm Colonel Hardie, General, War Office staff."

"Yes, yes, what is it?" The voice had a whining quality that surprised Hardie.

"I'm afraid"—Hardie smiled slowly—"I've come to give you some trouble, General."

Meade knew. In this politics-ridden army, at last it had happened. Someone, Hooker probably, had ordered him arrested on some baseless charge. "Rest assured, Colonel, my conscience is clear and I am quite prepared for whatever might come," he said with weary resignation. Meade swung his legs out of the cot to the ground.

Hardie lit the candle on a small table next to Meade's cot. "Not that sort of trouble, General, please read this." Meade stared uncomprehending at Lincoln's brief letter, waiting for his eyes to become accustomed to the candlelight.

He stood up, dun-colored underwear sagging about his lank legs. His face twisted in peevish annoyance. His prominent eyes protruded like hard, ivory orbs. He paced the tent. His voice took on an unpleasant petulance all too familiar to his staff. "Why me? Why not Reynolds? I don't know the Army's position. I don't know its plans. I don't know if it has any plans!" The eyes bulged accusingly at Hardie. "I am going to wire General Halleck my request to be excused." He sat at the small table and angrily seized a pencil.

Colonel Hardie leaned on the table and looked directly into those formidable eyes. "Sir, if I may say so, it won't do any good. There is not an objection that they have not already anticipated."

Meade's arms dropped to his sides. "Well," he said wearily, "I've been tried and condemned without a hearing and I suppose I shall have to go to the execution." George Meade had become the fifth commander of the Army of the Potomac.

Not far off, that same evening of June 28, Meade's counterpart, the Confederate commander, General Robert E. Lee, the soul of dignity, was suffering a severe bout of soldierly but undignified diarrhea. As the men put it, "Marse Robert has got the shits." Lee exhausted himself with endless trips behind his tent to the latrine in the woods. He had turned in early, worn out that night, but at ten p.m. was awakened by a sharp rapping on the tent pole.

"Major Fairfax, sir."

Lee fairly bolted from the cot and reflexively began buttoning his jacket. "What is it?"

The major spilled out his message. Lee frowned. The reports of spies were not the sort of information upon which Robert E. Lee liked to act.

"I have no faith in any scout, Major. What do you make of this Harrison person?"

"I don't know, sir. General Longstreet is quite high on him."

"I know, I know. Well, let's have a look at him."

The small, slope-shouldered man brought before General Lee wore a well-cut but now badly wrinkled, dirt-caked, and dampened brown suit.

From the saloons of Washington up through the Maryland and Pennsylvania countryside, during a long day blurred by heat and a night blackened by rain squalls, James Harrison had carried his incendiary burden, the knowledge which he alone possessed of the approximate strength and closeness of the converging Rebel and Union forces. Harrison had borne this priceless cargo through enemy towns, past Yankee farmers and Union troops, and, no less perilous, through the Confederate lines. Using his acting skills, he had fitted his role to the varying suspicions he had to allay. His art was an odd and unappreciated armament for a commissioned Confederate officer, Harrison had thought with a secret pride. Now he stood before an audience of one to perform a role made no less simple by the fact that what he spoke was truth. He could not help noticing that Robert E. Lee refused to look at him directly.

Harrison delivered his report to Lee concisely, unemotionally, with an understated authority. Still, the Southern commander found his characteristic courtesy taxed in dealing with the spy. "Very good, Mr. . . . Mr.?"

"Harrison, sir."

"Yes, of course, Harrison. Then I am to understand that the Union Army is well north of the Potomac?"

"Yes, sir. They crossed, I believe, the twenty-sixth. I caught up with them at Frederick. When I last saw them they had reached South Mountain."

"And General Hooker has been replaced by General Meade?"

"That's right, sir. He was informed early this morning," Harrison reported, repeating the rumor he had gathered on the journey north.

"Very good, thank you . . . ah . . . Harrison."

The spy hesitated an instant. His eyes searched Lee's face vainly for a flicker of approval. Then he turned and wordlessly left the tent.

With Harrison gone, Major Fairfax saw a rare look of anxiety pass over Lee's face. Maybe it was just the damned sickness acting up, Fairfax thought, as Lee excused himself and headed again for the back of the tent.

The new commander of the Army of the Potomac was a forty-eight-year-old West Pointer born, by accident of his merchant father's profession, in Cadiz, Spain. George Meade had shown no particular promise as either scholar or soldier at West Point. His appointment had been wangled by his mother, a clever, ambitious woman. She saw the academy as an economical yet socially advantageous way to educate her son after her husband had died, leaving the family in straitened circumstances. Meade married well after graduation and, with one brief civilian interlude, pursued his army career as a topographical engineer. Ten years out of West Point, George Meade was still a second lieutenant.

By the time the War began, Meade had risen to captain and was in charge of surveying the Great Lakes. He itched to get into a line command, where he knew the stream of promotion would run more swiftly. His own efforts to trade his surveyor's transit for a sword failed utterly. In the politically charged Union Army, Meade, a capable if colorless officer, still had to advance through influence. Through his wife's social and political connections, Meade landed command of a brigade of Pennsylvania reserves and a general's star. He demonstrated solid competence in the Peninsula campaign, at Second Bull Run, and at Chancellorsville, where he had argued for attack while his superior, Fighting Joe Hooker, counseled retreat.

The fratricide of civil war was literal in the Meade family. George Meade's two sisters lived in the South. One was married to a Confederate Navy lieutenant. The other was mistress of a Mississippi plantation which had been overtaken by the Union Army. One of her sons had been killed in the fighting of 1862. Another son died in battle against his Uncle George at Chancellorsville. Charlotte Meade Ingraham poured out her bitterness in a letter to a friend. With Lee now in the North, she prayed he would be "swarming and pillaging" Pennsylvania. "If only New York could be fired, I think I would feel better."

As a soldier, her brother was capable but not brilliant, more analytic than intuitive, more cautious than aggressive. Meade inspired respect, but little warmth. In the ranks there was open disappointment that he, and not the adored McClellan, was to be General Hooker's successor.

The new commander was tall, and aristocratically lean. Large, protruding eyes and a great Roman nose dominated his gaunt face. Meade was alternately frosty and reserved, or irascible and petulant. His habitual expression was that of a professor with nerves worn thin by rowdy students. To the staff officers who had to work closely with him, his random bursts of temper were like a bomb thrown in their midst, injuring guilty and innocent alike. He was known behind his back as "the snapping turtle." But since his rages were aimed, democratically, at all, they caused little personal animosity. He was able, brave, scrupulously honest, and within a tight inner circle of his aides he enjoyed a certain grudging affection.

The man now most affected by the character of George Gordon Meade said, upon learning of his appointment, "General Meade will commit no blunder in my front, and if I make one, he will make haste to take advantage of it." The knowledge that it was Meade that he now faced shaped Robert E. Lee's decision to halt his advance through Pennsylvania and to consolidate his forces near Gettysburg.

"Battery B fall in for rations," the company orderly sang out. "Cub" Buell felt too exhausted to join the ragged line standing with tin cups and haversacks in hand.

Cub had won his nickname with a single punch. The fresh-cheeked, dark-haired youth of nineteen was one of several volunteers mixed with longtime army regulars in Battery B, 4th United States Artillery. His face expressed a simultaneous innocence and pugnacity. His five-foot-seven-inch frame exuded unspent vigor. Buell's favorite entrance was to report to his position doing a handspring over the gun mount.

He also fancied himself a boxer. One afternoon, after easily out-boxing two other young volunteers, Buell decided to test a long-sim-mering ambition. Jim Cahill, an old army regular, bull-like, impassive, was easily the strongest man in the battery.

"Come on, Cahill," Buell had taunted the old gunner. "Let's see if you regulars really got the gunpowder in your blood."

"Ah, Buell, quit your gassing. I don't want to hurt you. You ain't nothing but a cub." Cahill began to walk off.

"I heard that excuse before."

Cahill turned, face still stony. He came back and slowly pulled on a pair of gloves. He ambled over to the crouching, dancing Buell. Cahill's fist struck Buell's beardless chin like a thunderbolt. The young volunteer staggered back six feet and crumpled into a heap. He was "Cub" Buell thereafter.

On this night, after the punishing march into Pennsylvania, even Cub Buell's well of energy had been drained. He wanted nothing but sleep. Another old regular who looked after the boy, Corporal Pat Packard, grabbed Cub's arm and pulled him into line. "Cub, you stay here and draw all the grub they'll give you, son. I expect we'll be fighting for a time and you won't get any more while that's going on." Cub drew the regulation twenty-seven cakes of hardtack, nine spoonfuls of sugar, nine of coffee, and a small piece of dried meat—rations for three days.

Packard and Buell took their rations and settled themselves near a fire. The conversation was desultory, the fragmented ruminations of weary, exhausted men.

"Pat," a man said, sitting down next to Packard, "think we'll get licked again?"

Packard sipped carefully at the scalding tin of coffee. "We? We ain't been licked yet, man for man. But we sure's hell been outgeneraled every time."

"Yes indeedy. Got a point there." The man nodded. "I don't call Burnside no general. He was a blamed butcher!"

"And," Packard snorted, "Chancellorsville was no battle, it was a massacre."

"This Army of the Potomac is being murdered by inches, I tell you, by stupidity."

The other man's voice lowered to a whisper. "If we get whipped here, and I pull through alive, I'm making tracks for home. And the provost guard be damned."

No one else seemed surprised, but such talk made young Cub Buell uncomfortable.

Over nine hundred horse-drawn ambulances accompanied the Army of the Potomac. One driver and two stretcher bearers rode each ambulance. The wagons were covered with white canvas stretched over bows. When parked together, the ambulances presented a billowy sea of white. A leather-upholstered seat ran the length of each side of the wagon. A similar seat, which could be raised or lowered, ran down the center. Thus, with the center seat raised, six to eight lightly wounded could be seated on the sides of the wagon. With the center seat lowered, three seriously wounded could be stretched out lengthwise. At the tail end of the wagon, under each seat, was a water keg with a protruding spout. The ambulance was supplied with beef stock, bandages, and medicines. Hanging along each side of the wagon was a canvas-covered stretcher.

Lee had not dared to gamble against the veracity of the report given him by the spy Harrison. If true, he had his own army now scattered over forty-five miles of Pennsylvania, while his enemy was massed in his rear not forty miles away. No longer did he face the irresolute braggart Hooker, but the sober, deliberate, intelligent Meade.

Lee paced back and forth before his tent. His officers eyed him silently, uneasily. He stopped and turned toward them. The concern that had briefly clouded Lee's face disappeared. He addressed them with his usual confidence.

"The enemy is a long time finding us, isn't he? Well, then, if he will not find us, then we shall have to find him. Gentlemen, tomorrow, instead of proceeding further north to Harrisburg as we had planned, we will go over towards Gettysburg and see what General Meade is after."

Lee fired off couriers to direct Ewell to reverse his march and rejoin the rest of the army in the vicinity of Cashtown eight miles west of Gettysburg. He ordered his other two corps commanders, Hill and Longstreet, to leave their refuge behind South Mountain and also to converge on Cashtown. Only Pickett's division was left behind to guard the supply train at Chambersburg. Lee's new intent was to coil the dispersed Confederates into a tight, hard muscle, draw out the Yankees, and deal them a death blow.

He turned away to enter his tent. He pulled General Heth aside. The anxiety returned to his face. "Harry," he pleaded, "where is Stuart?" Lee had not heard from his gaudy cavalry chief for days.

Heth could well understand Lee's apprehension. An army without cavalry was a groping man denied hearing and sight. Yet Lee was still determined to precipitate a battle. Even had Stonewall Jackson lived, Heth thought, Robert E. Lee was still the most aggressive man in the Confederate Army.

Most of the Union soldiers sat quietly as the young officer droned out General Meade's first order to the men of the Army of the Potomac. A few made sneering jests. Most listened carefully. This was a new commander speaking to them on a different battleground. ". . . The enemy is on our soil." The officer's reedy voice barely carried across the regiment. ". . . The whole country now looks anxiously to this army to deliver it from the presence of the foe. . . . Homes, firesides, altars are involved. The Army has fought well heretofore: it is

believed that it will fight more desperately and bravely than ever. . . .
Corps and other commanders are authorized"—the adjutant cleared
his throat—"Corps and other commanders are authorized to order the
instant death of any soldier who fails in his duty at this hour . . . by
command of Major General Meade."

"That last part sure makes a man want to fight for the Union," a
soldier muttered.

"Yes, it does indeed." His neighbor nodded. "If you don't get out
there and get shot, you're gonna be shot."

They both laughed, and then became silent, remembering what
they had seen months before. They had stood with the division,
drawn up into a hollow square, with only the desolate wail of the
bandsmen playing the dead march breaking the morning's silence.
Two flatbed wagons rumbled through an opening in one end of the
human square. On the back of each wagon a condemned deserter sat
on the edge of a pine coffin. Their shoulders were slumped. They
looked neither right nor left. If any expression could be read in their
faces, it was only a dull embarrassment.

The wagons halted before two fresh graves dug that morning. The
guard detail jumped off the back of the wagons and slid the coffins to
the ground in front of the graves. The guards blindfolded the prisoners and tied their arms behind their backs. A sergeant pinned a piece
of white paper over their hearts.

An officer read the sentence loud enough for the entire division to
hear. The chaplain whispered to each of the men, opened the Bible,
and read a prayer. Some of the troops bowed their heads stiffly. The
chaplain stepped aside. A firing squad faced each of the condemned
men. The provost marshal raised his arm in a ready signal. He
dropped his arm and the guns sputtered. One man fell writhing on
top of the coffin. The other man was not struck. A groan went up
from the troops. The unharmed man managed to work his hands free
and tore off the blindfold. He looked about, blinking and bewildered. The guards grabbed him, tied his arms again and replaced the
blindfold.

The wounded man was propped upright on the edge of the coffin.
The firing squad let go a second salvo. The wounded man fell, struck
again. The other man was still unhit, but now gibbering hysterically.

On the third salvo, the wounded man was killed and fell into the
coffin. The previously unharmed man was slightly wounded. He

struggled desperately to free his hands. The provost marshal, red-faced and fuming, ordered every man in the firing squad to come up individually and fire point blank at the prisoner's head. The condemned man flinched with the click of each trigger. Not a gun fired. Rain had dampened the powder. The provost marshal angrily yanked his revolver from its holster. He set it against the man's forehead and emptied the gun. The prisoner tumbled back into the coffin and lay motionless.

"No sir, I never want to see me another firing squad." The soldier shook his head. "I'd rather stick it out here. At least the Rebs would do a neater job."

The general's aide, curious to see the war through the eyes of the enemy, had bought the newspaper from a farmer coming up the road from Gettysburg to Cashtown. The aide sat down in the shade of the general's tent fly and studied the masthead of the weekly Gettysburg *Compiler,* dated June 29. He liked the subtitle, "A Democratic and Family Journal." The front page carried a story of Ewell's men driving the Yankees out of Winchester two weeks before. The aide was agreeably surprised at the objective treatment. Page three reported the "Invasion of Pennsylvania" and told of the Southern cavalry's penetration as far as Mercersburg.

The general's aide glanced at an ad for "The Excelsior Washer, the most perfect labor-saving washing machine ever invented. Price $8." More intriguing was the advertisement of R. F. McIlheny's store. The firm boasted a whole new line of boots and shoes, balmorals, Wellington boots, Congress gaiters, brogans. This, the general's aide thought, may be the most interesting news in the Gettysburg *Compiler,* He took the paper in to General Heth.

From Colonel Fremantle's diary:

> 30th June: *This morning, before marching from Chambersburg, General Longstreet introduced me to the Commander in Chief. General Lee is, almost without exception, the handsomest man of his age I ever saw. He is fifty-six years old, tall, broadshouldered, very well made, well set up—a thorough soldier in appearance; and his manners are most courteous and full of dignity. He is a perfect gentleman in every respect. I imagine no man had so few enemies, or is so universally*

esteemed. Throughout the South, all agree in pronouncing him to be as near perfection as a man can be. He has none of the small vices, such as smoking, drinking, chewing, or swearing and his bitterest enemy never accused him of any of the greater ones.

He generally wears a well-worn long gray jacket, a high black felt hat, and blue trousers tucked into his Wellington boots. I never saw him carry arms; and the only mark of his military rank are the three stars on his collar.

. . . We marched six miles on the road towards Gettysburg, and encamped at a village called (I think) Greenwood. . . . In the evening General Longstreet told me that he had just received intelligence that Hooker had been disrated, and that Meade was appointed in his place. Of course he knew both of them in the old army, and says that Meade is an honorable and respectable man. . . .

I had a long talk with many officers about the approaching battle, which evidently cannot now be delayed long, and will take place on this road instead of in the direction of Harrisburg, as we had supposed. Ewell, who has laid York as well as Carlisle under contribution, has been ordered to reunite. Everyone, of course, speaks with confidence.

From *At Gettysburg, or What a Girl Saw and Heard of the Battle,* by Tillie Pierce Alleman:

We were informed they had crossed the Stateline, then were at Chambersburg, then at Carlisle, then at or near Harrisburg, and would soon have possession of our capital. . . .

A week had hardly elapsed when another alarm beset us. "The Rebels are coming! The Rebels are coming!" was passed from lip to lip. And all was again consternation.

We were having our regular literary exercises on Friday afternoon (June 26) at our Seminary, when the cry reached our ears. Rushing to the door and standing on the front portico, we beheld in the direction of the Theological Seminary, a dark dense mass, moving toward town. Our teacher, Mrs. Eyster, at once said: "Children, run home as quickly as you can." . . .

I had scarcely reached the front door, when, on looking up the street, I saw some of the men on horseback. I scrambled in, slammed shut the door and hastening to the sitting room, peeped out between the shutters.

What a horrible sight! There they were, human beings clad almost in rags, covered with dust, riding wildly, pell-mell down the hill toward our home, shouting, yelling most unearthly, cursing, brandishing their revolvers, and firing right and left. . . .

Soon the town was filled with infantry and then the searching and ransacking began in earnest. They wanted horses, clothing, anything and almost everything they could conveniently carry away. . . .

Upon the report of, and just previous to this raid the citizens had sent their horses out the Baltimore Pike, as far as the Cemetery. There they were to be kept until those having the care of them were signaled that the enemy was about, when they were to hasten as fast as possible in the direction of Baltimore. Along with this party Father sent our own horse, in charge of the hired boy we then had living with us. They overtook the boys with the horses, captured and brought them all back to town. As they were passing our house my mother beckoned to the raiders, and some of them rode over to where she was standing and asked what was the matter. Mother said to them: "You don't want the boy! He is not our boy, he is only living with us." One of the men replied: "No we don't want the boy; you can have him; we are only after the horses."

About this time the boy's sister, who was standing a short distance off, screamed at the top of her voice to Mother: "If the Rebs take our Sam, I don't know what I'll do with you folks!" Thus holding us responsible for her brother's safety even in times like that. . . .

About one-half hour after this some of these same raiders came back, and, stopping at the kitchen door, asked Mother for something to eat. She replied: "Yes, you ought to come back and ask for something to eat after taking a person's horse." She nevertheless gave them some food, for Mother always had a kind and noble heart even toward her enemies.

Their manner of eating was shocking in the extreme. As I stood in a doorway and saw them laughing and joking at their deed of the day, they threw the apple butter in all directions while spreading their bread. I was heartily glad when they left. . . .

"What a filthy, dirty looking set! One cannot tell them from the street!" Mother said.

To the Southern cavalryman his horse was an extension of himself. Confederate cavalry charged with sabers slicing the air, a magnificent pageant. The drama was performed with consummate ease by men raised in the saddle. But to General John Buford, commander of the First Division Cavalry Corps, Army of the Potomac, a horse was strictly transportation. Buford was quick to see the inappropriateness

Advertisement in the Gettysburg Compiler, *dated June 29, 1863.*

of knightly horse warfare for Northern soldiers. Instead, he developed the concept of cavalry as mounted infantry.

Under Buford's method, horses sped the men to the scene of battle, where they dismounted. Every fourth man stayed in the immediate rear to hold four horses. Each horse holder thus freed three other men to form an infantry skirmish line. At an instant's notice, the men could run back to their horses and speed to new positions. The power of Buford's cavalry was further intensified by the new weapon many of them carried, the fast-loading Spencer repeating rifle.

The value of Buford's cavalry technique had been dramatically demonstrated just before Second Manassas when 3000 of his dismounted horsemen had stood off 27,000 Confederates for six hours.

Now his men and his methods were about to be tested again. The First Union Cavalry was headed for Gettysburg to provide the outer shield of Meade's army.

"Splendid, splendid," General Heth said when his aide pointed out to him R. F. McIlheny's advertisement in the Gettysburg *Compiler*. If there were shoes there, General Heth wanted them. He dispatched General J. Johnston Pettigrew's brigade to get them. Pettigrew's troops were then bivouacked eight miles from Gettysburg in tiny Cashtown.

The morning of June 30 was already hot as they started on the mission. But the journey was virtually a stroll after the forced marches the men had undergone over the past month. Halfway to Gettysburg, a courier came galloping up to Pettigrew. "General, there's enemy cavalry between us and the town." Pettigrew knew General Lee's instructions. Battle was not to be provoked prematurely. He turned his brigade around and headed back to Cashtown.

General Heth was bitterly disappointed. He wanted those shoes. In the evening he went to his superior, General A. P. Hill. The two men discussed the potential enemy strength at Gettysburg. Hill agreed that besides the cavalry detachments on reconnaissance, the only other likely enemy were local militia. Small obstacles, Heth ventured. He persuaded General Hill to let him make another try for the shoes the next day. This time he would send four brigades.

General John Buford's cavalrymen were stretched like a thin membrane between the main Federal army and the Confederate enemy northwest of Gettysburg. Buford's scouts had spotted some Confederates that morning coming down the road from Chambersburg toward Gettysburg. But the Confederates had turned back when they saw the Union cavalry. Knowing the enemy to be so near, Buford fanned his men out in a sweeping arc from the north of Gettysburg down to the west about a mile and a half from town. This five-mile perimeter stretched his three thousand men perilously taut. In a fight, a quarter of these men would be tied up holding the horses for the other men. Buford had only six cannon. If anything happened, he could conduct nothing more than a holding action.

3 | THE FIRST DAY

IT WAS 5:20 IN THE MORNING, July 1, 1863. Corporal Alphonse Hodge peered into a fine mist. First light was just beginning to define the trees and barns and the Chambersburg Pike, which he was guarding. Hodge's advance picket of four men would soon be relieved. Soon they could appease the hunger that had been building through the night. In a few minutes, they would fry up some hardtack in bacon and wash it down with a scalding tin of coffee.

All night Hodge had goaded his men to keep sharp, to fight off sleep. Several times he had gone to splash his face in the cooling waters of Willoughby Run. Out there somewhere to the west was the Confederate army. If it moved, its likely path was down this road. The pike of stone and gravel was one of the few hard-surfaced roads running into Gettysburg.

Hodge suddenly stiffened. His heart raced. His hand went automatically to his carbine. Out in the gray void something was taking shape. Hodge waited agonizing seconds to confirm his suspicion. He summoned the other three men with a loud whisper and carried out his standing instructions. He sent one man off to the right and another off to the left to warn the other picket posts. He rushed the third man to the rear to alert the picket line reserve.

Hodge then slipped across Willoughby Run toward the approaching shapes, following the edge of the road to conceal his presence. A shot whizzed past him and kicked up dust in the road. Hodge tarried only the split second necessary to verify his attackers beyond any doubt. He then bolted for the rear. His instructions were not to return fire but to fall back immediately and report. He ran back across the bridge over the creek. Hodge swung behind the abutment of the bridge, and yielded to his combative instincts. He trained his carbine on the gray shapes, now about half a mile off, and got off three quick rounds. The first exchange of battle had occurred.

From reveille, the men of the Iron Brigade had sensed something fateful in this day. The brigade had encamped on the Emmitsburg Road, five miles south of Gettysburg. They now gathered in small knots, habitual messmates crouched together around the campfires watching the coffee boil. The conversation was subdued. Colonel Dawes was telling his company commanders to make sure that the men got a full distribution of ammunition.

The chaplain approached him. "Sir, I wonder if I might call the men together for prayer this morning?"

"If you like, Chaplain. But make it brief. Have the men fall in for prayer," Dawes told his aide.

"Shall we stop passing out the ammunition?" the aide asked.

"No," the colonel answered, "there's no time." The enemy was known to be in force nearby. They were already late in carrying out General Meade's order to provide every man with three days' rations and forty rounds of ammunition.

The men kneeled in a grassy field on the side of the road, heads bowed, following the chaplain's incantation. " . . .Under His wings shalt thou trust; His truth shall be thy shield and buckler." His prayer was punctuated by the rumble of minié balls tumbling into cartridge boxes.

Cub Buell's battery halted on the Emmitsburg Road to let the cavalrymen pass.

"What's going on?" Cub shouted to the horsemen.

"We found the Johnnies. They're just ahead and off to the left. The woods is full of 'em."

As the dust settled behind the last cavalryman, the artillerymen prepared to move again. A grim-faced sergeant from a neighboring battery of the First Pennsylvania came over to Cub's gun.

"I know you're all New York and Michigan and the like. But, let me tell you, boys, it's different for us. We Pennsylvanians are fighting on home soil now. Why, I don't live more than ten, twelve miles from here. You don't know what it's like when maybe tomorrow you'll be fighting in your own back yard. It sure puts some iron in your backbone."

"Don't you worry none," said gruff old Sergeant Cahill, the man who had given Cub his nickname with that single punch. "We'll stick by you till hell freezes over."

"And if we have to," Cub added, "we'll die on the ice."

What a marvelous contrast, Tillie Pierce thought as she compared the Union cavalrymen riding by with the Rebel raiders who had passed through Gettysburg a few days before. This was an army, not a mob. More soldiers than Tillie had ever dreamed existed came galloping up Washington Street. They turned west on Chambersburg Street and headed toward the outskirts of town. Tillie and her girl friends stood watching from the corner of Washington and High Streets, so moved by the spectacle of these gallant horsemen that they burst into a chorus of "Our Union Forever."

It seemed to the young ladies of Gettysburg impossible good fortune that so many brave, handsome young men could be gathered at one time in one place. The girls threw flowers at the passing horsemen. The cavalrymen rewarded them with courtly salutes and dazzling smiles. The more daring blew kisses to the girls, who giggled and squealed.

Then, Tillie was aware of a dull, muffled thumping off in the distance—out the Chambersburg Pike, it seemed, beyond the Lutheran Seminary.

Not long after Corporal Alphonse Hodge had signaled the presence of the enemy, the Confederates began to emerge in a skirmish line spanning both sides of the Chambersburg Pike. The Rebels moving toward the dismounted Union cavalrymen outnumbered them at this point by at least two to one. And behind this first wave lay the bulk of the Army of Northern Virginia.

The first ranks of skirmishers came trampling through the fields of wheat, across pastures, guns at the ready. The Union soldiers silently trained their seven-shot Spencers, issued just days before, on the advancing foe. Just as they began to splash through Willoughby Creek, the Southerners met the terrific burst of the cavalrymen's new weapon. The Spencer automatic got off twenty-one shots a minute, ten times the firepower of the muzzle-loading rifles the Rebels carried. Private Henry Raison, Company B, 7th Tennessee, went down, the first man to die that day.

General Buford needed a better vantage point. Just behind his line, on the south side of the Chambersburg Pike, the chalk-white bell tower of the Lutheran Seminary poked above the trees and afforded a commanding vista. Buford rushed up the seminary stairs to the tower. The scene unfolding gripped him with foreboding. The Rebel infantry flowed forward out of the trees into the open like a human river escaping its banks. Menacing rows of cannon were unlimbered and swung around, their barrels pointed toward his men. If he could not get infantry to support his cavalry, and quickly, he could not hold. Buford sped a courier to the First Corps commander, General Reynolds, and another to the man now holding the job Reynolds had turned down, General Meade, the new commander of the Army of the Potomac.

"It's the Iron Brigade, I'll bet," Cub Buell said. Coming up the Emmitsburg Road, the artillerymen heard a strong, steady drumbeat, underlying the strains of "The Campbells Are Coming." The Iron Brigade appeared above the crest of a small hill, disappeared into a depression, and came over another rise, their blue uniforms and gun barrels producing the effect of a steel-crested wave coursing through a river channel.

"You fellers better stop here," Cub Buell shouted as the infantrymen passed by. "The weather up there don't sound none too good for such delicate creatures." Other artillerymen joined Buell in the ribbing.

No reply came from the grim-faced ranks of the Iron Brigade. They had heard about Buford's appeal for infantry and knew what lay ahead. The brigade marched to a point about a mile south of Gettysburg, then turned west and headed up a small rise called Seminary Ridge, toward the growing sounds of battle. Just before they reached the slope of the ridge, the order went out to load and fix bayonets. The metallic ring of steel against steel clanged in the summer's air. They advanced double-quick up the slope and headed north along the crest of the ridge toward the Chambersburg Pike, toward Buford's cavalry. They turned left forming an extended line of battle and began to move into the woods. The Rebels let them get within forty yards and then opened fire.

"There's the devil to pay!"

General Reynolds looked up in the direction of the voice coming from the belfry of the Lutheran Seminary and saw General Buford gesturing to him. "I'll be right down, General," Buford shouted. He disappeared and within seconds emerged from the doorway of the seminary. He quickly briefed Reynolds. Reynolds called for his message pad and scribbled a note to General Meade describing the advancing enemy force. He assured Meade, "I will fight him inch by inch, and if driven into the town, I will barricade the streets and hold him back as long as possible."

Reynolds wanted a closer look at the situation. He and Buford galloped toward McPherson's Woods. The highest-ranking Union officer on the field was now as close to the enemy as the humblest private. Reynolds grasped the gravity of the situation at once, and began directing his divisions in an arc roughly paralleling the fragile line that Buford had drawn with his cavalry.

The fresh infantrymen passed through the lines and lifted the burden of the fight from the badly bloodied horse soldiers. If Reynolds' actions were even more swift and resolute than usual, it might be because he was fighting on his homeland, less than sixty miles from his birthplace in Lancaster, Pennsylvania.

Privates Wood and Cox had become separated from their company almost as soon as the Yankees began firing into them. The fire was too fierce for them to do anything but run for cover. The two Confederates plunged down the embankment of an unfinished railroad cut and lay gasping on the ground as bullets crisscrossed the air above them. "We can't stay here, Frank," Cox said to Wood. Cautiously they climbed up the bank of the cut and peered in the direction of the Union fire. Wood crawled forward and took cover behind a fence, lying flat on his belly. He motioned to Cox to follow him. Wood pointed to a stand of trees down the Chambersburg Pike. "See 'em?" Cox followed Wood's finger to the edge of the trees. A few hundred yards off he could see a knot of Union officers on horseback near the trees. Private Wood rested his musket barrel on the lowest rail of the fence.

Wood sighted down the barrel. He tightened his finger on the trigger. His shot was echoed by a salvo of other Confederate fire in the direction of the mounted Yankee officers.

General Reynolds slid from his horse, dead before he hit the ground. The bullet had struck him in the back of the head. He lay there, his eyes half open, the finest general in the Union Army, some believed, Lincoln's choice for the job Meade now held. In the chess of battle, the Union Army had lost its queen in the opening move.

Battery B, 4th Artillery, reached a rise in the Emmitsburg Road. Before, the men had heard only the muffled, distant overture to battle. Now, on the hillcrest, the curtain lifted and the entire drama unfolded before them. The panorama staggered Cub Buell. He could see the city of Gettysburg and off to the left of it massed armies and smoking cannon presented a scene out of a Napoleonic tableau.

The 4th Artillery halted for an hour and watched the majestic drama unfold. At noon, they ceased being spectators and became characters in this spectacle. Half of the guns of Battery B were posted on the north side of the railroad cut, which paralleled one side of the Chambersburg Pike. The other half of the battery was positioned south of the cut near the Thompson farm. The guns pointed roughly west across Willoughby Run where distant masses of gray could be seen forming.

As the men stood anxiously by the guns, three hundred Rebel prisoners were herded past them toward the Union rear. Cub Buell studied their faces intently as though somehow he might find in them some secret to his survival. They were sullen, hard-looking men. If they were relieved that the war was over for them, it could not be read in their faces. They ignored the Union soldiers eyeing them so intently. One simple-faced Confederate stared at the lettering on the Union cannon and turned to a fellow prisoner. "These damn Yankees got about as many of them 'U.S.' guns as we'uns has."

Leander Warren and the other boys gaped in fascination at the ragged procession. "Jeez, Leander, did you see that one? His arm was blowed right off," a boy exclaimed. They were sitting on a fence rail late in the morning, watching the Union wounded stream past on their way to the field hospital. Few stretchers were on hand for this unexpected engagement. Most of the wounded were carried on army blankets, many with dark stains spreading over them.

"I got to be getting on home now," Leander said, swinging off the fence. He was fourteen years old, a tall, raw-boned boy, with an undisciplined thatch of red-brown hair and an easy lopsided smile. He walked back toward town alongside a pair of litter bearers carrying a man with a leg wound. The soldier had his arms propped under his head and, when not wincing from a particularly rough jolt, appeared reasonably content with his lot.

"Want to be a soldier, kid?" he asked.

"Sure." Leander grinned.

"After what you've seen today?"

"Don't bother me none, I'd duck."

A sudden pain stifled the cavalryman's laugh. "You figure I didn't duck fast enough, eh?"

Leander shrugged his shoulder and with a casual wave turned into his street.

A dozen soldiers were clustered around the window of the Warren home. His mother cheerfully ladled water out of a pail for the men.

"Oh God, that sure tastes good. Thank you kindly, ma'am."

"Least I could do. Got a boy in the Army myself," she smiled. "Leander, where've you been? You help your sister draw some more water from the well for these thirsty fellers." She wiped the perspiration from her damp brow with the back of her hand and beamed at the Union soldiers.

Two cavalry officers rode up with swords drawn.

"C'mon, you men, there's no time for water now." The soldiers sullenly dispersed and headed west toward the sounds of battle.

"Ma'am, I'd advise you to get your family inside, get down in your cellar. It's likely to heat up here real quick," one of the officers warned.

"You hear that, Leander," she said, "find your sister and father. Thank you kindly, young man."

The fighting was now divided between that going on south of the Chambersburg Pike and fighting north of the road. On the south side, the Iron Brigade had slammed hard into the enemy in McPherson's Woods. As the Union troops drove the Rebels back to Willoughby Creek, the Southerners realized that their hope for a quick romp through skittery Union militiamen was shattered. A Southerner crouched behind a tree shouted, "Here's those damned black-hat fellers again. It ain't no militia. It's the Army of the Potomac!"

The noose was tightening on the brigade that General James Archer commanded. The Confederates had gotten themselves hemmed in at a sharp bend in the creek, with the Iron Brigade closing on all sides. The Rebels began to throw down their muskets and raise their arms. Private Pat Maloney, a pugnacious Irishman, spotted his prize. Maloney could easily have dropped General Archer with a shot. Instead, he dashed among the surrendering Rebels and pinned the astonished general in a muscular grip. "You're coming with me, Mr. Big, do ya hear! You're Paddy Maloney's prisoner!" Archer struggled hopelessly as Maloney dragged him away to the accompaniment of the general's yelling and the astonishment of his men.

Lieutenant Dailey heard General Archer bellowing and rushed over.

"Sir," Archer fumed, "will you have this ruffian get his damned hands off me. What kind of people are you?"

"Maloney," the lieutenant barked, with poorly concealed amusement, "free the general at once."

Maloney relaxed his grip.

"Now, sir, will you surrender your sword to me?" The lieutenant held out his hand.

"Damn you too," Archer roared as he pulled down his rumpled jacket and composed himself after Maloney's manhandling. He flung the sword at the lieutenant and stomped toward the Federal rear on Seminary Ridge under escort.

Union General Abner Doubleday saw his onetime comrade coming toward him. Doubleday thrust his hand toward the prisoner-general and cried, "Archer, I'm glad to see you!" Archer refused his hand and sputtered, "Well, I'm not glad to see you, sir, not by a damn sight!"

Hewn through shale and trap rock, the roadbed of the unfinished railroad ran parallel to the Chambersburg Pike. Rebel soldiers poured into the protective depth of this stony trench and from it unleashed a withering fire at the Union soldiers south of the Chambersburg Pike. This Confederate position had to be silenced. The 6th Wisconsin of the Iron Brigade and two other regiments drew the assignment. The men were lined up parallel to the Rebels in the railroad cut. Only a wooden fence interrupted the open terrain between the two forces.

"Charge!" the order rang out. Among the blue-coated soldiers dashing forward was the boy whom Colonel Dawes had spared from the firing squad for sleeping on guard duty the week before. They clambered over the wooden fence. After they cleared it, bodies hung like broken dolls along the top rail.

The boy was over the fence and raced into the row of flame-tipped Confederate guns that rimmed the edge of the trench. The Union pressure became too great. The Rebels started to scramble back down the side of the cut. Too late. The men of the Iron Brigade stood on the rim firing into the trapped enemy at a range from which they could not miss. Bodies quickly piled up at the bottom of the trench. Men trying to scramble up the opposite side were shot through the back and tumbled down onto their comrades. Two Yankee companies spilled down into the cut to seal off any Rebel retreat. For eight eternal minutes a thousand men in the cut and another thousand on its rim butchered each other with muskets, bayonets, and swinging gun butts. When it was over, the sides of the trench were slippery with blood, the air rang with the screams of trapped and dying men. The Southerners began to throw down their arms.

The Iron Brigade marched 225 prisoners out of the trench. In it, they left bodies piled two and three deep. Dying men had clawed their fingers deep into the opposite side of the trench and hung there in a grisly frieze. The railroad cut had become a huge, open grave.

The Iron Brigade paid dearly for this audacious thrust. Four hundred and twenty men had come charging across the turnpike and over the fence. Of them, 240 reached the cut. They had covered 150 yards at a cost of more than one man per yard. One of those lives paid was that of the curly-haired youth whom Colonel Dawes had spared from execution. The colonel's compassion had extended the boy's life by one week.

Mrs. John Burns sat on the porch of her small, white frame house and listened to the sounds of war come rumbling down the Chambersburg Pike. She also heard strange rattlings from her parlor and wondered what the old fool was up to now. She had better take a look.

There had been a familiar fire in the old man's eyes ever since a Rebel raiding party had ridden into Gettysburg a few days before. As

John Burns.

town constable, John Burns had marched up to the Southern provost guard and bellowed that he, and not a bunch of gray-back traitors, was the law in Gettysburg. The Rebels laughed until they realized the old buzzard was serious, then promptly clapped John Burns into his own jail. As soon as they left town, Burns reasserted his authority. His first act had been to lock up Confederate stragglers who had tarried in Gettysburg.

In the days since this fracas, Burns had been remote, querulous, and short with the old woman. She left the porch now and entered the parlor, where she found her husband removing from the fireplace the ancient musket he had carried in the War of 1812.

"Burns, what on earth are you doing now?"

He turned his corded neck and jutted a lined and defiant chin toward his wife. "I ain't a'doin' nothing. It just occurs to me that some of our boys could use the old gun, and I'm just getting it ready for 'em."

The old man disappeared into the bedroom, and his wife returned to her rocker on the porch. Minutes later Burns came out, walked wordlessly past her, and went down the porch steps, wearing his Sunday-best swallow-tailed blue coat with the large gilt buttons. On his white-thatched head he wore a tall, bell-shaped hat.

"Oh my God!" His wife got up and trailed him down the stairs. "Burns, you daft old fool, where do you think you're going?"

Without a backward glance, Burns slung the rifle over his shoulder, swung into a creaking stride, and said, "Just going to see what happens!"

By noon the bleeding and exhausted armies, almost by unconscious agreement, broke off fighting to regain their breath and plot their next blows. At this point, Buford's tenacious cavalry, against heavy odds, had won the Union army two precious hours. These hours had permitted the First Corps to form a rough semicircle to the west of Gettysburg. The cavalrymen had bought time for other elements of Meade's army to begin moving on Gettysburg. The 11th Corps, under General Howard, arrived just before noon and was posted to the right of the First Corps and north of Gettysburg.

Under their packs, the men of the 11th Corps also carried the added burden of contempt heaped on them by the rest of the army for their past dismal performances, most recently at Chancellorsville. The Union 11th Corps included a high proportion of Germans. Their accents provided the butt of endless jokes among the other corps. "You fights mit Sigel?" "No, I runs mit Howard." Even Lincoln had to admit that he found the name of one of the 11th's officers, General Schimmelfennig, amusing. The rest of the line took small comfort from the fact that they now depended on the Germans for support on their right.

With the 11th Corps in place, the Union line now curved from McPherson Ridge on the left to a stream called Rock Creek on the right of the city.

The extreme right end was anchored by an artillery battery under a nineteen-year-old lieutenant, Bayard Wilkeson. The young lieutenant rode his white horse with a commanding coolness, shouting orders, completely exposed to the enemy. Also approaching Gettysburg at that moment was Samuel Wilkeson, a war correspondent for *The New York Times,* the lieutenant's father.

At midday, during the lull, the North could claim a short-term victory. The Rebels had been beaten back. Large caches of Confederate prisoners were streaming to the Union rear. Ironically, the battle of Gettysburg had begun with the Confederate army attacking from the north, and the Union army coming up from the south.

To Warren Goss, authority seemed oddly perched on the shoulders of his comrade, Old Joe from Beverly, Massachusetts. Since his ascension to corporal, Joe had revealed an unexpected pomposity. "Feeling his stripes," Warren put it.

The regiment was marching the road from Taneytown to Gettysburg. Off to the north they could detect a faint drum roll of cannon. Knots of Rebel prisoners marched past them, and they exchanged pleasantries.

"How ya doin', Johnny Reb?"

"It's dog eat hog up there, bluebellies."

"We got to lick them bastard Rebs this time, boys," Old Joe said with deep resolution. "And I say that as an officer now."

Warren looked at Joe from a corner of his eye, unable to subdue a grin. Yet, the thoughts Old Joe expressed were, nevertheless, those of all the men as they neared the enemy for the first time on home ground.

"If they get us down by the short hairs," Joe went on, "they'll be cutting up in Boston and calling the roll of their niggers on Bunker Hill—maybe even Beverly."

"Why, Joe," Wad Rider chided the corporal. "They ain't niggers. They're unbleached Americans!" Old Joe scowled.

The company came to rest beneath some shade trees. As they savored the idle minutes, a frantically gesturing Pennsylvania Dutch farmer ran up to them. The man waved a fistful of Confederate dollars in Warren Goss's face. Rebel bank notes bulged from his pockets. Warren's attempts to remain serious were sorely tested by the man's bizarrely accented English—a sputter of misplaced "d's" and "t's."

"Boys, do you think the government will give me good money for this stuff?" He was in his thirties, squat, with a peasant closeness to the ground that gave him the appearance of being rooted in soil.

"Where'd you get those bluebacks?" Warren asked.

"Ach," the farmer wailed. "Them Rebs took my horse, my cow, my potatoes and with this, they pay me. You think I can change it for Union money?"

Turning to the other men, Warren shouted, "Anybody want to trade this Dutchman some green for this Rebel wallpaper?" The men hooted and jeered.

"You are all the same," the farmer fumed. "Bunch of no good wiseacres. If I don't get real money for this, I'm ruined." Again he shook the bills in Warren's face.

Thinking of the dollar they had been charged for a quart of milk or a loaf of bread by Pennsylvania Dutch farmers along the way, young Wad Rider came up close and stared, hard-eyed, at the farmer. "Dutchman, you're lucky we're fighting for your God damn farms. Why the hell ain't you in uniform anyway?"

"Ya, sure," the farmer scoffed. "I get killed, who's going to take care of my wife and my kids, eh?"

"There's no flies on this fellow." Old Joe spat on the ground and turned away from the farmer. "These people make you want to puke out your gizzard."

"So! I pays my taxes and you fights for my land." The farmer stalked off with a triumphant logic that left the Union soldiers speechless.

"Who's your tailor, old fella?" . . . "Hey, grandpa! Was you at Valley Forge?" The arrival of John Burns snapped the tension that had silenced the men of the 150th Pennsylvania as they moved toward the fighting near McPherson's Woods. The old man ignored their taunts and fell into step with them, his jaw set determinedly. When they came to a halt, old Burns sought out the regimental commander.

"Colonel, I'm Burns, War of '12, Mexican War, and I'd be pleased to give a hand."

The colonel saw more than an absurd figure before him. He looked into two hard, cold eyes. "Can you shoot, old-timer?"

"Give me a chance, I'll show you who can shoot."

"We can do better than that relic you've got," the colonel said.
"Sergeant, give this man . . . what's your name?"

"Burns."

"Give Mr. Burns one of the wounded men's rifles and twenty-five
rounds."

John Burns stuffed the cartridges into the pocket of his best
Sunday coat, patted his new weapon affectionately, and marched with
the Pennsylvanians into the battle line.

The lull in the fighting had been seized by both sides to reset and
strengthen their lines. From the west came fresh Rebel regiments.
More Confederate cannon were wheeled into position. Buford's cavalrymen, still holding on as the northern arc of the Union semicircle,
could see a whole new Rebel column bearing down from the north of
town. These recent arrivals were advance elements of Ewell's corps,
which had been off capturing York and threatening Harrisburg. They
were responding to Lee's order to break off any further probes into
Pennsylvania and to consolidate near Gettysburg. Their return route
had fortuitously brought them to the north of Gettysburg, where
they linked up with Hill's corps streaming in from the west. The two
Southern corps thus formed a parallel semicircle around the increasingly outnumbered Federals.

In McPherson's Woods, the Iron Brigade passed the recess uneasily. Willoughby Creek ran in front of the woods, and somewhere
beyond the creek, unseen, the enemy they had driven off were
regrouping. In unbearable stillness, the Union soldiers listened to the
shrill song of yellowshafted flickers and watched the sun glistening
off the leaves and striking the ground in gossamer rays. They waited
in this peaceful green and gold arbor, poised to kill.

Then the brief truce exploded. "Here they come!" yelled the Iron
Brigade's skirmishers, pounding back across the creek into the protective cover of the trees. An undulating gray wave moved into sight.
The Confederate guns cracked and echoed within the woods. Bullets
slammed and split narrow trunks. Cannon exploded and great branches
crashed down, breaking skulls and fouling the muskets of the Federals. Awful shrieks now filled the air where birds sang moments
before. The human sea of Southerners rolled forward no matter the
Union fire poured onto it. The Iron Brigade drew back to the edge of

the woods, then drew back farther, then back farther still, closer to Gettysburg, each orderly retreat recorded by a precise row of blue-clad bodies.

Tillie Pierce had waited until the last soldier, the last wagon passed by before she returned home near noon. Her mother had prepared dinner for Tillie and the smaller children as usual, come Rebel troops or Union troops. They had eaten silently, looking nervously at one another with each thump and boom of artillery.

Then the pounding ceased.

Almost immediately, there was an insistent banging at the kitchen door. Tillie's mother cautiously opened the door to a highly distraught neighbor, Mrs. Schriver. She was the young mother of two small children. Her husband was away in the Union Army. "Oh, Mrs. Pierce, I can't stay home. I'm frightened to death for the children."

"Don't you fret none, dear, you just bring the little ones over here."

"Oh, no. I don't want to do that. I want to get them away from town. I want to take them down to my father's place."

"Did you want a bite to eat before you go?" Mrs. Pierce asked.

"No, I just wondered"—the woman fidgeted, hesitated—"couldn't Tillie come with me? It'll be safer for her too, don't you think, Mrs. Pierce?"

"Oh can I, Ma?" Tillie rose quickly from the table.

Mrs. Pierce wrung her hands and wished her husband were home. Finally, she gave in to her imploring daughter.

Young Mrs. Schriver and Tillie Pierce, with two children in hand, started down Baltimore Street at about one in the afternoon. They took the shortcut through Evergreen Cemetery, where sweating, cursing soldiers wrestled artillery into position. The men stopped and gaped at the petticoated party appearing in their midst.

A bare-chested young giant pushed his cap on the back of his head, put his hands on his hips, and, breathing heavily, shouted, "Ladies, just where do you think you're going?"

"Down the Taneytown Road, to the Weikert farm," Tillie answered.

"Well, I suggest you move right along or you're going to see a little more of this war than you bargained for." He pointed toward

Seminary Ridge. "I expect there's going to be some shelling up here before long."

"Oh my God," Mrs. Schriver cried and started running and dragging the two frightened children. On the Taneytown Road, they passed Mrs. Leister's house, teeming with Union officers.

"Mister," Tillie shouted to a young lieutenant, "can't you get us a ride in one of these wagons?"

"Where to, ma'am?"

"We're going about a mile and a half down this road."

"Just a minute." The officer strode into the middle of the road and held up his hand to an approaching wagon. "Hold up," he ordered the unshaven, red-eyed driver. "Take these women and children with you. They'll tell you where."

"It's the Weikert place," Tillie said. The driver shrugged his shoulder, offered a calloused hand to the women, and pulled them aboard. The young lieutenant handed up the children. The wagon was springless, and struck every rock and rut with bone-jarring force.

As they approached their destination, artillery shells began flying overhead. They saw a man riding a caisson coming toward them. Suddenly, the caisson disintegrated in a deafening, blinding burst. Tillie saw the driver flung crazily into the air and watched his body land in a wheat field. Two stretcher bearers rushed to the man and carried him into the Weikert house. Tillie held her arm across her face but could not tear her eyes away. The man's body was a blackened mass. There were bloody sockets where his eyes had been. "Oh my God," he muttered, "I forgot to read my Bible today. What will my poor wife and children say?" His lips were quivering as they carried him into the house. Tillie Pierce ran to the side of the house and retched violently.

Battery B had waited an interminable, nerve-fraying hour for the Rebel thrust. Then they heard the yelling, could see the flag tips rising above the small ridge before them, then the glittering points of bayonets. The endless gray ranks emerged, steady, tramping, shouting. The Southern battle cry had an unnerving effect on the Union artillerymen. It was a yelping, whooping, shrieking, savage cry—a distillate of hatred and blood lust, fiendish and terrifying. Yankee skins had first shivered at the sound of it at Bull Run in '61. Stonewall Jackson had told his men there, "When you charge, yell like furies!"

The insane shrieking made Cub Buell's scalp tingle. The men gripped hard at whatever they were holding, ramrods, lanyards, shells. Lieutenant Davison, commanding Cub's half of the battery, finally opened the floodgates of their pent-up tensions. "Load canister double . . . ready . . . by the piece . . . at will . . . FIRE!" Cub Buell felt a soaring ecstasy as he saw the canister tear into the enemy ranks. The shrill battle yell was now counterpointed by terrible screams as thousands of iron balls drove into hands and heads and eyes and chests. Still, they kept coming.

"Feed it to the bastards," Davison screamed. "Come on, boys, pour it into the sons of bitches. Shoot the God damn balls off 'em . . . come on . . . pour it on!"

The men had their jackets off, their sleeves rolled up. The Rebel bullets struck the guns with a ringing clangor and ricocheted wildly among the gun crew. Sharp splinters flew about as bullets smashed into wooden wheels and axles. The screams of the men were lost in the hideous whinnying of the horses as they plunged about, mad with wounds and terror.

Sergeant John Mitchell moved calmly from gun to gun, giving encouragement, shifting men, doubling their assignments to compensate for the fallen. Pat Packard kept wiping the blood from his eyes to sight the gun. The blood ran from a head wound, making red rivulets through the black powder smearing his face, giving Packard the aspect of a demon. A loader clasped his hands over his bleeding face and staggered away from the gun screaming, "I'm blind! I'm blind!" Sergeant Mitchell calmly ordered another man to pick up his duties. They were meeting well the artilleryman's highest test, loyalty to the gun.

All Cub Buell's fears evaporated. His consuming obsession now was to inflict injury upon his enemy. He felt an obsessive drive to conquer, much as he did in schoolyard fights as a boy.

Cub and the gun crew went through their individual tasks with the fevered precision of a clock that is both ticking and disintegrating at the same time. For the artilleryman, the shelter of a tree or trench did not exist. He stood in the open, his cowardice or his courage naked to the world. He was one gear in a machine. If he failed, the machine stalled. He knew that wherever he fought was vital ground, since the army did not engage its mightiest arms for small purposes. And so they stood and were slaughtered in their tracks.

A wagon driver, young, narrow-shouldered, and terrified, swung down from the seat of the wagon. Major Stewart, commander of the full battery, insisted, even in the heat of battle, that no driver was to dismount unless ordered. The boy felt something hard jammed into his ribs. It was Major Stewart's revolver. Livid, face reddened, the major shouted, "Get back on that wagon, do you hear, and die there if you must." The boy scrambled back up.

Lieutenant Davison was bleeding now from two wounds. His right ankle had been shot away, and one of the men held him up so that he could still direct his guns. They had blunted the enemy's frontal assault. But the Rebel mass was now merely circumventing their fire by moving around to their left. Lieutenant Davison shouted to the men to swing the guns around to the left so that they now aimed south across the Chambersburg Pike. The artillery had a clear field of fire across the open road. For seven minutes a desperate exchange exploded between artillery and infantry. With shells bursting, bullets hissing, horses stomping, iron and wood rending the air, and comrades falling, the men still fed the gun as rhythmically as in a drill. Each man now did the work of three and four.

On Buell's gun, Griff Wallace was both loading and sponging, but sponging only after every fifth load. With each round fired, Cub jammed the thumbstall into the vent. The heat in the barrel was burning the thumbstall to a crisp. "Jesus Christ, Griff!" Buell shouted. "Sponge the God damn gun!"

"Sponge your ass, you little bastard!" the blackened and sweating Wallace roared as he rammed home another charge of canister. "You stick to the vent. Hear?"

Buell kept pulling the charred thumbstall down further on his thumb after each round until the leather was nearly all burned off. "Griff," he pleaded, "sponge the gun! The vent is burning my skin off!"

"Thumb it with the bone, then, God damn you!"

It was 2:30 in the afternoon. At the point where Reynolds fell, the Union troops were being driven inexorably back. The 151st Pennsylvania, called the Schoolteacher Regiment, was ordered to plug a gap in the faltering Federal line. Nearly a quarter of the Pennsylvanians in this command had left teaching jobs for the Union Army. Company D had decimated the faculty of McAlister Academy. The school's former principal, Lieutenant Colonel George McFarland, was commanding the schoolteachers this day.

The regiment moved forward with parade-ground precision, Company D in front. A Rebel fusillade struck the front rank like leaden hail. The teachers of McAlister Academy dropped to the ground in a neat row. With half the regiment soon down, McFarland got word to fall back. He issued his last orders from the ground where he lay, shot through both legs.

The Schoolteacher Regiment, which had entered the field with 487 men under a lieutenant colonel, withdrew to Cemetery Hill with 121 men, under a captain. Almost all of Company D had fallen, thirteen dead and ten more wounded.

Farther to the north of the crumbling Union line, at a point nearly perpendicular to the Mummasburg Road, the 88th Pennsylvania waited its turn to receive the Confederate hammer blow. The Confederates advanced toward the Pennsylvanians in perfect formation, their guns at right shoulder, colors fluttering out front. Private John Vautier fleetingly forgot his fears and imagined he was watching a parade. Vautier could hear the Southern officers' orders, making the fine corrections that moved their men rhythmically, monolithically, forward. They were so close now that Vautier could pick out individual features. Red hair there. A beardless boy's face on that one. The tallest man. The smallest. Another limping slightly. Closer, closer. Buttons, torn sleeves, stubbled chins, crusted bare feet could now be discerned. At one hundred paces, the six Union regiments rose from behind a stone wall. In the first volley, one thousand cones of lead flayed the tightly woven Confederates. The first rank peeled to the ground like a falling leaf. The Union soldiers continued to pour their fire into the nakedly exposed Southerners and drove them back to the protection of a gully.

The Union soldiers kneeled again behind the stone wall or hugged the ground. Private Vautier watched while two of their best sharpshooters, Sergeants Evans and Whitmoyer, challenged each other to new heights of marksmanship. A Confederate color bearer flaunted his flag at them from the gully. Evans brought his gun to his shoulder and took careful aim. "Watch me give those colors a whack." Whitmoyer heard a dull thud. He turned to his partner. The life had drained from Evans' face. He lowered his rifle slowly and rolled over with a bullet in the heart.

The heavy fire nearly exhausted the Union soldiers' ammunition. Fingers groped frantically in empty cartridge boxes. Their commander detected the waning volume of gunfire. "We'll give 'em the cold steel!" he shouted.

The order went out to fix bayonets. The charge succeeded. The Yankees swarmed into the gully and rounded up nearly three regiments of Rebels. General Iverson, commander of these Southern troops, saw his men waving scraps of white, saw much of his line still lying down, and became enraged. But as the Yankees rounded up the prisoners, Iverson noted that the line which he thought had disgraced him was still lying motionless. Some five hundred North Carolinians lay dead and wounded in near perfect rows. In his heart, Iverson exonerated the surrendering survivors.

The Union triumph was brief. As soon as the Yankees dispatched their prisoners to the rear, a fresh flood of Confederates poured out of the woods. The Pennsylvanians fled back to the stone wall, leaving a trail of bodies en route. Wounded men began hobbling, limping, dashing to the rear. The regiment abandoned the wall as the Southerners threatened to engulf them. They fell back toward the railroad cut and, momentarily, stood firm.

"Ain't you scared to die in the prime of life, daddy?"

John Burns returned a contemptuous snort to the sergeant ragging him. "There's your business, son," he said, wagging a leathery hand toward the approaching enemy, "out there." The Rebels opened fire and the 150th Pennsylvania fired back. In the battle's heat and smoke, the Pennsylvanians were amazed to see the old man, standing, unprotected, rhythmically loading, ramming, aiming, and firing to deadly effect. Two Rebels, one an officer on horseback, went down under the marksmanship of the seventy-two-year-old Burns.

Burns suddenly doubled up, spun away, and staggered out of the line.

"He's shot, the old man's shot!" The soldiers ran to their newfound comrade. Suddenly, Burns stood upright, cackling with an ancient laughter. He pointed to the misshapen remnant of his metal belt buckle.

"God damn, God damn, I ain't shot. They just hit my buckle!" The creviced face crinkled with glee as Burns stepped briskly back up to the line and resumed firing.

*   *   *

The 149th Pennsylvania was posted nearly midway in the Union line, near McPherson's Lane, taking a hard pounding. A shell landed directly in the midst of Company B. One man, wounded by the blast, hopped along the line like a dog, on all fours, screaming, "I've been killed, I've been killed!" A colonel drew his revolver. "The hell you are. Get back in place, you weak sister." The wounded man rolled over and died at the colonel's feet.

Another officer had a scheme for stalling the expected enemy advance on the 149th. He would march the color guard forward, thus suggesting to the Rebels that the full infantry must be close behind. Brehm, Friddel, and Hammel were sent forward to enact the scheme. As Henry Brehm stepped out with the flagstaff raised high in his hand, he cast a sorrowful glance at the men remaining in the line.

The three men advanced in uneasy isolation and halted in the corner of a fence, waiting to be seen. Brehm heard something rustling in a wheat field. He cocked back the flagstaff. The other two men raised their muskets. Out of the wheat swept a Confederate skirmish line. A Rebel soldier leaped the fence and grabbed at Brehm's flagstaff.

"Gimme that, that's mine!"

"The hell it is!" Brehm roared.

The two men wrestled. The flag fell to the ground. Another Rebel seized it. Friddel from a foot away blasted a hole in the back of the Rebel who had taken the flag. Hammel shot dead another enemy soldier hurtling over the fence. Brehm grabbed the flag again, and the three Yankees started fleeing back to the safety of their own line. But there was no line. Their regiment was gone, had retreated. Instead, they rushed into the arms of the enemy. Friddel went down, shot through the chest, Hammel was shot in the stomach. Brehm abruptly changed course and had all but escaped when a Rebel shell exploded just feet away. It ripped the clothes from his body and flung him, mortally wounded, to the ground.

The men of the 88th Pennsylvania, now fighting from the north side of the railroad cut, had to fall back or be overwhelmed. They were ordered to retreat to Cemetery Hill. Two escape routes were open, across lots skirting the western edge of town up to the hill, or straight down the Chambersburg Pike and through the streets of Gettysburg to Cemetery Hill.

Those who avoided the city made it. Most of those who fled through the city did not. One of these was Lieutenant Beath. During the retreat, Beath had passed a wounded man propped against the side of a wall.

"Lieutenant, Lieutenant!" The man's cry was desperate. Beath turned back and recognized him, a private from his regiment. The man's lips were pale and trembling.

"Where are you hit?" The soldier lifted a blood-soaked hand from a wound in his abdomen. Beath shook his head.

"Please, Lieutenant, don't leave me. Don't leave me to them God damn Rebs!"

Beath was determined not to be captured. The wounded man clung tenaciously to his leg. "Don't go, Lieutenant, it ain't right to leave one of your own men."

Beath reluctantly took the private's arm and swung it around his shoulder. They began, one awkward step after another, edging toward town, passed on either side by fleeing bluecoats.

The Confederates had already set up an emergency hospital in a large house on the western edge of town. There was little Beath could do now but drag the private toward it. A Confederate soldier came over and took the now nearly unconscious man by his free arm and helped Beath get him inside the house. A Rebel surgeon examined the wounded man in his turn, without regard to the color of his uniform. The doctor was methodical, precise. He dexterously exposed the private's wound, looked to Beath, and said, "About two hours, not much more. There's nothing to be done."

The man snapped from his torpor. His eyes flashed wildly. "You low-lived son of a bitch!" he shrieked. "You're a'gonna let me die! You don't want to treat me . . . cuz . . . cuz I'm on t'other side. Lieutenant," he gasped exhaustedly, "don't let 'em leave me die!"

The Southern surgeon turned coolly to an orderly. "Give this poor devil a dose of laudanum." He then turned to Beath. "And now, my friend, what am I to do with you?"

Beath smiled. "I have one ambition at this point, doctor. I don't want to be a prisoner."

"I can't very well let you go, can I? Not that you'd get far. I'll tell you what. Surrender your arms. I'll provide you with a hospital corps arm band. You can help us tend the wounded. Then, when this battle is over, however it goes"—he gave a half smile—"you'll be allowed to return to your side."

"Doctor," Beath said, "you are the best of a bad breed."

The Civil War doctor, "surgeons" they were usually called, ranged from the brave and brilliant to drunks and quacks. The uneven quality was the result of political influence in the appointment of some medical officers and wildly varying state-to-state standards, running even to an absence of any qualifying standards in some cases. One state required no medical degree from prospective surgeons on grounds that "scholarship" was no "measure of practical ability," which may explain the former barbers and similarly qualified men occasionally commissioned as surgeons.

A substantial cut below commissioned medical officers were "contract surgeons" hired by both sides on a monthly fee basis and not officially members of the military. Contract surgeons were supposed to be medical-school graduates, though some who wangled contracts had never seen the inside of a medical classroom. Those contract surgeons who were trained were frequently the dregs of the profession, men who could not get an Army commission and who were failures in private practice.

When the war began, not a single woman in the country was trained as a nurse in the modern sense. In the field, regimental officers assigned soldiers to auxiliary medical duties. The tendency was to retain the best men in fighting units and to assign incorrigibles, the stupid, and the weak to nursing duties. Musicians were automatically made members of the medical detail during and after battle and proved to be the most resentful and resolutely inept nurses of all.

Just days after the War began, Dorothea Dix, who had won renown for founding insane asylums, threw her energies into creating a female nurse corps. Miss Dix's qualifying standards were designed to discourage anything from going beyond a medical relationship between nurse and patient. In addition to possessing good health, prospective nurses had to be over thirty and "plain almost to repulsion in dress and devoid of personal attractions." Age and ugliness, however, proved to be poor guarantees of nursing ability, and Miss Dix's standards eventually had to be relaxed.

Catholic nuns, called by the men "Sisters of Charity," proved successful nurses because of their disciplined organization and a tradition of obedience, which made them far more acceptable to surgeons than often outspoken and officious volunteer nurses from the secular world.

The one-woman marvels performed by Clara Barton have created an exaggerated notion of the role that women nurses played on Civil War battlefields. Few women actually served in the field. Most were posted to general hospitals well to the rear. Yet every great battle stirred a tide of volunteer nurses of both sexes, mothers, sisters, fathers, and brothers of the wounded men as well as local women moved by the suffering around them.

In spite of the soldiers' chronic griping against the "sawbones" and "opium peddlers," apart from the drunks and incompetents, the great majority of surgeons and those who aided them proved able and dedicated. Walt Whitman, whose service as a Civil War male nurse put him in a position to know, observed that all but a few of those who tended the wounded knew what they were doing and cared.

The Iron Brigade had now been driven back all the way to Seminary Ridge. Glancing over their shoulders, the men could glimpse the county courthouse and the cross-tipped spire of a Catholic church in the city of Gettysburg. Directly behind them, about a mile off, was Cemetery Hill, which tapered off to the south in a long stretch of land known as Cemetery Ridge. Alongside them now was the comforting presence of Union artillery, the 5th Maine Battery. The brigade had to stem the Southern advance here or face a rout. They watched the Confederate regiments close in on them from the base of the ridge. Every cannon was loaded, every lanyard tightly gripped. On they came. The Union forces choked back the fierce urge to open up. Not yet. A few more yards. A few more feet. The Rebel troops started up the slope.

"Fire!" Every lanyard was pulled as one. The Confederates literally withered away. When the smoke cleared, the front rank appeared to have been swallowed up by the earth. Immediately, another wave of Confederates took their place stepping into the gore of a hundred mangled and torn comrades, walking over rudely amputated heads and limbs, feeling the human offal under their feet. They pressed on. "By damn," Pat Maloney cried in disbelief. "We still haven't stopped . . ." His cry was cut off by a shot through the head. Maloney's celebrity at Gettysburg had been short-lived. The private who, hours before, had captured a general fell dead.

No course was left now but to make for the hills to the south of the town. As they retreated along the Chambersburg Pike, a Rebel column paralleled them, shooting down the fast dwindling numbers of the Iron Brigade and bagging scores of prisoners. The last man to reach town was a regimental color sergeant, still holding the flag high until he was felled by a blast of canister. His comrades picked up his bleeding body and laid him atop a caisson in the retreating caravan. He was still waving the banner as they joined the mounting bedlam in the streets of Gettysburg.

The Iron Brigade had been virtually killed in action this day at Gettysburg. Its stubborn stands and grudging retreats had been marked by seven successive lines of dead. Three of every four men in the brigade had been killed or wounded in eight hours of fighting. A brigade would bear that honored name through to Appomattox. But it would be an uninspired collection of conscripts, nine-month men, Easterners, a group of strangers gathered under a once proud banner. But the old, revered Iron Brigade, which entered the field at Gettysburg with 1883 men and came out with 671, died this day.

Cub Buell shouted through the noise to the man holding up Lieutenant Davison. "Can't you see he's out! Put him down!" The soldier set the lieutenant on the ground.

They could no longer stem the enemy tide. "Limber up!" the cry rang out. The men started hitching up the horses in the midst of the Rebel fire. A soldier hooking up a cannon and caisson slumped dead over the cannon's trail. No time now for fallen comrades. The man was flung aside, and another man finished hitching the horses to the gun. As they sped toward town, men were shot off the caissons and trampled under pounding hooves and crushed by iron-rimmed wheels. A shell fragment pierced a horse's abdomen. The animal shuddered but kept running, its entrails dragging from the wound. Two men cut the horse from the traces, and Pat Packard shot it through the brain.

At last, the panting and heaving survivors of Battery B gathered on the safety of Cemetery Hill south of town. The recruits, awed by the fury of their fiery baptism, babbled with a strident bravado of close calls, of proofs of courage, of the grisly comedy of battle. "Did you see that Reb's head go . . . could feel that ball graze my neck . . . he'd no sooner fell when I took up the ramrod and . . ."

The veterans spoke little. They said nothing of casualties, of friends lost. They muttered only biting commentary on the follies of leadership.

"It would have been different," Griff Wallace said, looking out over the ground they had just given up, "if they'd sent the Twelfth Corps up Seminary Ridge to back us up, instead of up here."

Sergeant John Mitchell, stretched out with his cap shading his eyes, chewing a long-stemmed weed, nodded sagely. "Griff, if you're so smart, how's come you ain't made officer?"

Old John Burns had uncomplainingly taken three painful wounds. He had been struck in his thigh, then in his arm. A third bullet had cut a deep path through his ankle. The colonel ordered him out of the line. "You've done your share and somebody else's to boot, old fellow, now get to the rear."

Burns gave the officer an exaggerated salute, laid his rifle down, and began hobbling toward town. The pain became intense. The sweat ran down the deep ravines in his face. Burns could manage no more than a few steps between rests. He reached a house where a yellow flag with a letter "H" on it hung from a window, signifying a Confederate aid station. Burns stood before the house, started to move again, stopped and reluctantly pulled himself through the doorway.

A harried Confederate surgeon looked up from the man he was treating at the old man before him. "What are you doing here? What do you want?"

"I'm here because I'm hurt, as any plain fool can see."

"Don't be so damn uppity, you old coot. How'd you get wounded? Who did it, our troops or yours?"

"I don't know," the old man snapped impatiently as he slid himself gingerly to the floor. "I only know I'm hurt bad."

"What's your business for being out? Our boys don't go shootin' old men for sport."

Burns looked up cagily. "It's my old woman. She's sick. I'd gone to get a girl to help care for her. Before I knew it, I was slam-bang in the middle of this fix. And here I am."

The doctor shook his head dubiously. "All right, let me take a look at that foot."

General Gordon was furious. His troops formed the far left of the Confederate line, northeast of Gettysburg. They had pressed forward steadily but were now stalled and paid a heavy price to a stubborn Union artillery battery for every foot they advanced. These four Union guns drew back slowly and hurled fire and hell into Gordon's infantry before every grudging retreat.

The problem was clear. The Union battery commander, nineteen-year-old Lieutenant Bayard Wilkeson, astride a white horse, rode fearlessly among his men, wedding them to their guns by the courage of his example. Even the Rebel soldiers admired the unruffled coolness of this officer in the midst of chaos.

General Gordon had had enough of Yankee heroics. He ordered two entire batteries, twelve cannon in all, to aim directly at the white-mounted officer. A tremendous thunder exploded around the young lieutenant. His horse was blown from under him. Wilkeson was thrown to earth, rent with horrible wounds. Now Gordon's Rebel infantry could roll. All along the Northern line, the Federal resistance gave way before superior numbers.

The Indiana man limped to the middle of the road and held up his hand to slow the approaching wagon. On the side of the road were five wounded soldiers of the Iron Brigade. The more seriously hurt lay prostrate, the less wounded were sitting up.

"What do you want?" the driver of the wagon snarled. "Let me through."

"We got to get to the field hospital. Take us in."

The man frowned and scanned the men on the side of the road. "Twelve dollars," he said.

"You no good bastard!" one of the wounded men cried.

"Get out of my way, you tramps." The farmer yanked at the reins and the two horses lurched forward.

"Wait up! Wait up!" the soldier in the road pleaded. He walked over to his wounded comrades. "Let's face it. Some of us are gonna die if we don't get help." They reached into their pockets, muttering and cursing. The man hobbled back to the driver. "Here's ten dollars."

"I said twelve," the driver answered sullenly.

The soldier limped over to an unconscious soldier stretched on the roadside and went through his pockets and knapsack. He came back and handed the money to the farmer.

"Here, you son of a bitch Dutchman." Tears of hatred streamed down his face. The farmer shoved the money into his pocket and jumped off the wagon.

"Thanks, boys," he smiled, "let me help you up."

Robert Stiles had arrived at Gettysburg toward evening. His battery was posted on the northern outskirts of town, guns loaded with canister should they have to clear the streets.

Burgoyne was a favorite with Stiles' gun crew. He was a huge, broad-shouldered Irishman, powerful, slightly bowlegged, with the quick movements of a cat. Burgoyne was never happier than in the heat of battle, sweat pouring down his muscled torso, some song of his Gaelic boyhood on his lips, ramming home the charge with powerful grace and joyful exuberance.

Eyeing Burgoyne on this day, from among the Yankee prisoners held nearby, was a magnificently structured and even larger Irishman. The man had caught Burgoyne's accent and shouted, "Hey, ye bloody bog trotter, what are ye doin' in the Rebel Army, eh?"

Burgoyne stalked over to the prisoner, eyes flashing.

"Be-Jesus, ain't an Irishman a free man? Haven't I as good a right to fight for the Rebs as ye have to fight for the God damn niggers?"

"I'll tell you what I think of the nigger, the same as I think of a Rebel," the Union soldier sneered. "You're both nothin' but shit asses."

Burgoyne reddened. "If I hear one more word from your ugly mouth, I'll knock your teeth down your ugly throat."

The Union soldier lunged at Burgoyne. Stiles eyed something white and red-stained amidst the windmill of swinging fists. "Hold it! Stop it!" He forced himself between the fighters. "Can't you see, Burgoyne, the man's wounded?"

A bandage had come undone on the Yankee's hand and exposed two badly shattered fingers.

Burgoyne offered profuse apologies. "Paddy, you're a real trump,

The Evergreen Cemetery Gateway.

give me your well hand," he said. "I didn't see your wound. We'll fight this out some other time." He laughed and went back to the battery.

Retreat had collapsed into rout among the 11th Corps. Its soldiers streamed through Gettysburg in mad confusion. They leaped back-yard fences, raced through alleyways, passed each other coming and going in the mounting pandemonium. The Rebels were into the north of town before the 11th could clear out of the southern end. They were tracked down like trapped beasts, shot clambering over fences, caught in blind alleys and easily dispatched.

The Yankees in reserve on Cemetery Hill watched the flight with deepening anxiety. The hill they now manned rose south of Gettys-burg a few hundred feet from town. It was crowned by Evergreen Cemetery. Here the Federal reserve troops sweated amidst monu-ments and tombstones digging rifle pits and emplacements for the artillery.

Here too, one gained a sweeping view of the Federal retreat. The Federal line had started to unravel first on the right, the part held by the luckless 11th Corps with its heavy German contingents. As this withdrawal north of town deteriorated into a rout, the remainder of

The view of Gettysburg from Seminary Ridge.

the Federal defensive arc, under the more disciplined First Corps, was inescapably doomed. The collapse on the right side of the line meant that the Rebels could get around and behind the rest of the Union troops, unless they, too, shrank their perimeter by falling back.

The men on Cemetery Hill watched the gloomy spectacle, the men on their left, the First Corps, dropping back with ordered discipline, the 11th Corps streaming through the city's streets in wild disorder.

For General Lee the fight had been premature. He had not wanted to engage the enemy in force until he had fully consolidated his far-flung corps. Now, at Cashtown, eight miles from the fighting, General Hill was telling him that some of his men, on the way to Gettysburg to get shoes, had collided with Federal cavalrymen. This force was under instructions not to force an engagement if it ran into Union infantry. But the echoing thunder of artillery spoke of far more than a skirmish. Lee headed down the Chambersburg Pike toward the sounds of battle.

Late in the afternoon, he was operating from a hastily contrived headquarters on Seminary Ridge from which the Federals had been freshly driven. The fury of the fight unfolding before him made clear

to Lee that he was fully committed whether he had yet wanted a full-scale battle now or not.

For a moment Lee's senses were caught up in the epic drama spread before him. He stood on a rim of fire that half girdled the town. He stood at midpoint on a great encircling arc of gray-coated men who spilled over small green hills, across fields, down roads, and up streets, driving back an ebbing sea of blue-coated men. The scene was vividly splashed by huge bursts of red, yellow, and orange exploding against the blue sky. Swirling trails of smoke traced endlessly changing shapes, while the earth shook and trembled. General Lee shook his head abruptly, shattering the spell. Once he had remarked to Longstreet at an earlier battle, "It's just as well war is terrible, or we might grow too fond of it."

With the Union army in full retreat, Lee recognized that boldness now could bring him swift and total victory. He dispatched his aide, Colonel Walter Taylor, with a message for General Ewell, who was in command north of Gettysburg.

Taylor galloped over to Ewell and conveyed Lee's belief that it was only necessary to press "those people" to win possession of the heights below Gettysburg. Taylor returned to Lee with a clear impression that Ewell would carry out Lee's wishes.

As the Rebel infantry overran the Federals' position and bore down on the town, litter bearers followed behind to pick up the refuse of battle. They knew the mangled Yankee lieutenant lying next to his dead horse. The animal's white hide was stained with its own bright blood. The young lieutenant was barely alive. In his hand he clutched a pen knife. He had used it to sever the last remaining shreds of flesh connecting his leg to his body. They gently lifted Lieutenant Bayard Wilkeson onto a stretcher, unsure of which parts of his broken body to grasp. "You don't scare easy," one of the men said to the Union officer. Wilkeson attempted a feeble smile. They took him to a hospital set up in a nearby almshouse.

Wilkeson asked for water. A Confederate attendant brought a tin cup to him. The wounded man next to Wilkeson whimpered, "For God's sake give me some." Wilkeson passed the man the canteen, and then died.

Few people of Gettysburg witnessed the chaos claiming their streets. They had mostly taken to their cellars, and the battle was to them only an unending succession of muffled cracks, bursts, and roars. Above them, one regiment of Yankees would collide with another escaping from an opposite direction until both were hopelessly entangled. Wagons, ambulances, and guns became enmeshed in the fevered rush to escape town. The Rebel soldiers pouring into the north side of Gettysburg found the fleeing Union mob an easy target. Thousands of Union soldiers surrendered unresisting in the streets. Brigadier General Alexander Schimmelfennig was forced to an ignominious refuge under a woodpile. Union soldiers broke into houses and hid under featherbeds and in pantries while Rebel troops searched them out from cellar to attic.

Major Gerber had ducked into a church, spied a surgeon's apron, quickly put it on, and busied himself carrying water to the wounded stretched out on the church pews. Striding toward him, sword in hand, came a Southern officer. Gerber was undone, he knew. The two men had known each other before the war. Captain Gilmor examined Gerber in disbelief. He clapped his hand on the Union officer's shoulder. "Gerber, where the hell did you study medicine?" Then, glancing quickly around the church, Gilmor leaned into Gerber's ear and whispered, "Play your game," and walked out of the church. Gerber quickly tore off the doctor's apron, slipped out the vestry door, and ran for Cemetery Hill.

From Lt. Colonel Fremantle's diary:

> 1st July (*Chambersburg, Road to Gettysburg*): At 3 p.m. we began to meet wounded men coming to the rear, and the number of these soon increased most rapidly, some hobbling alone, others on stretchers carried by the ambulance corps and others in the ambulance wagons. Many of the latter were stripped nearly naked, and displayed very bad wounds. This spectacle, so revolting to a person unaccustomed to such sights, produced no impression whatever upon the advancing troops who certainly go under fire with the most perfect nonchalance. They show no enthusiasm or excitement, but the most complete indifference. This is the effect of two years' almost uninterrupted fighting.
>
> . . . At 4 p. m. we came in sight of Gettysburg, and joined General Lee and General Hill, who were on the top of one of the ridges which form the peculiar feature of the country round Gettysburg. We could see the enemy retreating up one of the opposite ridges, pursued by the Confederates with loud yells. The position into which the enemy had been driven was evidently a strong one. His right appeared to rest on a cemetery on the top of a high ridge to the right of Gettysburg, as we looked at it.

Winfield Scott Hancock sat tall and imperial on horseback atop Cemetery Hill, the most commanding presence on the field. The impressive captain of Los Angeles two years before was now an imposing general and Meade's most valued officer on the Gettysburg battlefield. Hancock had arrived at Gettysburg with Meade's instructions to take command and to advise him of the suitability of this place for a final stand. Hancock remained the calm eye in a storm of chaos. Union troops were clambering up Cemetery Hill from two directions, the orderly retreat of the First Corps from the west, the pell mell flight of the 11th Corps from the streets of Gettysburg.

"Jesus, would you look at that," one of the retreating soldiers shouted as they sought the refuge of Cemetery Hill. They were passing under an arch leading to Evergreen Cemetery. On the gate a sign read: "All persons using firearms in these grounds will be prosecuted with the utmost vigor of the law."

The utter serenity of Hancock had a magical effect on the disorganized troops streaming up the hillside. He knew unerringly what he wanted done and gave his orders with calm, unbreachable authority. An appearance of order was fashioned out of pandemonium. A pack of fugitives was reformed into companies, regiments, brigades, and turned around again to face the enemy.

Hancock's eye swept over the terrain off to the right of Cemetery Hill where the land dipped into a saddle for about half a mile, then rose again in a rocky, tree-covered mass called Culp's Hill. Hancock sensed that Rebel occupation of Culp's Hill could be fatal. It must be manned.

Hancock rode over to where General Doubleday was reassembling the shattered fragments of the First Corps. He ordered Doubleday to get a division onto Culp's Hill. Doubleday reacted, "Why me?" His men had absorbed brutal punishment. They were low on ammunition. They were in too poor shape to defend Culp's Hill. Try someone else. Hancock riveted Doubleday with an imperious stare and shouted, "I am in command of this field. Send every man you have got!" Doubleday ordered a bitterly complaining division to occupy Culp's Hill.

The men now forming a ragged rim along Culp's Hill and Cemetery Hill could rightly be counted survivors more than an army. Northern losses had been staggering. Nearly twenty thousand Union men had gone into battle that day. By nightfall, no more than five thousand were gathered here south of town. The rest were dead, wounded, captured, missing. Four thousand men had been captured within the city alone. For all Hancock's brilliant regrouping, the Southerners were poised before a shrunken, bleeding remnant of an army which they could easily brush from the field in one bold thrust, if given the order.

Fifty-one men of the 88th Pennsylvania were captured retreating through town. They were herded outside a tavern where a Confederate colonel had set up headquarters. Of all the baggage of war, prisoners were the most useless. Prisoners must be fed, transported, guarded, all to no purpose but to isolate them from further combat. There was another way, which the Confederate colonel was proposing

to the senior prisoner, a young, rather effete lieutenant, who heard
the proposal with unconcealed enthusiasm.

"I am prepared to offer parole to your men," the colonel said.
"They'll have to sign the required oath not to bear arms or in any way
aid the enemies of the Confederacy in the future. You'll be given safe
conduct through our lines. And then you can all go home for good.
Now, take those terms back to your men."

The young lieutenant mounted a stairway in front of a house. The
prisoners of the 88th Pennsylvania gathered around him. "The colonel has offered us generous terms." He smiled and carefully outlined
the parole offer.

"Tell him to stick it," a sullen voice said.

The lieutenant looked stunned.

"That's right," another man agreed. "Tell that Johnny to stick it."
A chorus of approval rose from the prisoners.

"I want it made quite clear what we are considering," the lieutenant lectured. "It's a choice between Belle Isle or Libby Prison or
going home."

"Don't let 'em shit you, Lieutenant, we ain't goin' to no Belle Isle
or Libby. We're going to get retook by our boys if we just wait it
out."

"Besides, look at all the men they'll have to tie up just looking
after us," another man added.

"Then I take it, the feeling is to reject the offer of parole?"

"Stick it!" the man who initially introduced this response repeated.

"Yeh! Right!" they chorused.

The young lieutenant gazed at them for some time. Then he
squared his shoulders and marched back into the tavern. "Colonel, we
reject parole," he announced confidently.

Lee now paid dearly for his practice of allowing broad interpretation
of his orders by his commanders. In Ewell he had counted on more
leader than he had.

Throughout the day, Ewell had obeyed the letter of Lee's order.
Had not Lee ordered him earlier to avoid a major engagement until
the entire Army of Northern Virginia was assembled? Ewell had
complied. Now, Lee's aide, young Taylor, had come over with Lee's
suggestion that perhaps he could attack and drive the Yankees off the
hills. But Lee was *asking* him, was he not? Not *ordering* him? His

troops had been heavily bled already. They were worn out by twelve hours of marching and fighting. Ewell did not move. There would be no more fighting that day. The golden moment slipped through his fingers.

Late in the afternoon, a brilliant alumnus of the Iron Brigade was bearing down on Gettysburg from Taneytown. Had the war not come along, he might have lived out his days in Madison, Wisconsin, in a successful if unspectacular career in the law. He might have done some writing, too, because he had a vivid eye and a sense of drama. The war ended the law practice. It also filled his adventure-loving soul to bursting with endless opportunities to defy death in glorious confrontations.

Lieutenant Frank Haskell had been plucked from the Iron Brigade for duty on General John Gibbon's staff. At thirty-five, Haskell was a veteran of all the major campaigns of the East, and still as battle-hungry as a freshly minted second lieutenant.

As he rode up the Taneytown Road, approaching the cockpit of battle, his pulse quickened. He peered through the openings between the trees and could see off to the north white puffs of smoke losing themselves in the blue sky. The heat-saturated summer air trembled with the roar of cannon, and Haskell felt a feverish shiver down his spine. As he came closer to the town, as the booming deepened and the white puffs grew thicker, Haskell noticed a silence fall over the men who walked alongside him. They marched more doggedly. Their faces became taut, hard. They barely spoke.

At about five o'clock in the afternoon, a lone ambulance, accompanied by three mounted and grim-faced officers, came rattling down the road toward them. It could only be the body of General Reynolds under that white canvas. Haskell felt a sharp, piercing sense of loss as the wagon passed. He had known and revered Reynolds as a true soldier's general. This sad spectacle only fired Haskell's impatience to get onto the field.

Lieutenant Robert Stiles' gun crew stood poised for action on the northern edge of Gettysburg as the Yankees were driven through the town. Stiles chafed for the order to move forward. A major rode up and yelled to him, "Limber up and move to the rear."

"You mean to the front, don't you, Major?" Stiles looked puzzled.

"I said what I meant." The major spurred his horse toward the next battery.

The men cursed and grumbled. "Lieutenant," one gunner said, "some rear echelon bummer's lost his nerve."

"There's the truth," Burgoyne added, "we could crack that town like an egg and hardly a man of us would be the worse for it." He spat contemptuously.

"Take it easy, boys," Stiles soothed them. "I imagine the town's barricaded, and we'll just pass around it and catch the Yankees on their flank."

Instead, they were pulled back a full mile to a height offering a clear view of the hills south of town. They watched in helpless rage as the retreating Yankees now dug in and threw up breastworks on these hills so lightly defended just hours before. Stiles appeared outwardly cheerful. Inside, he felt a sinking fear that the Confederate failure to follow up the Federal retreat right through town and up those hills could prove fatal.

Mary and Martha, the MacAllister sisters, were spinsters. They had always been skittish, and counted the death of an elderly relative a tragedy and the killing of a chicken violence. Still, they had unhesitatingly answered the call for volunteers to tend the wounded soldiers at their church.

The church had taken on a nightmarish aspect. The screams of suffering men echoed endlessly in the church's vaulted arches. The pews ran red with blood. Through the open stained-glass windows, surgeons casually flung severed limbs.

After hours of lifting casualties, carrying water, running about, and enduring unimagined horror, the two utterly drained women sped toward the refuge of their home. The streets were alive with Union soldiers frantically leaping over the huddled bodies of dead comrades, flinging their arms aside. Wounded men pleaded for help, hobbled and crawled toward safer places. The sisters longed to get behind their doors and shut out the sight of war.

At their doorstep they lifted their skirts to clear a large pool of blood. They found the dining room crowded with Union soldiers, most of them wounded survivors of the Iron Brigade. Among them was Lieutenant Dailey, who had rescued General Archer from the crushing embrace of the now dead Paddy Maloney. The lieutenant had kept the sword he had demanded of Archer, and now asked the MacAllisters to hide it for him. The two bone-weary women accepted that there was no escaping the battle and resigned themselves to helping the fugitives as best they could.

They hid General Archer's sword at the bottom of a firewood box. They offered Colonel Morrow, the commander of the 24th Michigan, a suit of civilian clothes. But the wounded colonel explained to the ladies that a civilian found on this day with a bullet wound furrowed through his scalp might have trouble escaping the classic fate of captured spies.

Suddenly, a loud, tearing sound outside plunged the house into total silence. The lieutenant eased himself cautiously to a window. In the MacAllister back yard, a detail of Confederates was pulling down the fence. They noticed the curtain flutter where the lieutenant stood, and quickly surrounded the house. They took all but the wounded as prisoners. One of the Rebels warned Martha MacAllister, "You better hang out a red flag, lady, so's they'll know what you've got here." Martha rummaged through her closet and pulled out her favorite red shawl. She tied it to a broom handle and flew her flag of mercy from an upstairs window.

Old man Pierce, Tillie's father, had been away from town when the Rebel assault drove the Yankees back and through the town. He arrived just as the last of the Federals fled to the hills to the south, with the Confederates pouring in behind them. Pierce walked the street with feigned casualness, taking long, quick strides. A block from home, five Confederates pounced on him and flung him against a wall.

"Why ain't you in your house, heh?" A Rebel corporal bunched Pierce's shirt tightly in his fist and drove his knuckles painfully into the man's chest.

Pierce's breath came in hard gulps. "I was trying to get there as fast as I can."

"Fall in." The man spun Pierce around and shoved him into the road. "Take us there." Pierce stumbled ahead of them, goaded on by musket barrels jabbed into his back.

When they arrived at Pierce's house, the corporal snarled, "Now we are going to search this place of yours."

Pierce grabbed the iron railings on each side of his stairway. "Boys, take my word for it, you won't find any Union soldiers in this house."

They started to move toward him, their faces twisted and ugly. A burst of gunfire at the end of the street sent them diving for cover. "You better be telling the truth, old man," the corporal said as they moved off toward the shooting, "cuz we are surely coming back."

Pierce sank to the stairs. His heart raced furiously. He drew himself up and was starting up the stairs when another Rebel party came up and demanded a search.

Pierce stood up manfully. Again he gripped the railings. "It's against the rules of war to break into a private house. You'll frighten my family to death. And you'll find no Union soldiers here."

One of the men, a sensitive-looking middle-aged officer, said, "Don't you worry none, old fellow. I believe you."

The firing momentarily waned. The officer had started away but turned back to Pierce. "By the way, what are your politics?"

"I am an unconditional Union man." Pierce stood defiantly. "I'll go further. I am a whole-souled Union man."

"Well, we like you the better for that. What we hate are these milk-and-water Unionists. All the same, you had better get into your house and stay there."

Pierce waited until they were out of sight and then went up to his front door. It was locked. His insistent banging brought no answer. He went around to the back yard and tried the cellar door. It was open. In the cellar's darkness he heard unfamiliar voices and muted moaning. His wife was hiding five Union soldiers.

Old John Burns had managed to sneak the message out with a Gettysburg neighbor to his wife.

"I'm to go and fetch him?" the old woman cried. "The devil take him! The old fool. Going off to fight at his age. Getting bullet holes in his best clothes. And he won't be able to work for months. Leave him. The devil take you, John Burns!"

It had now been silent in Gettysburg for nearly half an hour. "Ma, you stay down here a while yet. Leander, you come upstairs with me. Let's see what's going on." Leander Warren followed his father out of the darkened cellar up the stairs and into a kitchen dimly lit by the low slanting rays of the late afternoon sun.

"They sure didn't leave much." The elder Warren shook his head ruefully. Drawers had been emptied and flung on the floor. Cupboard doors yawned open, some yanked from their hinges. Trails of spilled flour and sugar crisscrossed the floor. As the elder Warren stood studying a ransacked pantry, Leander called in an excited whisper, "Pa! Pa!" The boy was pointing out the front door, which had been left open. Sprawled face down on the stairway was a dead Union soldier. The father dragged the body into the street next to a dead horse.

"What's that you got there, Leander?" The boy was pulling something from the stiff, unyielding grip of a Confederate corpse across the street. It was a beautifully made English rifle.

"Says here, 'T. J. Knight, Company G, 12th Georgia Vigilants,' " Leander read off the stock.

"Hurry up," the father said. "Take it home and hide it behind the fireplace."

The boy stroked the gun and rushed back into the house. He quickly rejoined his father. They explored a few more blocks of the city in its unfamiliar stillness and disarray. When they returned home, they found a stern Confederate officer on horseback confronting Mrs. Warren, who belligerently barred her doorway.

"Sir," the Confederate said, turning to Warren, "is this your house?"

"Yes, it is."

"Is this lady your wife?"

"For better or for worse."

The shift from Mrs. Warren's hostility to her husband's amiability seemed to mollify the Confederate. "Tell me, sir, why you're not in uniform?" His question was more curious than accusing.

"Too old. But I do have a son in my place."

"Are you a Union man?"

"Oh, I'm a Union man. No doubt of that."

"Why couldn't you all let us have our own union, then?"

"Ain't quite the same," the elder Warren said. "If you fellows had your way, you would've split the country into a bunch of splinters."

"Well," the Southerner said, "all this talk isn't filling my belly. I'm so hungry I could eat the hind end out of a skunk."

"Ma, have we got something for a starving man?" He looked at his scowling wife, who still defended the doorway. She did not answer.

He asked again, "Do we or don't we?"

"You know well enough they've gone and took practically every crumb in the house." She looked at her husband as though he had left his senses. "I've got a family to feed with what little they missed."

"C'mon, Ma," he said gently, "he could be our boy, you know."

She shook her head and reentered the house.

The Rebel officer swiftly devoured the piece of shortcake she brought back, licking the last crumb from his fingers.

"You're a Christian woman," he said, giving the woman a smile she did not return. He shook Warren's hand and rode off.

"Hey, Pa," Leander called, pointing to the dead soldier his father had dragged off their stairway earlier. One of the loose pigs in the street was gnawing at the body.

"Come help me, Leander." His father grabbed the dead man's hand. "C'mon, boy. Take his other hand."

Leander gingerly gripped the dead man's sleeve. They dragged him behind the gate of a hay shed, out of the pig's reach.

Private John Casler had mixed feelings about the Pioneer Corps. He cringed at the scathing gibes the men in the fighting ranks unleashed whenever the Pioneers passed by. He felt a scorching humiliation that the Pioneers marched into battle with pickaxes and shovels instead of muskets.

Casler suspected that his transfer from the infantry to the Pioneers may have had something to do with his having skedaddled a few times, with his courts-martial, and with his having been caught swiping alcohol from the surgeon's tent.

But, damn! Casler thought, where would this army be without the Pioneers? Where would the artillery be if the Pioneers did not first clear away the trees and brush to open a line of fire? Who put the roads through the wilderness and floated the pontoons and built the bridges? Besides, wasn't it a whole lot better back with the Pioneers than up there with the other dumb crackers getting your ass shot off every fight?

But there was one duty of the Pioneers that Private Casler hated, and that was the work he and five other men had just set out on, the burial detail.

Tillie Pierce had spent most of the afternoon in the Weikerts' kitchen with Mrs. Schriver and her unmarried sister, Becky Weikert. Tillie had fussed continually over the Schriver children to divert her thoughts from the man with the blown-out eyes lying upstairs.

The artillery fire made her tremble with each blast. Late in the afternoon she heard shouting outside and went to the door to investigate. Several soldiers were coming toward the house. The first had a rag wrapped around a bleeding thumb. The red-stained bandage sent another wave of nausea through her. "Oh, that's dreadful." She turned her head away.

"Well, dearie, you'll see a whole lot worse before this day's over," the wounded man said cheerfully.

Soon the wounded were pouring into the Weikerts' and every other house, barn, and building that offered cover. Some arrived on foot with heads, arms, and legs swathed in makeshift bandages. Some were brought in on stretchers, others came by wagon, some crawled.

In the house, Tillie sat shaking, listening to the men speak of fearful losses, of wholesale retreat, of the capture of the city, of a rout.

"What will they do to the people?" Tillie asked unsteadily. Two men, whose wounds appeared slight, sneered knowingly. "He he! If them Rebs don't behave no better'n Willie here did in Virginia, I hope you ain't got no sisters up there, girlie."

"Or a good-lookin' old lady." The man called Willie grinned.

Tillie rushed tearfully from the house. Becky Weikert ran after her. "Oh, don't pay any mind to those brutes, Tillie, even the Rebs can't be as bad as them."

"I've seen the Rebels," Tillie sobbed.

As dusk fell, the orange-red light of hospital lanterns glowed from behind the Weikert house.

"My God, they've taken Pa's barn, too. Let's go look," Becky said.

The two young women stepped inside the barn door and almost immediately fled. A foul stench assaulted them. The bare ground was covered with wounded. Soft moans and sobbing filled the place.

"Please bring us some water. Please." The pleading man lay near the doorway with his head propped against the wall. He was flanked on either side by dead men.

Tillie and Becky stumbled in the dark to the well and filled two pails with water. Tillie could not bring herself to go into the barn again. She reached inside the doorway and left the pail near the man.

Tillie leaned against the barn, trembling. "I don't think I can take any more . . . can't take any more. She vomited again. Then they went back in the house. The nurses saw Tillie's sickly face, the reddened eyes and shivering body. Becky described the visit to the barn.

"Oh, don't take on so, dear." One of the nurses patted Tillie's cheek. "Most of those boys have just got themselves a ticket home. Isn't that right, boys?" She turned to the lightly wounded men crowded on the kitchen floor. "Sure enough!" they laughed.

"Why," one man said, "I knew a feller so scared of fighting he tried to shoot off his own toe—except he missed and hit the colonel's horse!" The nurses and the men all laughed.

Another man piped up, "If one of us was to run for office some day, there's nothing better than a little old limp from a war wound."

Again they roared with laughter. Tillie Pierce found she too was giggling, then laughing hysterically, uncontrollably at the feeblest jest, at anything that anyone said, laughing so hard that tears bathed her face.

Boisterous Rebels roving the streets of Gettysburg scarcely noticed the small, intent private striding purposefully down East Middle Street. This was one fine town, they had decided as they bought fresh milk, cheese, and soft, warm bread with worthless Confederate bills or pillaged whatever caught their eye. Some of the men—not many, because of General Lee's stern warning against improper behavior— had gotten drunk. Wesley Culp ignored them, stepped around them and kept moving. He scanned every familiar doorway, every church spire, every remembered name over every shop with welling apprehension.

Culp's unit, the Stonewall Brigade, had missed the fight that day. The brigade arrived on the field late and was posted to the extreme left of the Confederate line in a forested position all too familiar to Wesley Culp. It was called Culp's Woods, a fact he kept to himself. His tangled emotions this night needed no further abrasion from the gibes which this knowledge might provoke from his comrades.

As soon as they had settled into place, Wes went looking for Pendleton, General Walker's orderly. He and Pendleton had been friends back in Shepardstown. Wes was sure the orderly could help.

Culp did not know what Pendleton told the general, but it must have had something to do with Wes's loyalty, because General Walker had clasped his hand warmly, told him how delighted he was to find out he had a Pennsylvanian in the Stonewall Brigade, and, yes, of course Private Culp could have a pass to visit his family in Gettysburg.

Even in pitch dark, he had walked the two miles over narrow country lanes, down the York Road over Rock Creek bridge and into town with the assurance of a man unlocking his own door. On the way, he passed close by his Uncle Henry's farm near Culp's Hill.

His heart pounded furiously as he crossed to West Middle Street. He fought down the urge to sprint the final distance. A sharp, stabbing nostalgia swept over him. He began to question the wisdom of this visit. He stopped before the doorway, breathing heavily. His eyes traced the door jamb, the worn floor boards. He knocked hesitantly. No answer. He knocked again, harder. After a long wait, the door opened a crack.

"Who is it?" a woman's voice, hoarse with fear, called. She opened the door wider, and gaped at the alien, yellow-gray uniform and studied the bearded face.

"My God," she said. "It is you!" She turned into the house and shouted deliriously, "Julia, it's Wes come home!"

"Buell," Sergeant Mitchell said, "got a nice, soft spot for you. You're going on ammunition detail."

Cub Buell and the other men picked by the sergeant hitched up a wagon and moved down the Taneytown Road, just behind the Union line. They passed a small house where officers milled about the porch and couriers moved in and out in a constant stream. The Widow Leister's home had become Union army headquarters. They turned east on a crossroad that led to the Baltimore Turnpike. Cub Buell looked down the darkened road and felt ill. Every house, every barn, every yard they passed was claimed by the wounded. Some moaned, some raved, some cried like children. They swore, cursed, screamed, "Help me, doctor, don't leave . . ." "Oh please . . . shoot me, somebody, please be kind, shoot me . . ." "Say goodnight to Daddy, children, Daddy is going to sleep," ". . . the farm, Ezra, you'll get the farm now, won't you, Ezra . . ." "Somebody, somebody, get this dead man off me . . ." "Water! . . ." "Whiskey! . . ."

"Doctor! . . ." "Help . . ." "Oh God, let me live," ". . . God, let me die."

Litter bearers deposited wounded on the ground in an endless stream. Hospital lanterns hung from poles, from barn doors, from tents and houses, casting an unnatural glow over the scene. In one mile, Cub Buell passed by eight thousand wounded men. One thousand of them would die during the night.

Long years later, the men of the 20th Maine would recall the night of July 1, 1863.

"We was near to collapse. We had already done twenty-six miles that day. As we pushed along the road heading west, we could hear something up ahead. Sounded as though someone was beating on a big rug far off. It was artillery, of course. But we didn't know exactly where or whose. We'd gone into bivouac at Hanover. All of us were plumb wore out. Well, we no sooner stacked our arms and flung our knapsacks on the ground and was a'lookin' for some branches for tent poles, when this fellow comes riding in hell bent for leather. That horse of his was just a'drippin' sweat, and so was he. He rode up to where they was setting up the division headquarters. It wasn't too long before we got the drift of what he'd come to say. It seems part of the army had run into General Lee's boys fifteen miles to the east. We learned General Reynolds was shot dead in this fight and the rest of the army was pulling back onto some hills south of a town called Gettysburg.

"I don't think we ever heard a worse order than when they told us to get moving again. It had been better if we'd never stopped. We'd done pretty near a hundred fifty miles in five days. My leg muscles was actually twitching with fatigue once we'd stopped. But no use. We just got up and cursed the God damn Johnnies and cursed the God damn war and fell in again.

"A funny thing happened. As it got darker, it got a little cooler. And the moon was so bright that it lit up the whole sky a pale blue. Just beautiful. We'd never marched amongst any but the enemy folks before, which ain't a very warming experience. But on this night, our own people was a'comin, out of the houses. They was cheering, and waving flags, and shaking handkerchiefs. Girls was blowing us kisses. And bands played. It was like when we'd left Maine the year before. Only more touching really because these folks were scared and depending on us. I don't think any of us ever felt so needed. We were defending the home soil. Protecting women and children. The fatigue and the miles we'd done just seemed to melt away in the moonlight.

"But the cheering faded as it got later. We marched the fifteen miles to Gettysburg and got there after midnight. We posted a guard and the rest of us just collapsed on the side of the road where it was all wet with dew and slept."

The joyful, painful evening had to end. "You can't stay until morning, Wes?" his older, married sister, Annie, pleaded, stroking his black hair with a soothing touch.

He shook his head wistfully. "I can't do that, Annie. General Walker's a real fine gentleman. He's got my word."

As soon as the shock of his sudden appearance had passed, Wes, Annie, and his young sister, Julia, had quickly resumed their old open affection. They gossiped of what had become of former schoolmates, who had gotten married, jilted, jailed. Wes was especially curious about the regiments his boyhood friends had joined, the battles they had fought, as though asking of comrades rather than foes.

He had learned with some relief that he and his brother, Will, would not likely meet at Gettysburg. The Culp boys had already faced each other as unwitting enemies a few weeks before in the engagement at Winchester, Virginia, a thought which particularly horrified young Julia. Will Culp's regiment, the 87th Pennsylvania, was not among the Union troops at Gettysburg, Annie assured him.

Wesley told his sisters how he had learned that Will was at Winchester during his strange reunion with his boyhood comrade, the wounded Jack Skelly. He suddenly remembered that he had a letter which Skelly had asked him to carry to his fiancée, Jennie Wade.

"Too late now," he said. "But I'll come to see you again tomorrow and I'll take her the letter then. I hope Jack makes it," he said softly, unconvincingly.

Wesley forced himself up from the comfortable, worn horsehair sofa, and put his arm around Julia. "Little one, darned if you aren't almost as big as me." It was true, since twenty-three-year-old Wesley Culp was scarcely taller than most children half his age.

"Then we will see you again tomorrow, Wesley." Annie clasped her hands and smiled. "That is so wonderful."

"Oh, Wes," she said, disappearing into the kitchen, "now you just wait another minute."

She returned with bread and cold meats spread on a large napkin, which she deftly tied into a bundle. Wesley Culp took the package, kissed his sisters, and returned to the Confederate lines.

As darkness descended, a fetid miasma hung over the Chambersburg Pike. It rose from the bed of the railroad cut, from trampled fields of corn and wheat surrounding Seminary Ridge, from stained pastures, from thousands of bodies exposed long hours in a baking sun.

Overhead, buzzards swooped and wheeled over the harvest of the guns. From the time that Private Raison, 7th Tennessee, had fallen early in the morning until the gunfire faded that night, 14,700 men had become casualties at Gettysburg—9700 Union men and 5000 Confederates, dead, wounded, or missing.

The Confederate pickets listened to the clicking of crickets, the whirr of insects, the awful moaning of wounded men abandoned on the field. From Cemetery Hill and Culp's Hill, Ewell's men could hear other sounds that made them rage against their chief. On the modest heights which they could have seized so cheaply hours before, they could hear the clanking of spades, the echo of axe blows, the rumble of artillery caissons. The enemy had been given the priceless gift of time to dig in.

The Rebel private moved quickly from body to body. His pockets bulged with rings, money, watches, and pocket knives removed from the Union dead. He came upon another Southerner sitting on the ground next to a prostrate Union lieutenant.

"What'n hell you doing?"

"I'm a'waitin' for this Yankee to die so's I can strip him."

"You damn fool." The scavenger pushed the waiting man aside and began rifling the pockets of the softly moaning wounded officer.

General Meade never got closer than thirteen miles to Gettysburg during this first day's fighting. His original plan had been to deploy the Army of the Potomac in a defensive position along Pipe Creek, which ran about thirteen miles south of Gettysburg. The Rebel search for shoes, the stubborn stand of his own cavalry, fate, in brief, had decreed otherwise.

On July 1, Meade was headquartered at Taneytown near the contemplated Pipe Creek line when he was told at noon that Buford's cavalry had been engaged. An hour later he learned that General Reynolds was dead. Immediately, Meade dispatched General Hancock to Gettysburg to take charge and to determine the best place to stand: at Gettysburg, or to fall back to Pipe Creek. By 4:30, the flow of reports had forced Meade's decision before he had Hancock's recommendation. He began firing off messages to his other corps commanders to converge on Gettysburg.

But not until ten o'clock in the evening did Meade and his staff leave Taneytown for Gettysburg. The general arrived on the battle-field shortly after midnight and began, methodically, analytically, to position his men for the next moves. The old topographical engineer could see even by moonlight that he had good ground to defend.

All night long, the quiet on the elevations south of Gettysburg was violated by the creak of artillery wheeling into position, the low rumbling of supply wagons and ambulances, the tramp of regiments as they slotted into place—the sinews of strength of the Union army massing, unseen, in the dark. One out of every eighteen men able to bear arms in the North had converged on Gettysburg. With the Confederate troops, 181,000 men were now gathered here—104,000 Federals and 77,000 Confederates. By daylight, Meade had virtually his entire army deployed where he wanted it.

4 | THE SECOND DAY

THE TOPOGRAPHY OF THE LAND west and south of Gettysburg shaped the fighting. West of town was a gentle swell of land running north and south for about five miles, called Seminary Ridge. At its highest, the ridge was only 560 feet above sea level. Directly south of town, running more or less parallel to Seminary Ridge and about a mile from it, was Cemetery Ridge. At its highest point, this ridge was about 600 feet above sea level. Cemetery Ridge gradually tapered south of town for about a mile and a half, losing elevation and dwindling to practically nothing. At the south end of Cemetery Ridge rose two modest hills, Little Round Top with an elevation of 650 feet and, directly south, Round Top rising 785 feet. The hills and a rock-strewn area in front of the Round Tops, called the Devil's Den, were geologic intruders in this otherwise rolling, fertile countryside. These jagged rises were formed of shale and trap rock, chunks of rock jutting out above the scrubby growth of trees and bushes.

At the northern end of Cemetery Ridge was a knob called Cemetery Hill. Located on its crest was Evergreen Cemetery. To the east of Cemetery Hill, separated by a short saddle of land, was Culp's Hill, 620 feet above sea level.

The morning of July 2 found the Union troops strung out in a line beginning at Culp's Hill, then running west to Cemetery Hill, then bending south and running down to Little Round Top.

Roughly paralleling the Federal ran the Confederate line beginning northeast of Gettysburg, running through the town, then bending south along Seminary Ridge.

In terms of maneuverability and communications, Meade had the better of it. From the right edge at Culp's Hill to the left edge at Little Round Top, he could move his men and messages behind the lines along a chord only three miles in length. Lee's line, bent around the Union line, extended over nine miles, and it was behind this sweeping arc that he had to dispatch his orders and deploy his men.

"I got a feeling we're going to violate our oath again, Isaac." P. H. Taylor laughed as he swung his haversack to the ground. It was a private joke between the two former schoolteacher brothers who now served with the First Minnesota. Isaac and P. H. Taylor had actually signed an oath not to take up arms against the Southern Confederacy, or to aid or abet her enemies. It had happened almost a year ago to the day, when they had been captured at Gaines' Mill. The oath held good only if they were paroled, in which case they could have gone home for good, freeing the South of two less mouths to feed. But they had been exchanged for Confederate prisoners instead of being paroled. The oath was no longer binding.

Their regiment had been roused from sleep at three in the morning of July 2 and had arrived on the battlefield at 5:40 a.m. Isaac Taylor had snatched a few minutes to write in his small leather-bound diary. He thumbed through the most recent pages and relished again the events he had recorded. His brother, P.H., had a lively, winning spirit, a knack for instant friendship to sustain him through this war. Isaac had clung tenaciously to his love of nature as his refuge from the madness, the killing, the desecration of life he held so dear.

On May 13, Isaac noted in the diary that he had finished *Hitchcock's Geology*. On May 22, he had recorded that he and P.H. had managed to slip away for a successful geological expedition. They had found five "concretions" fixed in sandstone. On May 27, *Wood's Botany* had arrived in the mail. One of the last entries noted that he had sent an unusual rock specimen back home to the state museum for identification.

In the tiny confines of the diary, Isaac had pressed several unusual leaves and flowers. One page had a flattened flower with each petal lettered to spell out "My Maryland." The date, "June 27, '63," had been neatly worked into the center of the flower.

This morning there was little time for flowers. Isaac scribbled quickly, "Order from General Gibbon read to us in which he says this is to be the great battle of the war and that any soldier leaving the ranks without leave will be instantly put to death."

To Lieutenant Colonel Arthur James Lyon Fremantle of Her Majesty's Coldstream Guards, the spectacle was remarkably American. He had climbed a tree on Seminary Ridge that morning for a better look at the Yankee lines. Beneath him sat the commanding officer of the Confederate Army, General Lee, his chief lieutenant, General Longstreet, and Longstreet's subordinate, General Hood, all of them whittling. The rustic busy work helped temper edgy deliberations. Lee wanted to attack forcefully and soon. Longstreet wanted to attack not at all. Hood, as Longstreet's subordinate, said little.

The Englishman was well aware of Longstreet's misgivings. The night before, he had dined in Longstreet's tent and found the general a gruff but considerate host. Fremantle regretted that he had never known the Longstreet of old of whom the other officers spoke. "Pete" Longstreet, now forty-two years old, had been a soldier's soldier, handsome in a roughhewn way, a man who had enjoyed a drink, liked a party and played bold poker. Fremantle never knew that Longstreet. The officer he met had lost all three of his children during the winter before in a diphtheria epidemic. It was a husk of the old Longstreet that Fremantle saw, but still one of the most impressive men he had ever known on either side of the Atlantic.

In the dinner conversation the night before, Longstreet had openly expressed his objection to the invasion of the North. He explained to Fremantle that he had told Lee he favored bolstering the Confederate armies in the West in order to defeat Grant and thus relieve Vicksburg. His counsel had been rejected. Once the decision had been made to invade the North, Longstreet said he favored luring the Union army into attacking, as at Fredericksburg, instead of having the Confederates attack. Again, Lee ignored Longstreet's advice.

"Do you believe the enemy is strong here, sir?" Fremantle had asked that evening.

"Formidable," Longstreet answered, gravely. "And no doubt about it, they'll be entrenching themselves into those hills all the damn night."

The following morning, from his treetop perch Fremantle watched the Confederate commanders below sharpening sticks with their knives and arguing the next moves.

Longstreet had a last counterstrategy. He would avoid a head-on assault against the Union army. He wanted to swing around the southern shank of that Federal line and put the Confederates between the Yankees and Washington and Baltimore.

He argued his position doggedly. Lee, gentle of surface but unbending within, was determined that the army must finish the job at Gettysburg. The day before, when he recognized that he was fully committed, Lee's hope had been to have General Ewell's troops deliver the death blow from the north, against Cemetery Hill and Culp's Hill.

After he had sent his aide, Colonel Taylor, over to urge General Ewell forward, he had gone over personally to weigh the situation. Lee had been sadly educated to Ewell's lack of fitness. The Federals had been heavily reinforced, dug in too deeply, Ewell had argued, or rather, his subordinates had argued since Ewell sat listless, nearly wordless throughout the discussion, which depressed Lee most of all. This slumped, silent figure was the successor to the incorrigibly aggressive Stonewall Jackson who had been killed months before at Chancellorsville. Lee's outward composure masked the deep frustration he felt as he spurred his horse, Traveler, back from Ewell's headquarters to his own camp that night.

Now, this morning, even his faithful Longstreet was resisting his attack plan. The thought crossed Lee's mind that maybe personal tragedy had spoiled Longstreet's stomach for fighting. The loss of his children may have dulled his will to provoke more death. No, Lee dismissed the thought, Longstreet was still a fighter, a great fighter. But, unfortunately, a defensive fighter. Lee left Longstreet still whittling and made one last trip to Ewell's sector that morning to reweigh the possibilities for a major thrust from north of town. He concluded from this visit that he could expect no more than a coordinated counterpunch from Ewell. He left knowing that Longstreet would have to make the main attack against the southern-

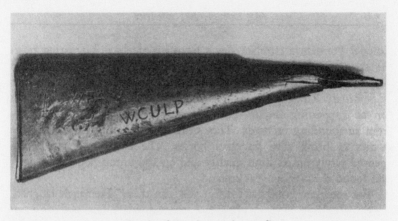

Stock of Wesley Culp's rifle.

most end of the Union line, down by the Round Tops. He gave that order to Longstreet on the morning of July 2 at eleven o'clock.

Like hostile beasts the Union and Confederate forces around Culp's Hill warily circled, probed, and pawed that morning. The main bodies of troops remained safely separated. But thin lines of rival skirmishers, maneuvering uneasily a few dozen yards apart, provided sharp claws for the armies to swipe at each other, to feel out opposing positions, to test relative strengths, to ward off surprise attacks. Wes Culp's company had drawn this skirmishing assignment.

The morning was deathly still. The sounds he made chewing the last crust of bread his sister had given him seemed dangerously audible. A slight flurry of movement. The lieutenant passed the word to the company. They were out of contact with the Yankee skirmishers. They would push farther up the side of Culp's Hill. Wesley was beyond reflecting on the irony of it. It was a hill. His Uncle Henry owned it. He was fighting to wrest it for an enemy invader. None of this occurred to him as he swallowed the last of the bread and began tramping with the company up the scraggly underbrush of the hillside.

Yankee and Rebel skirmishers exchanged a few shots as the Rebels neared. There were screams, some casualties. Then all was still again. The men of Company B tended to their wounded. They buried the one man killed. They had found Wesley Culp with a bullet in his head. In his hand he clutched a fistful of the earth of Culp's Hill.

*   *   *

Colonel Fremantle climbed down from his treetop observation post. He spent the rest of the morning wandering idly amidst the men preparing for battle. He and two Confederate officers rode the length of Seminary Ridge watching General Longstreet deploy his divisions for the impending assault. The officers gorged themselves on cherries from surrounding orchards. They ordered a grumbling Pennsylvania farmer to bring corn for their horses. The two Southerners commented wryly on its high quality and on the untouched wealth they had found throughout Yankeeland.

"But somehow, they can't defeat you, can they?" Fremantle laughed.

"So far, so far," one of the Southerners nodded, but with no great assurance.

They left the disgruntled farmer suspiciously examining a Confederate note. They rode south to where Seminary Ridge vanished into flat land.

The three men stripped off dust-caked uniforms and splashed happily in the shallow waters of Willoughby Run, Fremantle perhaps not as happily as the others. They were nearly beyond their lines and they could plainly discern the movements of Union cavalrymen alongside the Round Tops.

"Don't be concerned, Colonel," one of the naked Southerners comforted the apprehensive Englishman. "They won't bother us. We're wearing the universal uniform today."

By the time they had reached Gettysburg on July 2, the men of the 20th Maine had realized one of their deepest desires. The hard, demanding Colonel Adelbert Ames had been promoted to brigadier general and out of the regiment for his performance at Chancellorsville —"gone and forgotten," one of the men had gleefully noted, although the experience of combat had moderated their opinion of Ames' harsh methods. Indeed, Sergeant Tom Chamberlain seemed to mellow considerably toward the colonel after Ames recommended him for lieutenant. Still, wild enthusiasm had swept the regiment when Tom's older brother, Lawrence Chamberlain, was elevated to command.

On the field of Gettysburg, the 20th Maine and three other regiments formed the Third Brigade, under Colonel Strong Vincent. The men liked Vincent. He was intelligent and resolute, exuded confidence, and looked the leader of men. His bearing was erect. He had a handsome, sensitive face and was one of the few clean-shaven officers on the field, except for a pair of sidewhiskers which luxuriated down to his collar.

Lieutenant Beath, of the 88th Pennsylvania, moved freely among the Confederate soldiers. He had discarded his Union cap and now wore a Confederate hospital corps arm band prominently. He tended the wounded as he found them, his own kind or the enemy. Beath was working out of McPherson's barn, now designated a hospital. The term was a mockery. There were no doctors, no medicines, and until Beath came on the scene, no treatment of any kind. The dirt floor of the barn was carpeted with patients. Most of their wounds were festering badly. One man's arm, terribly mangled, had swollen to an enormous size and was turning black. Some of the men were stuck to the floor by their own blood. Some were dead.

Among these broken figures, Beath found one man in relatively good health, suffering only a slight arm wound, an illiterate, whining Virginian. The man had protested, but finally and grudgingly had agreed to carry water for Beath to the wounded.

Beath moved in an ever widening circle around the McPherson barn seeking out the wounded. He found sun-blistered men, mad with heat, dying from lack of water and food. They spoke delirious nonsense to him, called him "brother," "wife," "mother," "father." Others stared silently from voided eyes. Beath knew that his touch would be their last kindness on this earth. He gave them water, washed their wounds as best he could. He tore his own underclothes into shreds for bandages. He moved about the field in a state of almost euphoric well-being, humoring his ever complaining Virginian aide, whose sole philosophy of the War was summed up in his constantly repeated refrain, "They ain't no Yankee worth a pinch of shit!"

Among the reinforcements approaching Gettysburg was the 150th New York. These men had never tasted battle. They asked foolish questions. They reacted excessively, excitedly to every sudden sound. They had been in high spirits marching toward the field, fueled by a nervous tension that found release in horseplay and coarse repartee.

A particularly loud shell burst off in the distance. "Hey," a soldier hollered to the man ahead, "what's that big brown spot around yer drawers? You scared shitless already?"

"Kiss my ass, soldier."

"Ain't no point to worrying. When your time comes, down you go."

"Yeh." The soldier ahead turned and sneered. "Every bullet's got its billet."

Then, they quickly went silent. It had been only one man. He was among a group of stragglers streaming back from the front. The man's eyes were dulled. He held one bloody arm with the other. The men of the 150th New York looked at each other uneasily as he passed by and, thereafter, approached Gettysburg in silence.

In town that Thursday morning Jennie Wade recited the Twenty-seventh Psalm with a sense of rapture. The meaning was suddenly, shiningly clear.

"Though an host should encamp against me, my heart shall not fear. Though war should rise against me, in this I will be confident."

Never had Jennie Wade felt closer to her soldierboy, Jack Skelly, off with the Union army. Until these past two days, Jack's life away from her had been the stuff of girlish imaginings. Now, with the battle raging around her, Jennie knew what Jack was living. She was not horrified. She felt lifted by the unity of their experience. From now on, their letters would convey a shared communion. Yes, it was horrible, but it was a horror that her Jack will not have endured alone.

Jennie closed her Bible and bowed her head in silence. She was twenty years old. There was a simplicity to her face that denied great beauty. Yet she was striking enough, with a full, generous body. Her shining dark hair was parted in the middle and pulled tight against her head. The severity of the style was broken by a braid coiled across the top from ear to ear. Her eyes were bright and believing.

Jennie Wade had spent the first day of battle carrying water to wounded men lying in the streets of Gettysburg. She had also found time to bake a huge batch of cookies and felt a marvelous excitement at having them snatched up by blue-clad soldiers who came knocking at the door.

But, on this second day of battle, the Rebel soldiers commanded the streets of Gettysburg. The nearest Union men were sharpshooters perched around Cemetery Hill. Shots traded by both sides echoed endlessly through the streets. For two days the little brick house on

Jennie Wade.

Baltimore Street had been under constant fire. A shell had hurtled through the upstairs room, cracking walls and ceilings and showering dust and plaster on the family. They dared not move again. They had already left the Wade house on Breckenridge Street and had come over to Baltimore Street to the home of Jennie's married sister, Georgia McClellan. Jennie, with her little brother and her mother, had thought it best to stay at 'Georgia's place to help with

Georgia's five-day-old infant. The baby's father was off with the Union Army.

"Mamma." Jennie put aside the Bible. "I think I'll see to some bread." Her mother was cradling the baby, who slept oblivious to the sharp cracks of rifle fire and the thunderclaps of artillery.

Jennie stood in the kitchen kneading bread dough and singing softly to herself the half-remembered words of "Johnny, Fill Up the Bowl," a soldier song Jack Skelly had taught her. The serenity of the scene within the house, the sleeping baby, the rich smell of the dough being worked beneath her fingers blotted out the reality beyond the door.

Business had never been better or more unexpected than that Thursday noon at the Globe Inn. Two days before, the proprietor, Charley Wills, had hired two extra bartenders just to fill canteens as the Union soldiers came into town. Then, when the attack began on Wednesday, Wills had dutifully obeyed the army order to stop selling whiskey to the troops, and he had let the extra help go.

But that had been before the Yankee retreat. Now, every seat in the inn was filled all day long with Confederate officers. Wills had rehired the two extra bartenders to draw whiskeys from the continually emptying barrels behind the bar. He and his son, John, moved hurriedly, wiping tables, trying to decipher strangely accented orders and rushing steaming platters to the tables.

Wills was much impressed by the civility and good manners of the enemy patrons, a far cry from the frequent coarse comportment of the Union soldiers. When the Confederates had first come, he had been alarmed. He had raised the price of a dinner from thirty-five cents to fifty cents, and doubled a whiskey from a nickel to a dime. But these officers had never balked. They whipped out fat rolls of good greenbacks, even gold, and paid cash for every meal.

"Damn, Pa," young John Wills said to his father as they spooned fresh platefuls of lamb stew in the kitchen, "where are these Rebs getting all that good money?"

"That ain't our concern, boy," the old man said, kicking the kitchen door open and juggling four hot platters into the dining room.

That morning, at the southern end of Cemetery Ridge, General Daniel Sickles looked out, uneasy and unhappy, from the position assigned to his Third Corps. General Meade had directed Sickles to occupy the very last leg of the Federal line from the end of Cemetery Ridge down to and including Little Round Top.

Ridge, my foot, thought Sickles. The ground, higher and defendable at the northern edge of the Union line, trailed off to virtually nothing at the sector assigned to Sickles. The terrain in front of him was even more disturbing. About half a mile ahead of Sickles' line, the ground rose slowly to a peach orchard, slightly higher than the ground Sickles occupied. This was Chancellorsville all over again, Sickles feared. Confederate guns on that higher ground could pour fire down onto his men. Off to his left, in front of the Round Tops, the ground was badly broken. Great rocks, ravines, small hills, and patches of trees—a stretch of terrain known as the Devil's Den—provided a progression of covered positions for any foe moving up on Sickles' corps. He peered enviously ahead of him at the higher, unoccupied ground of the peach orchard. That is where I ought to be, before the Rebels take it, he concluded. He turned to his staff. "I am going to see General Meade."

On top of Little Round Top Union soldiers under General John Geary waited for Sickles. Geary had orders that his men were to be relieved by Sickles' men and then he was to move over to help defend Culp's Hill about three miles northeast. The impatient Geary had sent a messenger to Sickles to find out when he could expect to be relieved. Sickles, uneager to nail himself to the line he disliked so much, had sent Geary a temporizing reply. Geary now felt that he had waited long enough. He marched his troops off and left Little Round Top unoccupied, except for a few signalmen.

To Major Blackford, Gettysburg for the moment was a Roman revel in the midst of Armageddon. The major luxuriated on a plush, black velvet sofa, chatting idly with his fellow officers. Before them, piled on a handsome marble-topped table, were decanters of wine, meats, fruits, and cheeses. Outside they could hear the rumble of artillery and the occasional thud of a bullet against the house. The fashionably furnished parlor was much as its owners had left it, except that the wall facing south had been broken through. The parlor now opened directly onto the adjoining row house. The south wall of that house, too, had been battered through. And so had the walls of each succeeding house on the block, except for the last house, whose south side faced Cemetery Hill. In effect, the houses had been converted into a long interior corridor. This arrangement allowed the Confederates to move about without going outside and risking the fire of Yankee sharpshooters on Cemetery Hill.

From where he sat, Major Blackford could see through to the last house, where, on the second floor, he had positioned his three deadliest sharpshooters. In the stifling heat of the second-floor bedroom, the Confederate marksmen took turns firing from two windows into the rifle pits and artillery batteries on Cemetery Hill.

"Yup, it's that brick house at the end of the street with the gable facing us. I'd say the second floor," the young lieutenant with the binoculars said. "No doubt about it."

"Can we take her, sir?" Sergeant Mitchell asked.

"Go ahead." The lieutenant nodded.

They had eagerly searched for the Rebel sharpshooters' aerie. Since the day before, two men of Battery B had been wounded and one killed by this sniping. Sergeant Mitchell studied the house carefully. There were two windows on the upper floor. He turned to Cub Buell. "We'll use the new gun. Swing her into line, Cub." The weapon had the least-worn barrel in the battery and promised the greatest accuracy.

"Give her a round of case. Cut her for six hundred feet, Cub." John Mitchell, with slow, steady deliberation, sighted the gun. He stepped back. His powerful arm reached forward. He jerked the lanyard and the gun reared in recoil. The shot struck precisely between the two upper windows and exploded inside the house. It was the prettiest shot Cub Buell saw in the whole war. Major Blackford and his party felt the house shake. Plaster rained from sudden cracks in the ceiling and a cloud of dust whooshed through the corridor of broken walls joining the houses. Blackford jumped to his feet and made his way to the last house. The floor was deep with chunks of plaster and smashed brick. Coughing and gasping, one of Blackford's sharpshooters staggered down the stairway dragging another man by the arms. Both were dusted white by the powdery debris. The whiteness across the chest of the man being dragged was broken by a vivid, sprawling red stain.

The standing man dazedly waved his hand toward the stairway.

"Sergeant's still up there, Major. He's dead."

*   *   *

Everything that Dan Sickles said to George Meade had to pass through several filters of prejudice. Sickles was a politician, a murderer, a rake, worst of all, a political general. Indeed, Sickles was the only corps commander Meade had inherited who was not a career soldier.

"General Meade"—Sickles was straining hard at unaccustomed deference—"there is no stronger argument I can make for the untenability of my present position than to have you see it yourself."

Meade was agitated and preoccupied. He was expecting a Confederate attack from the north and this danger dominated his thoughts. He bowed over the papers before him, his eyes avoiding direct contact with the upstart general.

"Will you come, General Meade?"

Meade finally looked up at Sickles. "I have staked out the disposition of this army with some care, General Sickles. I trust I can expect you to follow your quite explicit orders."

Sickles persisted: Meade must come and see for himself the situation he faced.

"I'm sorry, I cannot."

"Can Butterfield?"

Meade's great Roman nose snorted. His chief of staff, he said, was too busy. Sickles planted his feet resolutely before Meade's table. Meade finally turned to General Hunt, his artillery chief. "Hunt," he ordered brusquely, "please accompany General Sickles. Report back to me what you think of the action he proposes." He turned back to the clutter of messages and maps before him.

"Can I use my own judgment, then, in deploying my men?" Sickles asked.

"Yes," Meade answered, without raising his head, "within the limits of the general instructions I gave you."

Sickles had already taken one precaution. Curious Confederate movements were afoot, around and behind the ridges a mile and a half in front of his line. Shortly before noon he had dispatched Berdan's sharpshooters to investigate.

"There go Berdan's boys. They'll sure'n hell stir up something," a Union soldier yelled out as the sharpshooters crossed the Emmitsburg Road at the peach orchard. They passed a farmhouse where a barefoot boy, thumbs hooked in his pants pockets, watched them warily.

"You don't want to go in there." The boy pointed to a patch of woods behind the farmhouse. "There's lots of Rebels in there. Whole rows of 'em."

"What's troubling you, boy, afraid we'll stomp your old man's corn?" They laughed and marched on.

They entered the woods. The sylvan stillness was broken only by the crunch of twigs and branches beneath their feet and the call of birds overhead. It was menacingly quiet.

The salvo exploded like a thunderbolt caroming off the trees. The first of Berdan's sharpshooters fell on the Gettysburg battlefield. His comrades took cover behind the trees and began pouring the superior firepower of their Spencer repeaters into the enemy. The Confederate skirmishers who had greeted them were quickly withered by the murderous Union fire. Once past this frail shell, Berdan's sharpshooters, some three hundred of them, pressed insolently against the nineteen thousand men of Longstreet's main body on the western slope of Seminary Ridge near Pitzer's Creek.

They had intercepted the Confederate troops on the point of moving south to position themselves for an attack on the left of the Union line. Berdan grasped their intention and sped Captain Briscoe back to warn General Sickles. He then ordered his men, now joined by the Third Maine, to advance firing. They had caught the enemy marching sideways to their fire. The best marksmen in the Union army were dropping the surprised and confused Southern troops with deadly frequency. Yet the sharpshooters were as so many fleas discomfiting the hide of an elephant. The Rebel force was a huge, horned beast that lumbered ahead, bleeding from a hundred places but still rolling on.

Berdan had fulfilled his mission. He ordered the bugler to sound retreat. The men pulled back, unhurried, deliberate, firing as they withdrew. Captain McClellan went down. Two of the men, Kipp and Nelson, unrolled a blanket and set the stricken officer on it.

"We got you, Captain, you're gonna be all right," a heavily panting Nelson said as they headed toward the Union line. "Gonna be all . . ." Nelson tumbled forward, a large, wet hole in his back. The wounded captain rolled off the blanket. Kipp hollered to another soldier to help him.

"Leave me, get out before we all get killed," the captain cried.

"All right, Captain," Kipp said, "we won't go no further. But I'll stay with you."

The wounded man and Kipp were quickly overtaken by three Confederate soldiers wielding bayoneted rifles.

"Get up and get to the rear," one of them ordered.

"I ain't going. I'm here tending the captain."

The three bayonets closed on him and pierced his skin. "We ain't fartin' around, soldier. Get to the rear."

A Southern officer came over and warned Kipp to obey. "Don't worry, I'll see that an ambulance takes care of your captain."

Kipp shrugged hopelessly toward Captain McClellan and started toward the rear with a bayonet poised inches from his back. He passed over the ground just contested and was appalled at the savagery. In some places, bodies were slumped over each other three deep. In the rear he found hundreds of Rebels being treated for wounds.

A Confederate surgeon asked Kipp, "What was that out there?"

"We're Berdan's sharpshooters."

"How many of you?"

"About three hundred."

The surgeon stopped bandaging and looked up in astonishment. "Three hundred! This is the worst fire we've ever faced."

The action had lasted twenty minutes. During that time, Berdan's marksmen had fired ten thousand rounds.

It was a lovely place. The men posted behind Ziegler's Grove on Cemetery Ridge prized a few hours stolen in the shade of its trees this steaming Thursday afternoon. To the west, across a gently sloping valley, they heard the strangely innocent popping as Berdan and the Rebels clashed. They could plainly define the enemy line, bordering a wooded ridge. But the distant Rebels formed only a dull gray strand in the green and golden panorama before them.

Six soldiers sat around a fire drinking coffee from tin cups, laughing and swapping tales of their last leave in Washington. A heavyset sergeant with three days' growth of thick black beard chided a blond, boyish soldier. "Okay, Newcombe, then what happened?"

The boy reddened, an impish smile crossed his face. "Then Lieutenant Tate told the nigger girl to get in the tent. He put me outside, kind of on guard duty for him. After a while he stuck his head out and he says, 'Newcombe, you come in here!' I went in and he didn't have no pants on, just his shirt. And this black girl is laying on the cot. Got her legs spread and she ain't looking at me or nothing, just staring at the roof of that tent. Then Lieutenant Tate ordered me to fuck her."

The men whooped and howled. "Ordered you? God damn, well, what did you do, Newcombe?"

Again, the small, satisfied smile. "Well, I fucked her."

They laughed hard again.

"Then," the blond soldier went on, "when the word got out, they held the court-martial on the lieutenant. But the colonel didn't do nothing to me."

"How come?"

"Because he said I was just obeying the lieutenant's orders."

They all roared. The sergeant smiled and shook his head. "God damn, boy, I'm surprised you knew what to do."

In town the Confederate provost guards rudely pushed a well-dressed middle-aged man forward. "We found this civilian up on the roof of the Globe Inn, sir." The man stood, unawed, studying the face of General Jubal Early, who sat on a slab of polished stone at the Cannon Marble Works on the corner of Baltimore and Middle Streets.

Early studied the man with a hard eye. "What were you doing on that roof, sir, if I may ask?"

"Frankly, General, I was enjoying the fireworks, watching your guns on Benner's Hill."

Early banged his fist against the unyielding marble. "Sir, the Army of Northern Virginia has not come to this town to conduct a circus. Nor are we here to molest the populace. We are here to defeat an enemy army. You put yourself in a situation where it's hard to tell the difference. Don't you know you were fair game for a sharpshooter, ours or theirs? My God, you're lucky you aren't a dead man. I want you to leave here directly and get yourself to a cellar, and don't come out until Lee is marching up Broadway."

"It's all mad, isn't it," the civilian said, smiling coolly.

Something in the sensibility of the man's voice brought a grin to the general's face. "Who are you, sir? What is your name?"

"I'm Cass Neely. I'm a lawyer here in Adams County."

Early laughed. "I'm a member of the bar, too, down in Lynchburg, Virginia. Strange way for men schooled in the law to resolve differences."

Neely nodded. "It's madness."

"What shall always puzzle me," Early went on, "is that all of you and Mr. Lincoln think that all this will somehow benefit the black man. That is cruel, sir, cruel."

Cass Neely raised his eyebrows.

"What will you do with the freed man?" Early asked. "Herd him into the sink holes of New York City? Will you wring him out in your sweatshops? He's ignorant, he's untrained. He has no skills. Cruel, sir, believe me, cruel." Again, Early pounded the marble slab.

Neely sighed. "I must confess to you that my ardor has cooled somewhat from the time I read Mrs. Stowe's book. Too many of our Adams County men have died for the black man's freedom. But the Union, General, the Union; to us, it is a sacred thing."

"So we all thought once," General Early shook his head. "Mr. Cass Neely, I will tell you something and no one else. If a dozen of the right men in the North and a dozen of the right men in the South had been hanged soon enough, we wouldn't have had this war." The Southerner extended his hand to Neely. "Now, do us both a favor. Go on home to your loved ones and take some shelter. There's been enough useless bloodshed in this business so far."

"I will see you in court, General," Neely laughed. He shook Early's hand and left.

General Hunt had to concede that General Sickles had a case. The higher ground of the peach orchard did offer a better field of fire than the ground assigned Sickles at the low end of Cemetery Ridge.

"Then I understand that I am to take the forward position and that you, as General Meade's representative, will so order?"

Hunt looked at the cagey Sickles and demurred. "I don't care to take that responsibility, General. But as soon as I can ride to General Meade's headquarters, you should receive his orders to do so. That order would have to come from General Meade himself. I think you recognize that, sir."

Sickles' patience was wearing thin with these hidebound military mentalities. He had no lack of confidence in the whiplike capacity of his own mind to sum up a situation, any situation, political, ethical, or military, and cut through surgically to the opportune solution.

If there had been any doubt as to what must be done, it was swiftly dispelled by the message Captain Briscoe now relayed to Sickles from Colonel Berdan, across Emmitsburg Road with his sharpshooters. Sickles learned that three columns of Rebel infantry were marching south behind Seminary Ridge. Their mission was apparently to swing around to the south of the Federal line, Sickles' sector of responsibility.

Sickles had to act, Meade or no. He gathered his division commanders and told them to prepare to advance immediately. It was nearly one o'clock in the afternoon.

Lieutenant Frank Haskell, the battle-hungry onetime lawyer from Madison, Wisconsin, sat astride his horse at midpoint on the Federal line along Cemetery Ridge. His body was drugged by a sleepless night of deploying freshly arrived regiments. Yet his senses burned keenly through the fog of soreness and fatigue. Haskell never felt more intensely alive than in the court of battle. He looked out across the shallow valley that separated the opposing armies.

It was quiet now except for the occasional popping of skirmishers out front. Haskell's eye ran along the interminable rows of stacked muskets spiking the crest like shocks of iron wheat. Between the guns, men slept, talked, made grisly jokes, and puffed contemplatively on their pipes. A young boy from the town, proudly drawing water for the soldiers, clattered under the burden of two dozen canteens.

Shortly after one o'clock, the afternoon's lassitude was shaken by a flurry of motion from the southernmost end of the Union line. Had Sickles gone mad? Haskell wondered. What was this preening exhibitionist up to now? Yet Haskell could not deny the magnificence of the spectacle. Ten thousand men, in perfect order, flags streaming, rolled majestically out from Cemetery Ridge. Cannon and caissons sailed the swells of undulating ground. A heavy line of skirmishers cleared the enemy away for the unhindered passage of the main body. Sickles' men marched toward the Emmitsburg Road, to the higher ground at the peach orchard the Union general had so coveted. There was a splendor in this unhurried, unbroken tide of blue. It absorbed all eyes on the Union front. The move was carried off with such authority that some of the officers began to wonder if they might have missed an order for a general advance.

Sickles aligned his men along the Emmitsburg Road, a half mile out front of the rest of the Federal line. At the peach orchard, he bent them back at a diagonal running through a wheat field as far as the craggy hillocks called the Devil's Den. There, Sickles ran out of men, leaving a gap between the Devil's Den and the Round Tops, which he had been ordered to defend. His line now formed a rough "V" with its point at the peach orchard and one wing running along the road, the other through the orchard. It had been an audacious stroke.

In spite of the pageantry of Sickles' maneuver, Lieutenant Frank Haskell noted uneasily that instead of one long, unbroken line, the Union army now formed two disconnected segments, with Sickles out front and the Round Tops unguarded.

When, at last, Jeb Stuart arrived on Seminary Ridge on the afternoon of July 2, Lee had not heard from his cavalry chief for seven days. Lee had counted dearly on Stuart to keep him informed of the enemy's position and movements. This was Stuart's major responsibility. Yet Lee had heard nothing while Stuart had been off on questionable diversions. Lee had been a blind man without his cavalry. Consequently, he had unexpectedly found himself with the Union army alarmingly close to his rear. He had also found himself drawn into a battlefield not of his own choosing. Yet, when the cavalry chief appeared, Lee, with Olympian calm, said only, "Well, General Stuart, you are here at last."

On the middle of the second day of the battle, their city had become an alien, hostile place to the people of Gettysburg. Union sharpshooters on Cemetery Hill made targets of every exposed window and every fleeting motion in the streets. Shells continually screamed over the town. Drunken Confederate soldiers roved the streets in ugly, marauding bands. Leander Warren's family decided to heed the advice of the now friendly Confederate officer whom Mrs. Warren had reluctantly fed the evening before.

"I know you'll lose everything, but you've got to leave," he warned, "or you'll lose your lives, too. Pack what you can in a wagon and go by the north side of town. I'll provide a man to take you through our lines."

Their escort was a musician, a pot-bellied, unshaven rogue of about forty, who carried a brass horn slung around his neck like a talisman that would protect him against the possibility of combat. He clearly relished this assignment, which would put even more distance between him and the Yankee rifles raking the town.

The bodies they passed in their retreat had lain in the streets for nearly two days. They had become discolored and swollen. Leander noticed that the pockets of most of the Union dead had been turned inside out.

Jake Cole had served with Colonel Elmer Ellsworth that fateful day in Alexandria in '61 when the colonel had bought immortality by being the first officer to fall for the Union. Cole had since fought in the Seven Days' campaign, at Malvern Hill, in the Peninsula, at Antietam, Fredericksburg, and Chancellorsville. Now, in the summer of 1863, he had turned sixteen.

From the moment they set foot on the field at Gettysburg, an unshakable gloom had seized young Cole. His closest friend, Andy Wilson, sensed it.

"You're damn still, Jakey."

"I know," Cole muttered.

"Scared?"

Cole glared at him. "Don't ever say that to me! I just . . . just got this funny feeling."

The brigade was held in reserve on Cemetery Ridge awaiting further orders. Jake Cole spent the time by himself working up the courage for what he had to do. He presented himself to Captain Favill, outside the general's tent. Favill, the New York City socialite, had not remained long in the ranks. Fortunately for his ambitions, the War had not lasted the few weeks which he had predicted in his diary back in 1861. Favill had had time to rise to eminence as General Samuel Zook's aide in the intervening years.

"Private Cole, requesting permission to speak with the general."

Favill knew the boy-soldier's record. He knew, too, Zook's empathy with his men. There was a deadly earnestness about the boy. "All right, Cole, go on in."

"General, I got some money here I want you to keep safe for me and send to my mother."

Zook dreaded what he would hear next.

"I got a feeling I'm going to be killed in this battle."

Zook put his arm around Cole's slim shoulder. "My boy," he said, "you mustn't give way to these feelings. We all have them. They mean nothing."

He studied the boy's solemn face. "But if you are afraid, I'll give you a pass to go into the ambulance corps."

Cole stiffened. "That isn't what I said, sir. I didn't say I'm afraid to die. I said I'm gonna die. I ain't cut dirt on the other boys before. And I won't now."

"Very well." Zook smiled sadly. "Leave your money with me."

General Meade's order for a council of war came at the worst possible time for Sickles. Authorized or not, he felt complete confidence in the wisdom of his move. His artillery now frowned from the rise of the peach orchard. He had a firm line along the Emmitsburg Road through the orchard, and the rest of his men enjoyed good protective cover in the jagged contours of the Devil's Den. Sickles himself was now headquartered in an ideally placed farmhouse just behind the point in the "V" that his corps formed. His staff had even recruited a pretty girl at the nearby Rogers farm, who was quickly and proudly engaged in baking biscuits for them.

One feature of Sickles' deployment violated traditional tactics. By pulling his corps out ahead of the Union line, he had exposed two naked flanks to the enemy. He had ruptured the continuity of the line that Meade had so assiduously constructed.

Now, Meade was ordering him to report to a council of war back at the tiny headquarters on the Taneytown Road. Sickles had already begged off once, informing his commander that he expected to be attacked imminently and dared not leave the field. But Meade had sent another messenger insisting that he attend just as the cracking muskets of the enemy skirmishers signaled the inevitable thrust. Sickles reluctantly put his subordinate, General Birney, in command. As he galloped off, Sickles heard the enemy artillery open up.

He pulled astride the house of Mrs. Lydia Leister, headquarters of the commander of the Army of the Potomac. Meade met him at the door. The volume of rifle and artillery fire swelled fearfully in the direction from which Sickles had just come.

"Don't dismount." Meade glowered. "I fear your whole line is already engaged. Return to your command at once. I will join you on the field." Meade adjourned the council of war and followed Sickles toward his sector.

As he rode down Cemetery Ridge, Meade stared with disbelief at what Sickles had done. His carefully pieced-together defense had been ruptured by this rash adventurer. With dearly purchased restraint, Meade shouted above the barrage, "Isn't your line too much extended, General?"

"It is, sir, but I haven't the whole Army of the Potomac. I have a wide space to cover. And this ground is more elevated than the ground I left."

"General Sickles!" Meade's face now turned a fierce red. "Indeed this ground is higher than the position to your rear. But there is still higher ground in front of you." He shoved his arm angrily toward Seminary Ridge. "If you keep on advancing, you can find continually higher ground all the way to the mountains."

"Does my position not suit you, then? If it does not, I will change it."

The crescendo of Rebel artillery mounted. A shell exploded close by. Meade's horse reared in terror, nearly throwing his rider. As Meade struggled to stay on the horse, he shouted at Sickles with all pretense of civility now vanished.

"It's too late! The enemy has already made that decision for you! If you need more artillery, call on the reserve. I'll send the 5th Corps and a division of Hancock's to support you." Meade rode off. Almost simultaneously, the Confederate infantry smashed into Sickles' line.

Longstreet's delay had sorely tried Lee's patience. Lee's plan possessed a classic simplicity. Longstreet's divisions were to attack the southern end of the Union line. Ewell's divisions, positioned in and to the east of the city, were to apply pressure simultaneously on Cemetery Hill and Culp's Hill at the opposite end. Between the two assaults, Lee hoped to buckle the right and left of the Federal line like a bent pin. He had given Longstreet his orders at eleven a.m. At 3:30 in the afternoon, the assault had not yet begun.

Longstreet stalled interminably. Two of his three divisions had to move south of Seminary Ridge to get into position. But in order to avoid observation from Round Top, they had first to march north in a long, looping route to get behind the ridge where the Yankees could not observe their southward intention. This was the maneuver that

Berdan's sharpshooters had unmasked. It was four p.m. before the Rebels were finally in position on a line crossing the Emmitsburg Road south of the peach orchard, facing Sickles' corps.

Longstreet's other division under General Pickett had not yet arrived on the field, so he had killed time whittling and catnapping. He knew the distress he was causing Lee, and it pained him. Longstreet had remarked to General Hood earlier, "General Lee's a little nervous this morning. He wants me to attack. I don't want to do so without Pickett. I never like to go into battle with one boot off."

It was now after four o'clock. He could delay no longer. With or without Pickett, the time had come to obey Lee's order. Fifty-four Confederate cannon crashing into the peach orchard launched the attack. Their fire tore the limbs off trees and men. Soon after, the Rebel infantry struck both wings and the point of Sickles' "V". In the north, General Ewell heard Longstreet's guns—the signal, at last, to unleash his own artillery.

Late, very late in the day for Lee, the second round of the battle of Gettysburg had exploded.

Ebbing and flowing across the wheat field and peach orchard, within the Devil's Den, the smoke and brilliant flashes of the guns blinded the men. Bursting shells shook their brains, made them deaf, stunned their perception. All was seeming chaos.

One day, no doubt, a chronicler of battle would map this place with neatly converging arrows, with precise white rectangles arrayed against equally precise black rectangles. It would all have a coherence, a logic that no man on this field now sensed.

Sickles' front in both the peach orchard and wheat field began to crumble under superior Confederate power. General Hancock ordered General Caldwell to get his division prepared to come to Sickles' aid.

"Fall in. Take arms." The orders rang out. The reserves who had been shielded behind Cemetery Ridge gulped down their last mouthfuls of coffee and fried bacon. Euchre games were abandoned and tattered decks of cards stacked and stuffed into knapsacks.

Among the troops called up to stiffen Sickles' collapsing line was the Irish Brigade under Colonel Patrick Kelly. This brigade had stripped whole neighborhoods of young men in the teeming Irish settlements of New York City, Philadelphia, and North Cambridge, Massachusetts. Colonel Kelly's men waited in taut silence for the word to move forward. A black-bearded Irishman came up to the colonel. He was the Reverend William Corby, formerly a professor at Notre Dame, now chaplain to the Irish Brigade.

"If there's time, Colonel, I'd like to propose a general absolution for the men." The custom was common in European armies. It had never been done in America before.

The colonel gazed into the not too distant inferno to which he would soon condemn his brigade. "I can't think of a better time for a man to be cleansed of his sins, Father."

The brigade came to Order Arms. A soldier quickly helped the priest into his vestments. Father Corby climbed onto a large, flat rock and looked out over the men. He raised his hand high and gained a silent oasis amid the rumble of battle.

"Men of the Union, yours is a sacred trust." His voice had a ringing, carrying clarity. "The object for which you fight is noble in the sight of God. Remember, my sons, Holy Mother Church refuses Christian burial to the soldier who turns his back on the foe, or who deserts his flag. Now, kneel before me and I will grant absolution of his sins for each of you who makes a sincere act of contrition."

There was a clatter of hundreds of rifles against the ground as the men knelt down, hands clasped, heads bowed. Here and there a Catholic from other regiments, watching the Irish Brigade, sank to his knees. A hum of prayer rose from the sea of bowed heads. "Oh, my God, I am heartily sorry for having offended Thee . . ."

General Hancock and his staff watched in respectful silence.

Father Corby raised his hand again as the prayer faded to a close. He began the absolution. "Dominus Noster Jesus Christus vos absolvat et ego . . .

The Devil's Den. Nature had chiseled a battleground here, then waited a million years for men to find it. Patiently, glaciers had broken away huge blocks of sandstone and shale, upended them, thrust them about at odd angles, driven them into the ground leaving corners, caves, crevices, holes, and fissures where men could take cover and shoot and hope to hide from death.

Near the Devil's Den, tough Colonel Cross made a speech to his men preparing for the assault. "Men, you are about to go into battle. You have never disgraced your state. I hope you won't this time. If any man runs, I want the file closers to shoot him. If they don't, I shall myself. That is all I have to say."

Moments later, Caldwell's division began tramping mutely toward the Devil's Den. As soon as they came within the Rebels' range of fire, a private dropped next to Colonel Cross. The man lifted his hand from his stomach and stared in horror at the blood on his palm. "Colonel," he cried, "I been shot."

"I know, my boy. Fortunes of war." Cross never looked back.

Up ahead, a commotion caught Cross's eye. The man was tall and brawny. His dash for the rear could not pass unnoticed. An officer had grabbed the straggler by the collar and tried to turn him around. The man was too powerful. He was now dragging both himself and the officer backward. The big soldier made whimpering, frightened, animal-like cries as he struggled to free himself from the officer's determined grip. Tears covered his face. Colonel Cross saw the two grappling figures and rushed over with his sword held high. "Hold the coward still, Lieutenant, and I'll cleave his head."

The man ceased struggling. He raised terrified eyes to the blade poised overhead. He slowly stood up, panting grotesquely. The lieutenant now grabbed him by the neck and the seat of his pants and shoved him toward the battle. The man began moving, stiff-legged, his musket dragging along the ground, terror frozen in his face. A bullet struck him in the forehead and he pitched over. Minutes later, Colonel Cross waded into the Devil's Den, where he too was killed instantly.

Not fifteen minutes had passed since Jake Cole had left his money with General Zook when he got word to report back to the general's tent.

"Yes, sir." Cole saluted. He found General Zook distracted, remote.

"Soldier, take your money. I can't keep it for you."

"But, General, you promised . . ."

Zook's voice was hollow. The gulf between private and general had dissolved. "I'm sorry I can't help you, Cole." Zook lowered his gaze. "I've got the same premonition you have."

Cole took the money and awkwardly withdrew from the tent. He asked the general's aide, Captain Favill, to hold his money.

*   *   *

General Meade bent over his maps snapping precise, impatient orders to his aides for stiffening his endangered left. In his total absorption, he had not noticed the angry farmer straining against two of his orderlies.

"General! General!" The man broke free.

Meade looked up. "What does this man want?" he snarled.

The man, a stout, bald Pennsylvania Dutch farmer, leaned over Meade's table. His anger nearly strangled his thickly accented speech. "These men, these men must stop! You, the general, must stop them!" he sputtered. "You are the government. They put shot-up soldiers all over mein house. Mein house is no hospital!" He shook his fist furiously. "They dig up mein yard. Bury dead men in mein yard! All over the yard, arms, legs! You are the government, General, you must tell them . . ."

Meade's cold fury finally silenced the man. He rose and moved his face close to the farmer. "You craven idiot! Until this battle is decided, you don't know—and neither do I—if you even have a government! If I hear any more from you, I will give you a gun and send you to the front line to defend your rights!"

The orderlies grabbed him and led the still fuming farmer away.

General George Pickett's division, spared the fight thus far, now marched toward Gettysburg. They had earlier been left behind at Cashtown to guard horses, cattle, and other spoils of the invasion. The pounding cannon and the faint sputter of musket fire became sharper as they moved down the Chambersburg Pike.

Among Pickett's ranks young Willie Mitchell and John Dooley marched, but no longer together. Slight, fragile John Dooley, who had spilled out his sickening fears of battle as the two lay together under the naked stars, was now a commissioned officer. Dooley had been elected a lieutenant by the men of Company C, First Virginia, the same company his father had commanded earlier in the war.

Dooley's commissioned status broke the web of constant companionship between him and Willie. The night of Dooley's election to the company command, Mitchell had come over to visit him.

"You know, it's funny, John, the way you've talked so much of the knot in your gut and your fears. But look what the men have gone and done for you. They know you have courage."

"Willie, if there's any courage out there, it's all mixed in with fear. We're all scared. Only the mad aren't. Bravery or courage or whatever you want to call it, it's nothing but sticking it out even when you're scared to death."

"Ah yes, what can't be cured must be endured," Willie observed solemnly. Dooley smiled to hear the boy spouting the wisdom of an old veteran.

On the march toward Gettysburg, Lieutenant John Dooley had been assigned to the rear guard, with the responsibility to drive stragglers forward. The heat, the exhaustion, the distractions of the rich Pennsylvania countryside were taking a fearful toll among the Virginians. The sergeant assigned to Dooley was a tough, grizzled man in his mid-thirties who towered over the new lieutenant. He reported to Dooley in a patronizing, paternal tone.

"You can show no mercy, Lieutenant. These sons of bitches will tell you every lie in their hearts to fall behind. If we don't bottle 'em up here, it's like a hole in a bucket. The whole army will leak out."

"I think, Sergeant, we can handle this well enough," Dooley answered curtly.

"Well, you just give me the word on any of these bummers and I'll kick their asses right to the head of the column."

Dooley found it unpleasant duty. Some of the men were obviously weakened by diarrhea. Others pleaded sickness but looked well. Some were felled by the sun's rays and collapsed. Others cried that they were sunstruck and feared they would die. Some held bare, bloodied feet up to the young lieutenant and pleaded to be left behind. But had they deliberately thrown their shoes away? Dooley loathed the assignment increasingly as the day wore on. The feeling that he was driving sheep to slaughter depressed him. He erred on the side of leniency, feeling that shirkers would be worthless in battle anyway.

At 5:30 in the afternoon of July 2, the regiment marched into a small copse of woods a few miles from Gettysburg where they would pass another safe night. Off to the east the cannon and muskets sounded, ominously close now.

General Zook and his polished aide, Captain Josiah Favill, had watched in disbelief the madly grand maneuverings of General Sickles' Third Corps. They had watched, too, as Sickles' reckless stratagem crumbled. Sickles' aide, Captain Tremaine, sweat-soaked and breathless, rode over to Zook and relayed his chief's desperate appeal for help.

Zook rode into the smoke-shrouded field and found Sickles near the peach orchard. He agreed to send his brigade to bolster Sickles' paper-thin left, which Longstreet's advance had now riddled.

Zook's brigade moved quickly toward the weakest point. The Rebel guns waited, let the new arrivals come closer. Then they exploded in a sheet of flame. The carnage among Zook's men was fearful. They attempted to press on, but the Rebel fire became a killing wall. They ran up and collapsed against it.

The smoke lifted, and Favill was stabbed with shock. General Zook was lying on the ground propped up by another officer. Favill ran to him. Zook looked up with distant, glazed eyes. "Favill," he groaned, "it's all up for me, tell Frazer."

Hesitantly, Favill withdrew from his fallen commander. He plunged back into the mayhem of bursting shells, the whip and whine of the bullets. He located Colonel Frazer and informed him that he had succeeded Zook as brigade commander. Frazer looked about at the sea of calamity. "Stay with me, will you Favill? I'll need your help."

"It's not possible." A shell burst drowned him out. His head ringing with the concussive blow, he shouted into Frazer's ear, "I've got to be with the general now."

Favill rode out of the boiling hell of the Devil's Den and found the wounded General Zook being carried to the rear by his orderlies.

Jake Cole's premonition seemed close to fulfillment. The two men to his right were blown to pieces by a shell blast. Cole felt something strike him, and he accused the man on his left of hitting him.

"I didn't hit you, you damn fool, you've been shot."

Cole felt only a tingling numbness in his arm, though he could see a red stain spreading through the torn fabric of the sleeve.

"You better get to the rear while you can," the man warned.

The air quivered with the hum of bullets. Harsh smoke scoured their nostrils. The beating of shell blasts against their ears dulled their hearing. They shouted at each other but heard only fragments of words.

"I ain't hurt bad enough," Cole yelled to his neighbor. He advanced a few more feet, then sank unconscious to the ground with his leg shattered.

"Damn fool," the man sneered, leaping over Cole's prostrate body.

*   *   *

Private Lokey raced past the colonel. There was little you could do for a man with half his head gone. The Federals were laying a heavy fire onto the Georgian troops from a small woods in the Devil's Den. Lokey grunted laboriously up a small hillside. He stopped midway and trained his Enfield on a Yankee springing from among the trees. As he gripped the trigger, a searing sensation scorched his thighs. Lokey sank to the ground, his gun clattering against the rock outcropping. The man he had been training on was coming straight at him. Lokey watched in helpless terror.

But the man was unarmed. Bullets struck and sent small spurts of earth into the air around the Confederate. "Don't be scared," the Yankee said. "Put your arm around my neck and lean all your weight on me."

Lokey had never seen the enemy so close. The man had a ruddy face and wore a good-natured grin. "This is a dangerous place. We got to hurry up," the Yankee said, dragging the groaning, half fainting soldier.

The air hissed with minié balls. A bullet crashed and split a small sapling as they passed. The Yankee pulled Lokey behind a rock, set him down gently, and wiped the perspiration streaming from his own face with his sleeve.

"God damn, Johnny," he laughed, "if you and I had to settle this matter, we'd settle it easy enough, wouldn't we?"

Lokey answered gamely between heavy gasps. "Well, Yank, since you're about to become a prisoner and I'm wounded, damned if I don't think we could."

The rear guard came up and hauled the Yankee away. As he left, he gave Lokey a wink. Damn, Lokey thought, and I almost killed that fellow.

The three Union men stood waist deep in the golden grain of the wheat field, firing in unison. One of them groaned, doubled up, and fell to the ground. His face turned pale. He gasped and whimpered, "I'm shot in the gut. That ends me."

Through the zinging, twanging, banging noise, the man next to him hollered, "No, crawl to the rear!"

"I tell you I've gone coon. I'll die here." The man rolled over on his back and stared hopelessly at the sky.

The second man kept firing. Suddenly, he began hopping on one leg yelping like a dog. He stopped, tried to kick his leg out, and found, happily, that he could. He tore away the ripped pant leg and studied the wound intently.

"You better go to the rear," the third man in the trio said.

"It ain't bad enough." The injured man hobbled back up to the line. They continued blasting across the golden spikes of wheat. The wounded man let out another astonished yell. He dropped his rifle, clutched at his left arm, and fell back behind the line. Again he examined the wound, grabbed the rifle, and recommenced firing.

"You're having a bad run of luck," his companion pleaded between shell blasts. "Go on back."

The twice-wounded man sighted his muzzle and shook his head. "Not yet." He resumed his fire. His head jerked violently. He fell to the ground. Got up, fell again, and rose to his knees. A stream of blood, teeth, bone, and bits of tongue began to spill down the corner of his mouth. His lower jaw hung slack like a trap door sprung by the bullet which had passed through his mouth. The man looked around, bewildered, uncomprehending. He tried to speak but could not. He flung the rifle down and hobbled toward the rear.

Throughout the wheat field, men who were hit ripped the clothing from their wounds, tore shirts open, and poked gingerly at bloody sites with their fingers. For some, this exploration produced relieved smiles. Others recoiled at the sight as though from a blow. Men accustomed to battle developed a sure sense of which wounds were mortal, even their own.

It was going badly for Sickles, General Meade feared. He dispatched his trusted and able chief engineer, Brigadier General Gouverneur K. Warren, to reconnoiter the area. Warren rode up Little Round Top, which afforded a commanding view of the field. When he reached the top, he was aghast. Warren stood upon possibly the single most strategic point at Gettysburg. Whoever held this height controlled virtually the whole of the Union line. Yet not a fighting man defended Little Round Top. Only a handful of signalmen were there, and they were packing up to leave as Warren arrived. He ordered them to hold fast and keep waving their flags furiously to deceive the enemy as to how vulnerable the hill was.

Warren sent word down to a nearby battery commander to fire a single artillery round into the woods in the direction of the enemy. It worked. The Rebels turned in the direction of the shot, and the sun caught thousands of brightly polished gun barrels, clearly signaling the Rebel position to Warren. The knowledge chilled him. They were obviously moving south to outflank the end of the Union line via the Round Tops. Warren galloped down the hillside to search out reinforcements. Luckily, he ran straight into Colonel Strong Vincent's brigade marching just north of Little Round Top on its way to bolster Sickles' failing line. Warren had no authority over these troops. But the urgency in his voice was unmistakable. Colonel Vincent unhesitatingly diverted his men up Little Round Top.

If General Sickles had any qualms about the position he had chosen, a studied calm concealed it. From his vantage point near the Trostle farm, he watched from horseback as his men took fierce punishment from right and left. His twelve thousand troops were absorbing the brunt of Longstreet's thirty thousand charging, yelling Rebels. The Yankees were giving way slowly, yielding their lives inch by inch. Sickles surveyed the carnage and pandemonium with unruffled serenity.

The shock of exploding shells pounded their eardrums. The acrid, smoky air tinged their nostrils and burned their eyes. A shell exploded and shook the earth with unusual ferocity. The officers' horses reared and shrieked. When the smoke cleared, General Sickles was sliding to the ground. Sickles' pants leg was torn off. His leg swayed aimlessly at the horse's side. Two of his men caught Sickles before he fell from the horse. They carried him to a wall near the Trostle farm. He was ashen. Only his eyes betrayed the pain he bore in silence.

"Get something on that leg. Quick, before I bleed to death." His voice retained its crisp edge of authority. One of the men buckled a saddle strap tightly above his knee and stanched the heavy flow of blood.

Major Tremaine rushed over to his fallen commander. "General, are you hurt badly?"

Sickles attempted a smile. "Man proposes. God disposes. Tremaine, tell General Birney he is in command."

Two bearers came up and began lifting Sickles onto a stretcher. One said incautiously, "General, we all heard you were a goner."

"So?" Sickles' eyes hardened. "Private, reach inside my pocket. There, good. Now light up that cigar for me and be so kind as to put it in my mouth."

Brigadier General Daniel Sickles was borne off the field, the cigar clamped between bared teeth set in a hard, tight grin, producing the desired effect among the admiring men he passed on his way to the rear. The cigar was removed only to ladle generous dosages of brandy down Sickles' throat, the customary treatment for shock.

At the field hospital, General Sickles went to the head of the line of waiting patients. He was placed directly on the operating table. The Third Corps medical director, Dr. Sims, made a deep, swift incision above the knee and reached for the saw.

The severed legs of high-ranking officers were not flung on the growing heap of other limbs. Sickles' leg was carefully wrapped, marked, and put aside for whatever later disposition he might have in mind, should he live.

A scant half mile behind the battle line, Tillie Pierce felt that she had become hardened to the sight of broken bodies. Yet this latest sight unnerved her. The wagons pulled up to the Weikert yard late in the afternoon. Four men jumped off and started unloading coffins on the side of the road. A wounded man stretched out on the grass hollered to them, "You fellers taking orders on them boxes?"

A fat, sweating wagoneer replied, "You figuring on needing one?"

"Christ, at the rate we're going here, I'll consider myself lucky if I get one."

The Alabamians were gasping and gulping for air with a desperation that sounded like sobbing. Their pounding hearts threatened to burst against their lungs. They rolled on their backs and groaned pitifully.

"The water. Where's them bastards with the water?" The panting, heaving figures on the larger Round Top, just south of Little Round Top, had marched twenty-eight miles since they were rousted out at three in the morning. They had marched under a searing sun with no water. They had been ordered to storm this sharply banked hill across a boulder-strewn clearing where an unseen regiment of Union sharp-shooters, men who could drill a target at six hundred yards, felled them with terrifying regularity. They had reached the base of the hill and had been flung against its flesh-tearing rocks, through its lacerating underbrush, and up its lung-splitting steepness, loaded with muskets and ammunition, all the while facing the crack Union shots. Their path to the top was charted by the bodies of comrades who had been shot or who had fainted in the heat.

Now the Confederates lay gasping, cursing the men they had left behind to fill the regiment's canteens. They did not know that those men had stumbled into a nest of Yankees and had been captured.

Their commander, an imposing Alabamian, Colonel William Oates, walked among them offering encouragement and praise. Yet Oates felt intensely frustrated. He now commanded from Round Top the best view of any Confederate officer on the field. He stood upon the highest elevation within miles. Off to the north he could see the steeples and rooftops of Gettysburg. He could see the entire Union spine on Cemetery Ridge. He could see a huge area bulging with Federal ammunition trains. God, if he could only get artillery up Round Top, he could dominate the field. Hardly a point of the main Yankee defense could escape the sweep of Confederate guns fired from here. But he had no authority to carry out such a plan. His orders were to get around behind the Union rear and start rolling up the Yankee line. Only Little Round Top now stood between him and execution of this mission.

He ordered his officers to get the men ready. The troops staggered to their feet, muttering, cursing a fate which had subjected them to this punishment, with no drop of water to slake parched throats. Soon they were wordlessly stumbling down the rocky decline of the hillside.

It was late in the afternoon before the 20th Maine had been dispatched to aid Sickles. Before they arrived at the swaying battle lines, the regiment had been ordered to halt at the edge of a field. Up ahead the men could see several officers around Colonel Vincent gesturing excitedly toward Little Round Top. They saw Vincent spur his horse up the side of the hill. Minutes later, Colonel Chamberlain ordered the 20th Maine up Little Round Top, too.

The hill was raked continually by Confederate artillery fire. Shells bursting on the rocks sent shards of granite and chunks of iron whining through the air. Shells exploding among the maples and pines made great, fearful, cracking sounds, and huge falling branches brained the soldiers below.

Three brothers, their horses riding abreast, led the 20th Maine up the hillside—Colonel Chamberlain, commanding, Tom Chamberlain, now his adjutant, and John Chamberlain, a third brother who had arrived on the field with the Christian Commission to help tend the wounded.

Colonel Strong Vincent quickly positioned the 20th Maine and his other regiments around the slope of Little Round Top, facing generally south. With these men deployed on the hillside, the Union line at Gettysburg was now complete. It began at Culp's Hill, bent around Cemetery Hill, ran south along Cemetery Ridge, jumped forward at Sickles' embattled salient, passed through the peach orchard and wheat field, and ended on Little Round Top. At the southernmost tip of the entire five-mile Union line, the last of the Union troops, was the 20th Maine.

As the Union men dug in on Little Round Top, the force of Rebel soldiers had just come down from neighboring Round Top. The Confederates moved quickly across the shallow valley toward Little Round Top. If they could swing around this far end of the Union line, they could break into the rear of the Union army, which was already badly battered from the front. The Federals would be caught in a fatal embrace from front and rear. Never had the Confederacy been closer to victory at Gettysburg.

Colonel Vincent rode over to Lawrence Chamberlain. "Your position is the extreme left of the entire Union line, Colonel," he said. "You understand you are to hold this ground at all costs." Chamberlain nodded.

Jake Cole of General Zook's brigade awoke to a red, searing, unbearable pain. He looked up at the Confederate officer towering over him. The huge, bull-necked man eyed Cole with a cruel smile. His foot was planted squarely on the boy's wounded leg. Pain ripped through Cole's body like the serrated edge of a knife.

"Aaagh! Aaagh! Please, please! Get off, get off!"

"You little Yankee pisspot, I'll cut your heart out." The Southerner raised his sword. His swing was interrupted by a strangled cry. The man's neck exploded in blood. The shot had been fired from the direction of Little Round Top. His great body came tumbling onto Jake Cole and pinned the wounded Yankee to the ground.

Strange how in the midst of it all, as he confidently barked his orders to the men girdling Little Round Top, the refrain spun in Colonel Strong Vincent's head. The thought had first struck him days before on the march north. A man could do worse, he had mused, than die in his native state for the old flag. The thought would not leave him.

Now, in the battle's roar, the idea seemed to spin faster and rise to almost a shriek just as the minié ball drove deep into his groin and dealt a mortal blow to the senior officer on Little Round Top.

He was a proud man, the sharpshooter from Georgia. He could put out a candle at one hundred yards. He liked to work out of a tree, tying himself into place so that he would not fall to the ground if wounded. There were few trees big enough here in the Devil's Den. But there were plenty of rocks. He took cover between two huge, angled boulders which converged almost to a point, leaving only a brief opening in the front.

Even late in the afternoon, with the sun well down behind him, the sharpshooter from Georgia soaked his coarse wool shirt with sweat as he and two comrades lugged rocks into place to block the open space. They laid the last stone into position. The two other men left. The sharpshooter leaned against the cover they had built, panting heavily, his hands rubbed raw from the rocks, streams of sweat seaming his face. He rested his musket on the uppermost rock and from this steady position began a deadly, sure fire on the distant figures on Little Round Top, especially the artillerists silhouetted along the crest. A shell blasted overhead and drove the Georgia sharpshooter to the earth as if struck by a hammer. When he regained consciousness, his head pounded with a bursting beat. He raised his hand and could feel the hair matted with blood around the outline of the wound. He rose dazedly to his knees. He unrolled his blanket on the ground and stretched himself out in his rock haven. He searched fitfully for a painless angle to rest his broken head. He must stay awake until the stretcher bearers found him. He fought to keep his eyes open, but a heavy dullness began to ease the pain in his head. He slipped into a sleep never to be broken.

Along the southern perimeter of Little Round Top, the men of the 20th Maine waited in agonizing suspense at the end of the entire five-mile Union line. Nature whipped their bodies into battle readiness. The heart rushed blood through the arteries; the lungs dilated, reaching for every molecule of oxygen; the intestines shrank. Tension coursed along the line from man to man like an electric current. The silence was hard, tangible.

Then the quiet was shattered. The wild, yelping, screeching enemy cry raised the hair on their necks. A cold shudder rippled their skin. They could see them now, fierce, hard, lean men unleashing that unholy yell, plunging toward them fearless and unhesitating.

"Fire!" The command brought blessed relief as they poured their tensions into the business of killing. A frantic jangling and jamming of ramrods rang out along the Union line. "Load at will . . . load . . . fire!"

As his men pumped fire into the smoke that quickly enveloped the enemy, Lawrence Chamberlain heard a cry that chilled his blood. "Colonel! Colonel!" Chamberlain turned to see Lieutenant Jim Nichols standing on a rock peering into the acrid cloud enveloping the enemy. "The Rebs are moving to our left. They're going to outflank us."

Through the shifting mists of gunsmoke, Chamberlain detected the shadowy forms drifting to his unprotected side, the left anchor of the Union line. He settled on a desperate mid-battle gamble. With bullets smashing into his men and a hellish din filling the air, he gave the order.

"On the right by file into line!" The parade-ground commands had an absurd ring amid the gunfire and the hoarse screams of dying men. The men at the far end of the line were confused. "Are we skedaddling already?" Chamberlain was bending half of his regiment back at a right angle to meet the Confederate drive now sweeping around his end. The companies moving to form the new front stumbled over the rocks, fanned out to circle around scrub oak and pine, boulders and bushes. Then they closed again. Men were hit, screamed and tumbled to the ground only to be trampled by men behind, who cursed and twisted their way through thick patches of undergrowth. Yet, within this man-made hell, an undercurrent of order was at work. The 20th Maine was now bent back to meet the expected Confederate assault on its left.

A few hundred yards off, a young Confederate lieutenant deployed his men into line. "All right, boys, we got 'em by the short hairs now," he whispered vengefully. "We're going to catch 'em with their drawers around their ankles." His men were breathing heavily. The feint to the Federal left had not been purchased lightly. They looked at the lieutenant, trusting, hopeful that this next lunge, as he assured them, would not be too bloody and would win them a merciful respite.

"When you hear that order to charge, be loaded, give 'em the yell, and run right up their backsides."

Chamberlain's realignment had already frustrated their hope. Instead of striking a naked, off-guard Union flank, they rushed forward to catch a storm of lead. Every rock, every tree spat death and mutilation at them. Chamberlain's gambit was working. A pattern repeated itself on the hillside: a shot, a horrified groan, a Confederate body tumbling into bushes.

The charge was momentarily blunted. The Southerners clambered back over the bodies of their fallen comrades. For now, they had to ignore outstretched hands and pitiful pleas. They regrouped and dashed forward again. This time, they broke the line of the 20th Maine. The Federals had no time to fix bayonets. They grabbed their muskets by hot barrels and swung them wildly. A Maine backwoodsman brought his gunstock down with a practiced axe-swing on the head of a young Rebel, as he would have on cord wood, and with the same effect. The boy's skull cracked, his eyes rolled heavenward, and he fell to the ground uttering a small whimper. All about were the sounds of steel clanging against steel, of snapping bones, battered flesh, the shrieks of maddened men.

A disarmed Southerner leaped forward and buried a rock in the face of a Union soldier, muffling the man's scream with the mashing blow. The Yankee soldiers farther back swung their cartridge boxes around in front of them, flaps open, and rammed cartridges home with frantic speed. They tried to pick the right targets from the roiling mélange of blue and tattered gray before they fired. Often they chose wrong.

In the seemingly shapeless confusion, the 20th Maine was being driven back. Sergeant Stede staggered to his company commander. "I am going, Captain." The captain saw a gaping hole in Stede's abdomen and lunged to grab him. The man fell, dead before he hit the ground. A private was struck in the head. He rolled over on his back, raised a clenched, menacing fist to the sky. His arm dropped to his chest, and he was gone. A young corporal lay prostrate, air bubbling up through the red hole in his chest. His eyes were open wide with disbelief. "Mother, I am dying," he gasped.

The line of the 20th Maine was bent back so sharply that the men were taking fire from the Rebels charging their own front and from those assaulting the center of the Union line.

"Ammunition! Ammunition!" the cry rang out. The men jerked cartridge boxes from the belts of the dead and wounded. These rounds were quickly exhausted. Men with empty cartridge boxes now looked desperately to Colonel Chamberlain. Chamberlain made his second gamble of the day. "Fix bayonets," he ordered. The men looked at him, disbelieving. "Fix bayonets!" he roared. The surviving company commanders echoed the order. The clang of steel shanks sounded against steel barrels. The Yankees with their empty, bayonet-tipped guns rushed forward. The Rebels, caught off balance, reeled backward. They stumbled again over the bodies strewn on the hillside, and slipped on the blood and gore coating the rocks. As they tumbled backward, a hidden force of Federals rose from behind a stone wall and began to fire into their backs. Now they were squeezed front and rear. A man was shot simultaneously through the head and through the back. A bullet tore through another man's throat. He looked down to see the blood geysering over his arm and musket and fainted.

The Southern commander, Colonel Oates, abandoned all hope of an orderly retreat and ordered his men to flee as best they could. Among the men he had to abandon on the side of Little Round Top was John Oates, his young brother, dying of his wounds.

The Union soldiers pounced on the disorganized Confederates and took four hundred prisoners. "War's over, you dumb crackers." A wild-eyed private grinned, pin-pricking Rebel prisoners with his bayonet to speed them to the rear.

Lawrence Chamberlain felt one overwhelming sensation as his tightly coiled senses began to unwind. He was emotionally drained and, suddenly, voraciously hungry. He told his brother Tom, his adjutant, to order the men back to the original line.

As they retraced their steps up the slope, their mood was sober triumph. They had turned back the advance. But they had paid dearly. The ground they covered was littered with 280 bodies in an area a man could cross in two minutes. Some of the bodies quivered. Others were still. The less severely wounded begged for help. Some men sat quietly against trees braced for death. They asked for no help. Many of the dead lay like torn dolls, contorted into ludicrous postures. Others were frozen into firing position, their guns still trained on some absent enemy seen through sightless eyes.

Streams of blood trickled down the slope and collected into small red pools in the clefts and depressions of the rocks.

The men were awestruck at the havoc they had inflicted. The trees on the hillside were stripped naked their first six feet, gouged with fresh, white wounds and draining sap. Smaller trunks had been chewed clear through by bullets and toppled. Every tree was pocked with bullets. Over forty thousand rounds of ammunition had been fired in these desperate minutes.

A Union private stood looking at a tangled pile of four dead Southerners. At the bottom of the heap lay a man, his face turned skyward. Blood from one of the bodies flung on him had trickled over his cheeks and jaw and stained his sparse blond beard. His wide-open, dead eyes looked up in protesting horror. The Union soldier tore himself from the sight and started picking his way among the other corpses. "I don't understand why." He shook his head. "I don't understand why."

Colonel Lawrence Chamberlain understood why. A college professor, less than twelve months removed from the classroom, had blunted a potentially fatal thrust of the enemy through brilliant, bold initiatives. The 20th Maine, along with the other regiments of Vincent's brigade, had climbed Little Round Top, had dug in, and had held it. They had arrived there just ten minutes before the Confederates would have found this crucial high ground naked.

Just around the curve of Little Round Top and facing west, Ellsworth's Avengers manned the line. Now, with the Confederate advance blunted, they eagerly seized the chance for rest. They lay on their backs, panting heavily in the sheltering shadow of trees and rocks. Among the Avengers was Company E, called the Normal School Company. A year ago they had all been students at the teachers college in Albany, New York. Professor Husted, their teacher, was now First Lieutenant Husted, their commander. Out in front of them, Rebel soldiers had taken refuge behind rocks and trees on the hillside, so close to the Union line that they could neither go forward against the murderous Yankee fire nor pull back without exposing themselves to peril.

Suddenly, handkerchiefs and hats were waving above the rocks. The men of the Normal School Company gaped in surprise. Lieutenant Husted knew they had to seize this opportunity quickly. "Five volunteers to take prisoners!" he called out.

The men looked out skeptically over the jagged landscape from which, minutes ago, a killing fire had raked them. No one moved. Sergeant Consider Willett finally stood up and walked to Lieutenant Husted. Willett said simply, "I'll take them, Lieutenant." Four other volunteers followed Willett's lead.

The party stepped gingerly from behind the protection of their own line. They were sickened at the close-up evidence of their fire. It was difficult to walk without stepping on the dead and maimed. They reached the surrendering men and saw their feared and vaunted enemy face to face. They were puzzled by their raggedness, the seemingly fleshless bodies, the bare feet. But in the Rebels' lean faces there was no weakness, even in surrender. Instead, the trapped men exhibited the tenacity and cunning of half-starved animals.

The five Yankees took ninety-seven prisoners. They hurried them back toward their line before the main Confederate force could realize what was happening. Sergeant Con Willett quickly passed by imploring wounded men. "Hold on, you'll be picked up later. Don't worry. It'll all be over soon." One Rebel he could not pass. The wounded man pleaded desperately, "Cut it, Yank, please, just cut it." The Rebel soldier had ripped the clothing from around a deep wound in his side, but the leather strap of his cartridge belt bit deeply, excruciatingly into the wound. He had no strength to remove it. Willett set down his gun, peered uneasily over his shoulder, and cut quickly through the strap with a pocket knife. The man gave out a pained gasp as the strap fell loose. "God bless you," he cried, tears welling in his eyes. "Now get out of here quick." He waved Willett away. The Yankee sergeant clambered up the hillside to catch up with the rest of the party.

The Union men still back on the line cautiously trained their muskets on the surrendering Rebels rushing toward them. One came up directly in front of Lieutenant Husted crying, "Don't shoot me! Don't shoot." A bullet from the Confederate line tore through the man's back and he pitched forward dead at Husted's feet.

Lieutenant Jack Adams had fallen in the effort to relieve Sickles. Private Callopel carried him piggyback to the field hospital. The tent was a bedlam of screams, staccato orders, and furious motion. The private eased the officer to the ground. "Can I go now, Lieutenant?"

"No, wait, wait a minute." Adams grimaced in pain. He was a tough-faced youth of twenty who had risen from private to lieutenant

in a year of swift proofs of military aptitude. "Don't go till I get some
attention, do you hear!"

The private shuffled his feet impatiently, looking about at the
mangled forms with obvious distaste.

"Surgeon! Surgeon!" Adams' insistent yells at last stopped one of
the doctors rushing past. "Check my wounds," Adams demanded.

"Can't you see I'm busy." The surgeon began to move off. But
Adams held the man's wrist in an iron grip. The doctor swiftly
examined the youthful lieutenant. One wound was in the lower
abdomen, with the bullet still lodged in the body. Another ball had
passed through Adams' hip. "You won't live twenty-four hours," the
doctor said curtly and started away.

"Wait up, you could at least stop the bleeding, you could be
wrong."

"Really, I'm sorry. We just don't have time to spend on hopeless
patients."

Private Callopel had heard the verdict and had quietly slipped out
before Adams noticed he was gone.

Near the point on Little Round Top where Con Willett had herded
his prisoners there rested another company of Ellsworth's Avengers,
under handsome Captain Lucius Larrabee, of Ticonderoga, New York.
The startling good looks of the twenty-five-year-old officer were
steeped in melancholy. He was speaking softly, impatiently to two
other Avenger captains, Bourne and Kimberly. "Don't be silly, Lou,"
Kimberly said to Larrabee.

"Damn it, I haven't much time. Do as I say. Take these things and
see that they get to my brother in Chicago. The address is on this
paper." Reluctantly, Captain Kimberly took from Larrabee a gold
watch, some money, and several daguerreotypes.

"I've known ever since the last battle that I'd get it the next time
we came under fire."

"And cheat the ladies of their prettiest soldierboy?" Bourne laughed
hollowly and clapped Larrabee on the back. "We all get that feeling,
Lou."

Larrabee turned away and walked up to the line. He was to stake
out a party of skirmishers two hundred yards in front of the Union
position on Little Round Top to hold the stalled Rebels at bay. He
formed the men into line and returned to his two friends. He put out

his hand. "Good-bye to you, Billy. You, too, Frank, I won't see you again." Awkwardly, uneasily, as the men watched, the officers reached out and shook his hand. Larrabee returned to the head of the skirmishing party. He started down the slope and signaled the men to follow.

They had neared the bottom of the hill, Larrabee still in the lead. From a clump of bushes he heard a faint rustle. "Captain!" a corporal cried out. Larrabee stood frozen. The bullet struck him in the center of his handsome forehead. Hours later, when his body was recovered, it had been stripped naked.

General Hancock had to buy time. He would pay for it in lives. "Why are our men falling back?" Hancock shouted to General Gibbon as he saw a flag approaching. But it was a Rebel flag leading an enemy column, less than one hundred yards away. Hancock ordered the First Minnesota. "Drive those people away." The men charged ahead, bayonets fixed, to blunt the Rebel spearpoint. Among the charging Minnesotans were the Taylor brothers, Isaac and P.H. The regiment marched straight into Confederate artillery fire. The concussive power of exploding shells hurled them about like cloth bundles. Blinding bright flashes seared their sight, dust and smoke enveloped them, hot metal riveted their bodies. When the smoke lifted, 47 men were left unscathed of 262. P. H. Taylor, gasping and choking, gathered the shattered survivors about him and led them, shocked and stunned, back to the Union line.

The sun was setting quickly and a stillness descended over the battlefield. P. H. Taylor sat alone, his head buried in his knees. His shoulders trembled imperceptibly. Most of the wounded from the First Minnesota's charge had been retrieved. His brother, Isaac, was not among them. He and 215 others, dead, wounded and missing had bought Hancock his time.

"Jack, old fellow, they say you are going to die. We thought you'd like a canteen of coffee before you cashed in."

The jovial visitor to Lieutenant Jack Adams was Mose Shackley. He and another friend named Younger had learned of Adams' fate from Private Callopel who had carried the wounded man to the field hospital.

Adams was weak but still truculent. "These butchers want to bury me alive," he said, twisting continually, vainly seeking a less painful posture.

"Don't you have anything to lay on, Jack?" Shackley asked.

"Only Mother Earth."

Shackley left the tent. Outside he found a wounded Rebel lying on a rubber blanket with a wool blanket over him.

"There's a damn sight better man than you with no blanket at all," Shackley muttered, tearing the blanket off the bewildered Southerner.

Shackley and Younger gently worked the blanket under Adams, who fought back the urge to scream in pain.

They finished their coffee. "Like to stay with you right to the end, Jack," Shackley said. "But there's still lots of fun up there." The two men left.

The shaming sense of uselessness, of boys watching men work, continued to plague the 150th New York. All they had seen of war thus far was one soldier with an arm wound. They were now positioned in reserve behind the looming security of Culp's Hill. They sat writing letters, mending clothes, talking, trying to piece together the fragments of events of which they formed an insignificant fringe.

In mid-afternoon they heard the firing begin, followed by a curious sound. It started as a prolonged, distant, wavering yell. It swelled in pitch, higher and louder, until shrieks and gun shots competed for dominance of the air.

"What's that noise?"

"That's the Rebels," an old veteran answered. "Means they're charging!"

The reports of musketry grew louder, closer, thicker. Then a new sound rumbled toward them, a deep-throated "Hurrah!" that rolled out in waves.

"Now, that's the sound of men," the old veteran said, "not a damn pack of hyenas. That's our boys. Means the Rebs didn't make it that time."

A black phaeton suddenly pulled up in their midst and diverted the men from the echoes of battle. The driver was clad in black, wore a black bowler and a black string tie looped over a soiled shirt. He looked out at the men who gathered before him with a joyless smile. His teeth clenched a dead cigar. He flicked the cigar away.

"What are you selling, mister?" a soldier asked.

"Dignity, boys, and peace of mind for your loved ones."

The men stared uncomfortably. The grin held fast.

"You know what can happen on that field, don't you? God forbid. But you're all big boys. Do you know what happens if you haven't made any"—he paused—"arrangements?" The eyes narrowed and he looked hard into their faces one by one.

"What kind of arrangements?"

"Boys." The smile dissolved. The voice went solemn. "I can't imagine anything that will break a mother's heart quicker, I can't imagine anything sadder, than to have a hero lying in a nameless grave—stripped of his dignity, not to mention every stitch and every valuable on him."

He paused. The men swayed uneasily, yet stood rooted.

"The smallest foresight," he went on, "can avert that unnecessary tragedy."

A leathery corporal looked up at the man in black. "How much?"

"Depends on your rank." The mechanical smile resumed. "I guarantee embalming and shipment of the body home starting with twenty dollars for a private on up to a hundred dollars for a . . ."

The embalmer suddenly stopped and eyed a captain standing outside the circle of listeners. The captain had drawn his pistol. He clicked the hammer. "Get out, you scum," his voice hissed. "Do you hear me? Get out!"

The man's smile sickened. He turned away from his audience, pulled the reins hard, and the phaeton went bounding off.

The officer sheathed his gun. "Men, I hope to have some fresh rations up to you before long." He put the gun in its holster, gave them a smile, and walked away.

The men settled back to listening to the alternating Rebel yell and Yankee roar off toward Cemetery Ridge. At nightfall, the last Rebel cry went unanswered by the Union cheer. "That means our line," the old veteran sighed, "has been driven back."

The fighting along the peach orchard, the wheat field, the Devil's Den, and the Round Tops raged for four hours. The battle lines ebbed and flowed like the tides of a blood-red sea. Six times the

Confederates captured a small plot of earth planted in wheat. Six times the Federals took it back. When it was over, the golden ears were trampled underfoot, the ground was soaked and stained, and this small plot had become the grave of five hundred Confederates alone.

Yet the Rebels had chopped Sickles' insolent advance to pieces. Of nearly twelve thousand men, the Third Corps lost in those four hours 4211 killed, wounded, and missing. In one regiment, the colonel in command fell. The major replacing him was wounded immediately. A captain took charge and died. Down they went, until, in the end, a corporal led the regiment off the field. So badly had Sickles' corps been mangled that it would never again be rebuilt as a fighting body.

When the fighting in this sector ended, the new Confederate line ran roughly from the peach orchard diagonally across the wheat field, along the Devil's Den to near the base of the Round Tops.

The wisdom or folly of Sickles' audacious thrust was hotly argued around the campfires winking along Cemetery Ridge that night. Lieutenant Frank Haskell cut short a fellow officer who allowed as maybe Sickles' maneuver did have some merit. Haskell dripped scorn. "I hope that man may never return to the Army of the Potomac, or anywhere else where his incompetence might destroy thousands of men again."

The crushing vise that Lee had hoped to clamp around the two ends of the Yankee line had failed to grip. At four in the afternoon, General Ewell had finally heard the exploding artillery introduce Longstreet's attack on the Union left. This was the signal for Ewell to strike the Yankees on their right.

But snarling Yankee artillery on East Cemetery Hill threw off Ewell's timetable. Not for another three and a half hours did he dare send Johnson's division against the Federals. He could not know that, by then, Longstreet's end of the pincer had jammed against Little Round Top and stalled.

As the Federal cannonade waned, Johnson flung his men against the steep hillsides bristling with trees and rock. While the Stonewall Brigade assailed Culp's Hill, the Louisiana Tigers, never before rebuffed in a charge, struck Cemetery Hill.

From Cemetery Hill, Cub Buell had a view, at once majestic and frightening, of the Confederate tidal wave flowing toward them. His battery was positioned in front of the cemetery gate. Lower down the slope were posted troops of the 11th Corps, who had fled so ignominiously through town the day before. The artillerymen took small comfort from the presence of these troops as their shield.

As the lowering sun grayed the golden afternoon, the long Rebel lines seemed to float across the flat land before Cemetery Hill. Federal batteries waited the agonizing minutes to get them into killing range. Then they exploded with the crash of a thousand trees falling to earth at once. Canister tore into the gray ranks with appalling effect—forty-eight iron balls from every cannon's mouth every time the gun fired. Unwavering, the Confederates moved through the killing rain and swarmed over the forwardmost Union infantry. The Union artillery had to cease fire as Rebel and Yankee soldiers mixed indiscriminately. Then the gunners resumed fire as the Confederates drove on up the hill.

"Fire by piece. Fire at will." The enemy was now so close that the Union artillery batteries were having trouble depressing their gun barrels low enough to fire down the hill on them. The Rebels reached the first Federal gun emplacements. Artillerymen lashed at the enemy with handspikes, ramrods, stones, and bare fists. A Confederate lieutenant sprang into Rickett's battery and wrestled the guide-on from Private Riggen. Riggen killed the lieutenant with a revolver, then fell dead himself. Another Rebel laid his hand on the barrel of a cannon and demanded surrender of the battery. A wiry Yankee spun around with a handspike and dashed the man's brains out. Still the Rebels poured in. Victory was within their grasp. Then, off to the right, another battery of Union artillery swung sideways and began pouring a scathing fire of double canister into the unprotected flank of the Rebels at virtual point-blank range. Screaming, shrieking, cursing voices rent the air. The Confederate advance flagged as bodies piled on the ground in heaps. Just as the Louisiana advance ground to a halt, a fresh Union infantry brigade boiled over Cemetery Hill, slipped between the Union cannon, and struck the Rebels with guns blazing. With infantry bearing down in front and artillery gouging their left side, the Confederates broke and staggered back.

Nearly 1700 Louisiana Tigers had set out to take Cemetery Hill. Over 1200 fell in the attempt. The once unstoppable brigade had been destroyed as an effective unit.

*　　*　　*

Instead of the triumphal entry into Gettysburg which he had imagined, Robert Stiles found himself moved farther from the battle. A suspicious force had been sighted well to the north of the Confederates' position near Culp's Hill. Two brigades had been dispatched to scout the unidentified force. Stiles rode with them. The reconnaissance force concluded that the troubling shadow was only an element of Stuart's long-missing cavalry. Someone would have to inform General Johnson, the commander of the division, to reassure him that no enemy was about to stab him from behind. Robert Stiles seized the opportunity to return to the battle lines. He volunteered to carry the message by horseback to General Johnson. By now, the terrain over which the scouting brigades had passed had exploded into a killing ground between Yankee and Confederate cannoneers.

The early distance which he covered was shielded from the enemy guns by small hills. But Stiles soon broke into open land. He could see projectiles well ahead of him, most of their propulsive force spent, sinking almost lazily to earth. As he pulled within range of the enemy guns, he could feel his horse shudder under him with every explosive shriek. The horse hugged the ground and Stiles hugged the horse.

He rode past a battery of Rebel artillery which had been trading fire with the Federal guns on Culp's Hill. The cannon had been blown backward from their positions on the rim of a crater into the crater bottom. The guns were heaped and twisted, barrels bent, carriages broken and splintered, ammunition chests shattered, limbers crushed. Amid smoke and flames, the maddened horses, trapped in their harnesses, reared and plunged, their hooves dashing out the brains of men entangled in the wreckage. Cannoneers with pistols drawn were wading amid the carnage and shooting the horses to save the trapped men. Stiles paused briefly before this small hell and pushed his horse onward.

He arrived at his destination, leaped off the sweating, foam-flecked horse, and tumbled out his message to General Johnson. Johnson grumbled a barely audible "Very well" and walked away. The general's thoughts now were absorbed in the assault he had unfurled against Culp's Hill. For Robert Stiles the ride was his last useful act at Gettysburg. He saw no action for the rest of the battle.

The Confederate attack against Culp's Hill fared scarcely better than the blunted thrust against Cemetery Hill. Three times the Rebels had charged. Three times they were repulsed. By ten o'clock, when darkness foreclosed the fight, Southern dead littered the hillside. The Rebels had clawed their way into some lower Union entrenchments at a staggering human cost. But the Yankees still held the crucial brow of Culp's Hill.

The second day's fighting at Gettysburg had ended all along the line. The Union army, even afrer Sickles' promontory had been smashed back, still held a continuous line intact from Culp's Hill on the far right, over to Cemetery Hill, down Cemetery Ridge to Little Round Top at the southern end of the battlefield. The Confederates now held much of the Emmitsburg Road, the peach orchard, and part of the Devil's Den. At the other end of the line, they held the town and that dearly purchased but highly useful patch of Culp's Hill practically behind the enemy line.

The distance was short, but the work was heavy all the same. Most of the Union dead had fallen on the western slope of Little Round Top. They had to be lugged through the thicket of brushes and scrub oaks over the sharp-edged, chafing rocks. The burial detail stumbled in the fading light. The men sweated and cursed as they dragged their burdens up the slope, around the crest, and down the other side. There, the company commanders held lamps to the faces, some half gone, some blood-caked, some peaceful, and directed the burial detail to an appropriate row of still figures—Company F here, Company A over by the big tree, Company G over to the left of A. The light was failing quickly. No time for ceremony. The bodies were quickly covered over with dirt. By nightfall the job was done.

Captain Charles Billings, an original member of the 20th Maine, Waterville contingent, was carried off the slope of Little Round Top late in the evening. Billings was taken to a barn sheltering sixty-five other badly wounded men. The litter bearers set him among several of his own men.

Minutes after his arrival, one of them died. Billings wept as the man was dragged away. He was responsible for the man's death, he said. He wailed and beat his fists against his head. "All my fault! My fault!" Two orderlies, with great effort, calmed him and pressed him back to the floor. Then another man died. Billings pounded the floor and sobbed inconsolably. When they carried out the lifeless body of a third man who had fought under him, Billings summoned some hidden reservoir of strength from his failing body, rose, and began to lurch among the wounded, raving, tearing at his clothes, screaming, shaking his fists to heaven. Five men wrestled him to the ground. His eyes finally lost their maniacal blaze. His body went limp.

The surgeon ordered Billings taken to a small, empty room and went in to examine him. When he came out he found the Reverend Robert Parvin of the Christian Commission waiting outside. The minister looked up expectantly. The doctor shook his head. "If they had done a primary amputation in the field immediately, maybe"—he shrugged—"but now, there is no hope."

"May I see him, doctor?"

"Certainly, Reverend."

The Reverend Parvin entered the small room. Billings now appeared quite calm.

"Reverend, tell me, what did he say?" Hope hung in the wounded man's eyes.

"Captain, he says you are a critical case."

"I know, I know that," he said testily. "But does he think I'll live?"

The minister was silent, then said, "The doctor thinks it hardly possible."

The captain covered his face with his hands and cried aloud. "Reverend, you must promise me something. Out on the field, someone took my money from me. Will you have my body embalmed and sent home?"

The Reverend Parvin nodded. "Of course, Captain."

"Stretcher bearer, take me! Take me next!" The voices pleaded piteously. "I'm Company C. Please, please help me." Arms reached out to clutch at the men carrying the wounded back to the field hospital. A soldier with a blanket over his stomach cried to two bearers, "Me next, it's my leg." The bearers approached the man. One ripped away the blanket. "Damn you, you got one in your belly, too. We got no time for you." The man uttered a hopeless cry and buried his face in the ground.

The bearers knew all the tricks of the wounded. They had their orders. Bring in the best prospects first, the men who can be saved by a quick amputation of a leg or arm. Men shot in the belly are going to die. So are men shot in the chest or the head. Don't waste precious time.

*   *   *

"You want what?" Major Pearson roared.

Undaunted, the spokesman for the delegation of farmers repeated, "We want money. We want money for the straw your men took."

Union soldiers had helped themselves to straw in neighboring barns to use as crude beds for the wounded. The rightful owners now confronted Major A. L. Pearson of the 155th Pennsylvania near Little Round Top, long after the fighting had ceased.

The farmer spoke again. "We want the money now. We won't get nothing when this army leaves. We know!"

"Get out of here immediately, do you hear! Get out before I send my men to burn your God damn barns to the ground. I will have you court-martialed for disloyalty and inhumanity. Get out of my sight."

The farmers turned impassively and stalked away. They trudged down the slope and up the road. They stopped at a field hospital. Outside, a burial detail was busy returning Union dead to the earth. Inside, the surgeons were treating the wounded in the dim lamplight. The head of the farmer delegation poked his head into the doorway. "You took our straw. We want pay for it. Now!"

The litter bearers carried the wounded man through the barn doorway. The doctor glanced up from the operating table at the dangling leg and motioned with a red-stained knife for the orderlies to put the patient near the door.

The bearers lifted the wounded soldier off the stretcher and set him on a dirt floor. Seven men lay between him and the operating table. Actually, it was no table, but a door suspended over two wooden horses. Six more improvised tables crowded the barn, each soaked crimson. The army had operating tables and hospital tents. But this equipment had been parked twenty-four miles away. It would not be available for days.

The patient was a sturdy, blond-haired eighteen-year-old. He had been stunned and silent on his arrival. But the screams of the other patients, their wild thrashing on the operating table, the sound of men crying, their terrified curses, had awakened and unnerved him. He gaped toward the table in mute terror. It was dark in the barn except for a few lanterns, and he stared at the surgeon through a funereal light.

The surgeon worked furiously and quietly except for curt, cryptic signals to the nurses. His shirt sleeves were rolled up and his arms bloodied up to his elbow. He was soaked in sweat. Sweat beaded his face and pasted his spattered shirt to his body.

The wounded soldier watched the mutilated forms before him being carried on and off the operating table.

"Next." The surgeon grunted with fatigue. He was breathing heavily and swabbing his forehead with a dry corner of his apron.

Two orderlies lifted the blond soldier onto the table. He was whining softly, like a small, terrified animal, "Nooooo, nooo, nooo, nooo, nooo."

The doctor ripped off the pants leg and exposed the site where the minié ball had smashed the knee. The surgeon reached into a bucket of clouded water and pulled out the sponge he had used all day. He dabbed at the wound a few times. The boy tried to lift himself onto his elbows, and craned his neck to see what was happening. The surgeon ran his finger into the wound, searching for the bullet. The boy screamed in agony. The surgeon wiped his hand on his apron. He clapped a towel over the soldier's nose and dribbled chloroform onto it. The boy's head sank back. His body went limp. The surgeon sighted the knife above an imaginary line a few inches above the boy's knee. He knew that the further the incision was from the trunk, the greater the patient's odds of survival. But he dared not cut any closer to the wound. His hand was trembling with fatigue. He brought the knife down in a guillotine whack across the thigh clear down to the bone. He dropped the saw into the incision, and its teeth bit into the bone with an odd, whirring whine. The surgeon threw the severed leg onto a growing heap of limbs at the end of the table.

The surgeon next moistened the tip of an oiled silk thread to a point with his tongue and threaded it through a needle. His trembling fingers sutured the arteries with surprising dexterity. He left the ends of the silk thread long enough so that they could be removed in a few days with a simple tug. He dressed the wound with rags from a nearby pile.

The patient began groaning. His eyes began to open. The attendants pulled him to a sitting position on the table. His head lolled from side to side until his eyes fixed on the site where his leg had been. He let forth a chilling scream and fell back in a faint.

The boy had been on the operating table for nine minutes. The surgeon waved to the attendants to remove him. He wiped his knife on his apron.

"Next," he said.

The sun had long disappeared below Seminary Ridge, setting a purple mantle over the sloping, silhouetted hills. The night was warm and muggy, and the moon, partially obscured by a haze, cast a sickly light over the battlefield. A regiment of Vermonters had spaced themselves out in a skirmish line well beyond the main Union force behind the Codori house where Sickles' men had fought that afternoon.

They had never been under fire. The harvest of the day's fighting lay scattered around them—bodies, singly and in clumps of twos and threes. It was the wrong introduction to war for men who had never fought and who soon would. Men who must face the cannon and the musket for the first time were not buoyed by the mangled bodies and pitiful cries of those who had. An appalling gloom gripped the field. If there is glory in war, it must fade with the last shellburst and return only in some artist's eye. Here on this field all that remained was the refuse of conflict.

Stretcher bearers from both sides picked their way among the dead seeking the still living, guided by low moans, the cries and mindless babble of men deranged by suffering.

A pair of Confederate stretcher bearers paused by a nervous Vermont skirmisher.

"Hey, Yank, take a look at that feller behind you, is he ours or yours?"

The Vermonter backed toward the body, never taking his eye from the enemy. He jerked his head around quickly and spied a rolled blanket over a butternut shirt. "He's yours."

The stretcher bearers came around to the prostrate form.

"He is, you God damn fool, but he's dead!" They quickly moved on to the next huddled shape.

A prisoner was brought to Lieutenant Colonel Nichols, who commanded this tense, untried line of Vermonters.

"This prisoner says there's somebody out there we ought to get," a Yankee sergeant snorted.

"Sir," the man said earnestly, "General Barksdale's out there in front of your line. He's wounded."

Nichols did not hesitate. He turned to the sergeant. "Vaughn, take a detail out there and bring the general back."

"Mud, blood, and shee-yut!" Vaughn muttered. He gathered a party of eight unwilling Vermonters and jabbed his musket into the Rebel prisoner's back. "Okay, boy, take us to the big bug."

Nichols spent twenty anxious minutes listening to the mournful chorus of the wounded, waiting for the return of his men. He heard footsteps approaching and could make out darkened forms hauling a stretcher.

"We got him," Sergeant Vaughn said grudgingly.

"Get him back to the field hospital, Vaughn."

"This is General Barksdale. He commanded a whole slew of Mississippis," Vaughn announced upon depositing the wounded general before an exhausted Union surgeon in the hospital tent.

General Barksdale opened his eyes to thin slits. He turned his head slowly away from the light. His pants legs were caked with stiffened blood. The rough bandages over his wounds had come loose and trailed from the table. Through his chest was a large bullet hole.

"I'm Barksdale." His long white mane was matted and snarled. He wore white, soiled gloves, which he peeled off with excruciating slowness. He handed the gloves to Sergeant Vaughn.

"Give these . . . to one of your . . . officers . . . my lad. I would like them . . . sent to my wife." His lips labored over each word. "Tell my wife . . . I fought like a man . . . and I died like one." He closed his eyes and passed easily from life.

"Take him out and bury him," the surgeon ordered. "Mark the spot clearly."

"Yes, sir," Sergeant Vaughn said. "He seemed like a real fine gentleman.

Had the Confederate cannon still been firing late that night, a well-placed shell could have severed the head of the Army of the Potomac. They had crowded into a room of Widow Leister's house on the Taneytown Road, General George Meade, his personal staff, and his ten commanders. Twelve generals occupied a room roughly ten by ten. Cigar smoke clung to the warm night air. The room was pungent with the odors of close-packed men, their clothes impregnated with the smell of horses, gunpowder, smoke, the sweat from heat and fear. General Meade had gathered his lieutenants for a formal council of war. They would debate, then vote on the next moves of the Union army.

General Meade sat in one of a half dozen straight-backed, rush-bottomed chairs. At his side was a small table, on it a wooden pail of water and a tin cup from which an officer occasionally drank. A candle had been fixed on the table in its own tallow, and its flickering light threw an unflattering color over Meade's dour countenance. He had slumped, stoop-shouldered, in his chair, with his glasses poised on that great nose. Meade said little, but continually wove and unwove his fingers. Other officers sat on chairs, on the floor, on the edge of a small bed, or leaned against the walls.

General Warren, exhausted and suffering a painful neck wound, had stretched out in a corner and fallen asleep. His quick judgment that afternoon in arming Little Round Top explained in large measure why they were here in this room plotting the next day's battle and not scattered in defeat on this night.

The only officer in the room whose appearance belied the day's experience was General Winfield Scott Hancock. He was, as ever, impeccable. Neither dirt nor sweat sullied his uniform. His boots shone and immaculate linen cuffs peeked from his coat sleeves.

"Frankly, withdrawal is out of the question," Hancock said with his customary authority.

General Newton, an engineer with a peacock strut, paced a few steps and shook his head vigorously. "Disagree. This is no place to fight a battle."

"Newton, this is good ground." Hancock's voice became deeper, firmer. "By holding it, we invite Lee to mass and attack us. And that is all to the good."

The debate rose and fell. General Meade remained wordless but was increasingly agitated and impatient.

"Butterfield, let's bring it to a vote," he said to his chief of staff. Meade took a piece of paper, wrote something on it, and handed it to his aide.

"I'll read the general's question and then we'll go around, from the junior officer on up," Butterfield said. "Each of you will please state where you stand." The first question was, "Should the army remain in its present position or take up some other?"

Butterfield looked directly at General John Gibbon, acting commander of the Second Corps and the junior officer present. Gibbon felt a tightness in his throat. This was his first council of war. He had not wanted to speak first. He had heard the respected Newton say that this was not a good place to fight. He had heard the awesome Hancock say it was. He breathed deeply and spoke in carefully weighed phrases. "I say remain here, and make such corrections in our position as necessary, but take no step which even looks like retreat." Butterfield made a rapid notation on the paper and turned to the next officer.

By the time they had all spoken, General Meade had framed his next question, "Should the army attack or await the attack of the enemy?" The answers came in curt, soldierly phrases. Butterfield scribbled the tally. With few variations, the council of war had decided—hold the present position. Do not attack. Await the enemy's attack. Meade, for the first time, relaxed slightly. He looked up from folded hands and said, "Such, then, is the decision. That will be all tonight, gentlemen."

As the boot heels of the departing officers drummed on Mrs. Leister's porch, General Meade rose and went to the doorway. "General Gibbon," he called out. Gibbon came back. "Yes, sir?" Meade leaned in the doorway, his arms folded. Protuberant eyes examined Gibbon. Meade knew Gibbon's family circumstances, not all that different from his own. The thirty-six-year-old North Carolinian had three brothers in the Confederate Army. They had disowned him.

"General Gibbon, if Lee attacks tomorrow, it will be on your front."

"Why do you say so, General Meade?"

"He has attacked our right flank and failed. He has attacked our left flank and failed. If he tries again, it will be on our center where you are."

"I hope he does, sir."

"Yes, yes, Gibbon," Meade said distractedly and turned back into the house. He dropped his lean frame into a chair, squeezed his temples tightly between his hands, and breathed deeply.

"Hey, Yank, you got any water?"

The voice startled the Union private. He peered out into the darkness. It was nearly midnight. The fighting for Little Round Top had stopped four hours earlier. The soldier and his company had been sent on picket duty as the forward antennae of the Union position.

"We won't hurt ya." The cracked voice uttered a joyless laugh. "Christ, we couldn't.

The private could now make out three shapes on the ground, illuminated by the moonlight, not twelve feet from his post. He unhitched his canteen and flung it toward the Rebels. The faltering movement of the arm that reached toward the canteen reassured him of his safety. He came up close and helped the Confederate guide the spout to his mouth.

"Thanks, Yank." The man drank deeply and pushed the canteen aside. "Here, give some to him." The man prodded another man near him. "Hey, we got a good Yankee here brung us water." The second man awoke slowly. He attempted to sit up, groaned deeply, and fell back down. The Union soldier put the canteen to his lips, and the man gulped avidly. He finally opened his eyes wide. "Damn, this here's a Yankee!"

"It's water, ain't it?" the first Confederate answered.

"What about him?" the Union private said, pointing the canteen toward a third figure.

"Give him some. But it ain't much use. He ain't gonna make it."

A tearful, childish whine rose from the third man. "God damn you! Don't you say that no more, y'hear?"

The first Confederate pointed toward the man's abdomen and shook his head in resignation. The Yankee private went to the third man and brought the canteen to his mouth. He seemed no more than sixteen. His eyes were barely open. He lay on his back. He had ripped his shirt open, revealing a soft, girlish trunk, smooth and pallid in the moonlight. The hairless white skin was broken by a purple hole near the navel. The Union soldier knew he should not give water to a man with a belly wound. But death was written in the boy's face. He tipped the canteen generously down his throat.

He then busied himself collecting blankets and haversacks from the plentiful dead around him. He gently inserted the haversacks under the heads of the three Rebels and covered them with blankets. He sat down next to the man who had spoken first.

"Where ya from, Yank?" the Confederate asked.

"New York state."

"What's yer name?"

"Henry."

"What did you do before you started fightin' for the nigger, Henry?" He said it matter-of-factly.

The Union soldier frowned long before answering. "I helped my pa do some tenant farming," he answered, and added, slowly, "and I ain't fighting for the nigger."

The Rebel ignored the harsh note. "Tenant farming? I didn't think you rich Yankees did that, just us poor Rebs. What do you plant?"

"Oh, corn mostly, some beans."

"We raise a lot of corn, too. Leastways we used to. I don't know who's doing anything now. My pa, he's sixty-eight. My brother got killed at Sharpsburg."

"Your brother? Damn." Tears began to well in the Union soldier's eyes. "I lost my little brother just a while back . . . Fredericksburg . . . with that God damn butcher, Burnside."

In the darkness, the two men studied each other's faces.

"How many niggers are you fighting to hold onto, Reb?"

"Shit." The man grimaced and raised two powerful-looking hands. "Here's the only niggers ever worked for me." He dropped his hands to the ground and coughed in pain.

"Ain't you learned yet, boy? This here's a rich man's war and a poor man's fight."

"Where you hit, Reb?"

"Where a man's a man." He patted the junction between his thigh and groin.

"Is it bad?"

"Can't tell."

"Better let me see."

The Rebel gingerly opened his legs. Henry cut away the torn and blood-soaked fabric and exposed the wound. Even in the dark he could detect the spreading stain that had seeped outward dampening the crotch, matting the hair. The grass beneath the Southerner was damp with his blood. Henry took a rag from his pocket and soaked it with water from his canteen. He daubed gently at the wound and cleaned it as best he could. He made a compress of part of the man's ripped trousers and pressed the cleanest part of it over the wound.

The second Rebel stirred again. "Hey, Yank, got any tobacco?"

"Don't use it."

"You deadbeat son of a bitch," the man whined.

Henry heard footsteps approaching. He heard the sergeant calling out the names of the picket detail.

"I gotta git."

The first Rebel grabbed him with unexpected strength before he could get away. The man grasped his hand warmly. "Good-bye, Henry."

"Good-bye," the Union soldier murmured, scurrying back to his post in the picket line.

The first faint light of the morning sun was dissolving the gray cover over the base of Little Round Top. A fresh company arrived to relieve the Union pickets. Henry had dozed off. His relief came up and shook his shoulder. He stood up, stretched himself, picked up his musket, and headed back. Suddenly he stopped. He turned around and retraced his steps of the night before. Again, the three forms. The man who had asked for tobacco was now sitting up, but refused to look at him. The Confederate he had talked to and the young boy were dead.

5 | THE LAST DAY

Few and short were the prayers we said;
And we spoke not a word of sorrow,
As we steadfastly gazed on the face of the dead,
And bitterly thought on the morrow.

A Soldier's Poem

THE MEN OF THE New Orleans Washington Artillery, weary and hungry, wheeled their cannon into position at two a.m. on July 3. Their gun barrels pointed roughly toward the middle of the Federal line on Cemetery Ridge. The ground around them was scattered with Union dead, most of them the victims of Sickles' impetuous deployment of the day before. As they rolled their cannon and caissons into place, one of the lumps they passed over emitted a mournful wail. "Jesus, Willy, watch out," a soldier hollered at the driver. "You just ran over a live one."

"What do you expect? It ain't lit up like Bourbon Street out here."

With the guns in place, the artillerymen dropped, exhausted, to the ground and felt the pangs of hunger, until then quelled by activity. They had marched the entire day and into the night. They had spent themselves hauling the guns over hills, out of ruts and through tangled brush. For two days they had eaten nothing. A gaunt sergeant, his eyes glistening, approached the battery commander. "Cap'n, I'd like permission to take a party foraging."

"Foraging? Have you lost your mind? Where are you going to forage in the middle of the night?"

The sergeant pointed toward the lifeless heaps on the field. "Out there."

The captain shook his head wearily. "I suppose so. Take five men."

The sergeant started toward the front, tapping men on the shoulder along the way. "C'mon, Nap, grab your haversack."

Nap Bartlett, onetime journalist, sometime lawyer, who had long since forgotten that the original cook of the Washington Artillery had been Edouard, chef of Victor's famed restaurant, found himself in a Pennsylvania pasture scavenging the bodies of dead men for his food.

Nap returned with the foraging party and helped distribute the confiscated hardtack and salt pork. As he sat gnawing greedily, he looked out at the once human rag piles they had just plundered. Bartlett thought, What is the difference between them and me? Days ago, hours ago, they too lived. Do we just add hours and then I join them? But I can't accept that. There has to be some mysterious difference between them and me. Something must explain why they are out there, misshapen and rotting, while I am here, whole, all life, my heart pumping, my mind whirling with thought and sensation. Or is it just time, the difference between us just the passing of some hours?

Earlier in the day, a dead cart had passed them as they wheeled their guns forward. One corpse sat upright with an arm stiffly held out front. This mute comrade, Nap thought, had pointed directly at him, as the wagon passed. What was that outstretched hand signaling? he wondered.

The buglers sounded reveille for Pickett's division at three a.m. The men rose, yawning, stiff-limbed after the long forced march in the beating sun the day before. They had snatched a few hours' sleep in a copse off the Chambersburg Pike, about three miles from the battlefield. They totaled fifteen regiments, all Virginians, a young army, average age nineteen. Many had never been under fire. They had been held in reserve at Fredericksburg and at Chancellorsville, and the fighting was over before they had arrived on those battlefields.

Young Willie Mitchell had come looking for John Dooley the night before, after they had encamped. The boy was uneasy but determinedly cheerful. He tried to talk to Dooley of some of the insect life he had discovered and catalogued on the previous day's march.

"But I lost the microscope."

"Lost it?"

"Well, not really, I think somebody stole it."

"God!" Dooley said. "We've got some scum in this army."

Willie attempted a feeble smile, his eyes turned toward the ground. "I'm a little scared, John."

"You and me both, Willie." Dooley clapped his hand on the boy's shoulder.

"Yes, but I know you won't run, John."

"Neither will you."

"How do I know?" The eyes pleaded for assurance.

Dooley shook his head sagely. "Willie boy. For one thing, it's not all that simple."

Young Mitchell looked up, wide-eyed. "Not easy to cut?"

"It's not all a matter of being brave. For one thing, there's those file closers behind you. They've got orders to shoot if you cut. They're back there jabbing your hindquarter with their bayonets if you even straggle. Besides, everyone in the company is looking out the corner of his eye to see who is fixing to run. I tell you it can take more guts to go backward than to go forward. Willie, you go back to your outfit now and get some sleep. They'll be rousting us out before you know it."

Willie smiled openly, warmly now. "Thank you, Johnny. I feel a bit better."

When Reveille sounded, it was still dark. Battle flags hung limp in the windless night air. The men lit fires, made coffee, munched on hard crackers if they had any. It was stonily silent. Just before daylight, they were ordered to fall in and march out to the Chambersburg Pike. They formed a gray, blind snake a mile long.

John Dooley felt the light, bodiless sensation overtake him again. How can I not fear death? he wondered. In every battle I see, it takes us in unexpected forms, in grotesque mutilations. I am terrified to have survived and then to face it again. Yet, an unthinking momentum propelled him. He missed no detail of what must be done. His orders carried a quiet assurance. "Column of fours . . . fall in . . . company . . . forrwaard . . . march."

As they swung onto the road, Dooley saw in the faint light of dawn the commander of the Army of Northern Virginia, alone, watching the men stream from the woods. General Lee sat athletic, erect in the saddle. From a distance he looked a man of forty. Up close, the snow white beard and patriarchal expression aged him beyond his fifty-six years. As they filed past, Lee, it seemed to Dooley, lacked the serenity that always seemed to possess him on the eve of victory.

On the far right of the Federal line at Culp's Hill, each side faced the other, waiting only for a glimmer of daylight to illuminate the enemy. All through the night the sounds echoing through the trees on Culp's Hill had suggested a logging camp. Union soldiers chopped down trees, piled the trunks into stout breastworks, and dammed every ravine, gully, and rock formation that offered shelter. They would need the protection. The troops coiled to strike them were led by the vaunted Stonewall Brigade. Rival commanders, impatient to seize the advantage, could not wait for daylight. By four a.m. Culp's Hill was ablaze with flaming cannon and flashing muskets. A magnificent oak forest that had shaded Gettysburg's favorite picnic grounds was being smashed into kindling.

The Union cannoneers met the first Rebel infantry advance with shot and canister. The Federal guns ripped off parts of men and flung them around the hillside. The blows stunned and stopped the Rebels. They reformed and charged again. This assault, too, was checked. But each fresh advance was launched farther up the hillside than the previous attempt, as the Rebels ground out gains measured in feet and demarcated by small rivulets of blood.

The men of the 150th New York found war a swift school. Twenty-four hours before, they had quailed at the sight of one bloodied arm. Now they loaded and fired oblivious to comrades dropping beside them. Musicians and other noncombatants transported bleeding, mangled bodies with a cool detachment that suggested years rather than a single day in combat. It was only work, the men concluded, work that one does when it must be done.

They knew their foe. The enemy repelled and now stalled before them was the Stonewall Brigade. That they had met the Rebels' finest and stood fast emboldened them.

A small white cloth waved from behind a boulder. The guns went silent. Every rock and tree yielded up a Confederate soldier. Over two hundred of them came leaping over the Federal breastworks to surrender. One of the prisoners crouched quickly behind the Federal rampart.

"What's the matter, Johnny, too hot for you out there?" a four-hour combat veteran asked.

"Lordy, you bastards had us between a shit and a sweat." The Rebel wiped his brow.

"What did you quit for?"

"We couldn't take no more heat from you fellers up front, and there's another rank of our boys behind us. And they weren't about to let us skedaddle. So's the only thing we could do was wait for enough smoke to hide our asses and git!"

Repelled three times, the officers of the Stonewall Brigade now called for a fourth charge. The men ordered to make it were numbed, mute beasts. No sentient being would have yielded to these repeated invitations to die. They gathered on the side of the hill, jaws slack, eyes haunted with no thought of how many years, hours, minutes remained of their lives.

A wild-eyed young lieutenant stomped among them, haranguing in a high, hysterical twang, "One more time, men. One more time'll do it. Just one more time."

Then they began moving straight up the hillside. There was no thought of seeking protective rocks or trees. Only the bang and the winking of the gun briefly revealed the enemy behind their sturdy ramparts. They shrieked the Rebel battle cry, stumbling forward, scraping legs on jagged rock, stepping on lifeless comrades, climbing toward the gun flashes. They crashed against an unforgiving wall of fire and fell back.

On this hill the greatest bloodletting thus far had taken place at Gettysburg. The slain lay in great mounds. Here the blood of brother was mixed with brother and neighbor with neighbor. In the early days of the war, each side had recruited regiments from the same part of bitterly divided Maryland. Now a perverse fate had thrown the Marylanders from both armies at each other here on a small Pennsylvania hillside.

The Rebels had been stopped for the last time in this sector. By eleven a.m., seven hours after the first cannon had barked, it was quiet across the Gettysburg battlefield. Lee's hope for a coordinated assault by Ewell from the north and Longstreet upon the Union center had vanished. The fighting on the Confederate left had ended. The fighting in the center had yet to begin.

P. H. Taylor of the First Minnesota, out in the fields before Cemetery Ridge, could hear the fighting on Culp's Hill. But it was not his war. P.H. blotted out time, erased thought that morning, working quickly at what had to be done. He had buried his brother, Isaac, himself. He wanted to dig the grave deeper, but the sergeant had hurried him. He carefully measured the spot, 340 paces west of the Taneytown Road, about midway between the houses of a farmer named Hummelbaugh and a black man named Fisher. He wrote the distances down in one of the little leather diaries he had found in Isaac's knapsack. He stared briefly at the flower pasted in the diary with the words "My Maryland" and the date "June 27" circling the petal.

P.H. wrapped the diaries carefully in a handkerchief, then in an oil cloth, and stowed them at the bottom of Isaac's knapsack. He had one last task. He pried a board from an ammunition case and began carving into it. Most of the men had inscribed the headboards in pencil. P.H. took the time to carve the marks deep into the wood. Rain would wash penciled letters away, and he would have to find this place some day. The finished headboard read:

> *I. L. Taylor*
> *1st Minn. Vols*
> *Buried at 10 o'clock a.m., July 3rd, 1863*
> *by his brother*
> *Sergt. P. H. Taylor*
> *Co. "E" 1st Minn. Vols*

Robert E. Lee looked out over the enemy terrain with an engineer's practiced eye. Sitting astride his horse on Seminary Ridge, Lee played his binoculars over the softly sloping ridge opposite him. He fixed his gaze on a clump of oak and chestnut trees that rose near the middle of Cemetery Ridge, the part of the enemy line that his troops had not yet tested.

What Lee saw heartened him. About a half mile distant, along the Emmitsburg Road, the land began to ascend in a gentle swell up to the Federal defenses. It was uphill, but not too steep to deter infantry, he decided. Besides, troops firing from an elevated position have a tendency to overshoot. Lee studied the stone wall that skirted much of the ridge. It was low, barely a foot or two high. And the ridge terrain would be too rocky to allow any deep entrenchment. As he strapped his field glasses back into their case, contentment shone in his face. His aide, Colonel Taylor, rode up and saluted. "Good morning, sir." Lee returned the salute almost cheerily. "Colonel, call my commanders together as soon as possible, please."

A rueful smile played across the usually gruff soldier's countenance of General Lew Armistead. He sat on a tree stump looking out toward Cemetery Ridge, where as dear a friend as he had ever known was among the enemy. If only for an hour he could suspend this blamed war and go over and talk with Win Hancock the way they used to in the old days. Then he would come back happier and they could resume this profession of killing like the old soldiers they were.

It was over two years since the night Armistead had left Winfield Scott Hancock's farewell party in distant Los Angeles and had left the Army to which he had once pledged his allegiance. His already sparse hair had become thinner and flecked with gray. He wore it in a Nero fringe, easy to maintain, no fuss, unlike the elaborate coiffure of his curled and pomaded superior, General Pickett.

Lew Armistead had followed faithfully the star of his new nation. Having made the wrenching decision, he never looked back. Yet, the star-spangled banner, the very flag that flew over Fort McHenry, the fort which Armistead's uncle had saved from the British in 1812, was still a treasured Armistead family heirloom. Lew Armistead now marched, unquestioning, under a different banner. Strange, he thought, that so many who had served so long under the old flag had died fighting against it. He could hear again the painful sweet song of General Johnston's wife the night they had left, ". . . it may be for years and it may be forever." That good and gallant soldier was gone, too, dead at Shiloh, fighting against the old flag. It was more than Lew Armistead's plain, soldier's mind could comprehend. He shook the confusion from his head and rose to check on his men.

Here on the field at Gettysburg, Lew Armistead commanded a brigade under Pickett. His unhesitating obedience to orders, his expectation of the same from his men, his immersion in the cult of discipline might stamp another man a martinet. Instead, gruff Lew Armistead was revered by his men.

On Baltimore Street, a sharpshooter's bullet struck a kitchen door with a splintering crash. A baby shrieked. Mrs. Wade rushed to the kitchen. "Georgia!" she screamed above the baby's wailing. "Your sister! Your sister! She's shot!"

Georgia rushed for the kitchen. Jennie Wade lay on the floor, her hands still powdery, a red spot swelling beneath her body.

After they had the baby quieted down, they located Jennie's favorite quilt, the one she had pieced together as a child. They wrapped her in it and carried her body to the cellar. Her mother heavily reclimbed the stairs to the kitchen. She stood several minutes, staring dumbly into the bowl holding the swelling lump. She ran her hands alongside her apron and began kneading the dough.

Lee and his chief lieutenants gathered near a place they called point-of-the-woods. This slightly higher ground, about midway along Seminary Ridge, offered a clear view of the Federal position and provided a protective backdrop of trees, concealing the Confederate officers.

Longstreet knew Lee's intention. He knew, too, that the commander's dysentery had continued to plague him and had eroded even Lee's infinite patience. Longstreet would have to get his case out quickly.

"General Lee, look at what's between us and the Yankees. There's that fairly steep grade, and the fences. They've laid out a heavy skirmish line as well. We will be passing over a mile of open ground. That field is going to rain with canister."

Lee's face tensed. Longstreet's assurance faltered, yet he went on. "But we still have an excellent opportunity to move around to the right of Meade's army and maneuver him so he'll attack us." Lee's face now reddened. Longstreet knew that he was pressing the outer limits of his commander's tolerance. "I could send Hood and McLaws south around the big mountain beyond . . ."

Lee's fierce stare cowed him. The commander pointed toward Cemetery Ridge and with the faintest tremor in his voice said, "The enemy is there, and I am going to strike him." All were silent. Lee then laid out the plan.

Eleven brigades of infantry, fifteen thousand men, would form along Seminary Ridge, the entire front measuring about a mile in length. In front of the infantry, General Alexander, Longstreet's artillery chief, would mass his guns, 176 of them. The artillery would lay down a heavy barrage, knock out the enemy's artillery, and demoralize his infantry. The fifteen thousand men would then advance up the slope of Cemetery Ridge, concentrate their force on the clump of trees, and break through the Federal center.

If the plan of the day before had been to crumple the Federal line with pressure at both ends, today's plan was to snap it in two at the middle. Lee looked at each of his officers. But it was Longstreet's approval he sought. An awkward silence reigned.

Rising, pacing, head down, looking at no one, Longstreet finally spoke. "General, I have been a soldier all my life. I have been with soldiers in couples, by squads, companies, regiments, divisions, and armies. I know as well as anyone what soldiers can do. It is my opinion that no fifteen thousand men ever arrayed for battle can take that position."

The other officers stole uneasy glances at Lee. Longstreet had veered close to mutiny. Yet that Olympian serenity had returned to Lee's face. He appeared to have heard nothing.

"That will be all for now, gentlemen," he said quietly. "General Longstreet"—he smiled—"will you take a ride with me? I want to give you the plan of attack in detail." Longstreet felt sick with hopelessness.

The objects of Lee's design, the men on Cemetery Ridge, waited, under an oppressive stillness, behind the stone wall, performing the perennial pastimes of soldiering. They wrote letters, mended their clothes, read newspapers, played cards, traded accounts of drunkenness and sexual conquest. Mostly they complained of the lack of food.

"Do you think they'll ever get the rations up here?" a private whined.

"Ain't you learned nothing about this army yet?" another man smirked. "First the negro, then the mule, and then the white man."

"Don't worry, boys," a New Hampshireman piped up. "The day's not too distant when the white man will be as good as a nigger."

The hungry private spat on the ground and grumbled, "I'd as soon fight 'em as fight for 'em."

A soldier sitting alone with his back to the wall thumbed through the Bible given to him by the American Tract Society. On the flyleaf

was a picture of an American flag, and onto the folds of the banner
had been printed, "If I should fall, send this to ————." He reached
into his pocket for a pencil and wrote his mother's name in a neat
hand in the blank space.

Some men dozed off in the languorous heat. Others gazed out
toward the enemy. The landscape between them and the Rebels a
mile off to the west was gentle and undulating, much of it covered
with clover and almost completely open. It was a lovely vista.

As they rode along the front, General Longstreet threw one last
obstacle before General Lee's plan. "You know, I can't commit two of
my divisions to this assault. I've already got Hood and McLaws cheek
by jowl with the Federals. There's no pulling them out without my
right collapsing."

Lee was unruffled. "You will have some of Hill's people to compensate. I'll detach men from Heth's and Pender's divisions to your
command for the assault." Longstreet swallowed hard, but said nothing.

As finally determined, the charge against the center of the Federal
line would be mounted by one division of Longstreet's corps under
Pickett, one full division from Hill's corps, and two brigades from
another of Hill's divisions. Lee, perhaps thinking in terms of the
arrival strength of these units, expected that he would strike the
Federals with fifteen thousand men. But effective men, those who
would actually carry muskets up Cemetery Ridge, discounting wounded
and stragglers, likely numbered closer to 10,500.

On this morning, the men of the 8th Ohio were far closer to Robert
E. Lee than they were to their own commander, George Gordon Meade.
The afternoon before, while other men had bled and died in a peach
orchard and a wheat field, the 8th Ohioans had lolled in the shaded
serenity of Ziegler's Grove, hearing the muffled reports of the guns
with scant interest. Their turn would come, they knew, all too soon.

From a corn field not a mile away, Rebel sharpshooters were
picking off exposed Yankee artillerymen with murderous accuracy.
The corn field had to be cleared. By four p.m. the Ohioans had
formed in evened ranks, colors fluttering overhead, and with the
cheers of those staying behind to spur them on, had marched to the
Emmitsburg Road toward the redoubt of the Confederate sharpshooters.

Most of the regiment remained in the protective declivity of the roadside ditch. One company was sent forward in skirmisher formation into the corn field. Barely ahead of them, the Union artillery dropped shells among the Rebels with pinpoint accuracy. The Rebel soldiers fled the corn field and disappeared behind fences and farmhouses. The company up forward was posted seventy-five yards ahead of the road. They had the protection only of the piled-up rails of a dismantled fence. Each company would man this fragile point of intrusion into the enemy's territory for a few perilous hours, then be relieved by another company from the ditch.

Lieutenant Tom Galwey commanded one of these companies of 8th Ohio infantrymen. Young Galwey had left the family farm outside Cleveland, lied about his age, and had originally enlisted as a private for three months. That had been two years ago. Now, perhaps an inch taller than his five-foot-four-inch enlistment height, with sparse silken hairs springing from his chin and cheek, Galwey was, at turns, a boy with an easy manner and laughing dark eyes, then, instantly, all officer as he barked orders which were obeyed unhesitatingly by men years his senior.

Now, on the morning of July 3, on his company's third tour at the dismantled fence, Lieutenant Galwey found that the dead had accumulated and were now crowding the living behind the meager protection of the fence rails.

Thirty yards ahead of them stood a lone tree. It concealed a Rebel sharpshooter who regularly banged away at the main Union line. Then he was unexpectedly silent. A softly accented voice called out from the tree. "Don't fire, Yanks!" Heads rose cautiously above the rails. The Rebel sharpshooter, his musket now slung over his shoulder, swung from a low-hanging branch and dropped to the ground. Twenty Union rifles trained on him. The man held a canteen in one hand and raised his other hand in a gesture of truce. "Don't anybody shoot," Galwey ordered. The sharpshooter walked half the distance toward them. He knelt beside a wounded Union soldier lying in no man's land and tipped his canteen to the Yankee's mouth. The Union skirmishers stood up for a better look. A private hollered out, "Bully for you, Johnny." Now the Rebel skirmishers were standing, too. All shooting stopped. The sharpshooter finished his errand and went back to the tree. He turned toward the Union line and shouted, "All right, Yanks, y'all get back down, now. We're going to start firing again."

They obeyed instantly.

A cannon was ordinarily fired by a crew of nine under the direction of a "gunner," usually a corporal. One man would carry a powder charge and a projectile from a caisson to another man posted near the muzzle of the gun who would first place the powder charge into the muzzle. Another man would ram the charge down the length of the barrel with a ramrod about six feet long. Next, the projectile would be placed in the muzzle of the gun, either solid shot, exploding shell, canister, or grape. The projectile was then rammed down the barrel. During these loading steps, a man was assigned to keep his thumb tightly over a small hole in the rear of the gun barrel called the "vent." Preceding discharges of the gun often left a burning residue of powder in the barrel. If the vent were not sealed, the ramming actions might create a sufficient draft from their embers to ignite the powder charge prematurely, which could cause serious injury to the man working the ramrod. The man plugging the vent wore a piece of leather over his thumb, called a "thumbstall," to protect his hand from the heat in the vent.

With the gun loaded, the man removed his thumb from the vent and jammed a spike down the vent to puncture the powder bag and thus expose some of the gunpowder. Another man dropped a small metal device into the vent called a "friction primer." A long cord, the lanyard, was attached to the friction primer. The man who set the primer and lanyard in place dropped back at an angle about twelve feet away from the gun. The gunner sighted the gun from behind the barrel and then gave the commands, "Ready—Fire!" On the command, "Fire," the man yanked the lanyard, which caused the friction primer to make a spark in the vent. The spark caused the gunpowder to explode, which drove the projectile out of the barrel.

After the discharge, the crew rolled the gun back into position, since it would likely have been driven backward by the force of the recoil. The opposite end of the ramrod held a sponge. The man working the ramrod then drove the dampened sponge end of the rod down the barrel to extinguish sparks before reloading.

Rebel skirmishers hugged the ground east of the peach orchard. They were posted well in front of the main body of troops filling the woods behind them, and well within range of Federal skirmishers. Private

Garth Johnson, 18th Mississippi, was startled by the well-booted feet strolling casually among his prostrate comrades. He looked up and recognized the white-bearded figure and his own corps commander. Bullets sang through the air as Private Johnson warned, "General Lee, you're running a terrible risk."

Lee appeared not to hear. He turned to Longstreet and pointed to a slight rise in the ground in front of them. "You'll mass your artillery behind that hill. At the signal, bring the guns to the top of it and turn them loose."

"Hear that?" Garth whispered to his neighbor. "Damn if I didn't," the man answered. The skirmishers immediately began scooping the ground with bayonets, with sticks, with anything that would move dirt. The Yankee artillery would surely begin to return the bombardment they had just heard Lee announce. Just as surely, the shot would land where they lay, unprotected and exposed.

The grandest results are obtained by the reserve artillery in great and decisive battles. Held back out of sight the greater part of the day, it is brought forward in mass upon the decisive point, when the time for the final effort has come. Formed in a crescent a mile or more in extent, it concentrates its destructive fire upon a comparatively small point. Unless an equal number of guns is there to meet it, half an hour's rapid firing settles the matter; the enemy begins to wither under the hailstorm of howling shot; the intact reserves of infantry advance, a last sharp struggle and the victory is won.

Appleton's New American Cyclopedia, 1858

Like a spiny reptile, the Confederate artillery stretched along Seminary Ridge; it then cut across the Emmitsburg Road and terminated near the peach orchard. In all, Longstreet had deployed 176 heavy guns, mostly brass, smooth-bore 12-pound Napoleons, named for the French Emperor Louis Napoleon. The gun crews worked furiously building up piles of solid shot, spherical case, hollow projectiles, and canister around the guns.

The Federals confronted this Confederate power with fewer cannon. From Cemetery Hill to Little Round Top, 103 guns pointed toward Seminary Ridge. Of the 176 Rebel guns, 102 of them were trained on a virtual pinpoint, the clump of trees on Cemetery Ridge. This object of Rebel attention was defended by only 31 Union guns.

*　　*　　*

A stench clung to the slopes of Cemetery Ridge. It rose from the bodies of Rebels who had almost reached the stone wall the day before. It seeped from the rotting carcasses of dead horses, from great mounds of garbage, and from fetid latrines which tens of thousands of men had used for two days. All during the morning the sun had passed in and out of the clouds. Now, at high noon, it had come out blazing, unobstructed. A miasma of gunsmoke and vapor still hung over the field from the earlier fighting. The whole Federal line lay under a pungent, soiled fleece. No faint breath of wind disturbed this oppressive cover.

At the north end of the line, on Cemetery Hill, artilleryman Cub Buell lay in a half daze, his head propped against the wheel of a cannon. Honey bees buzzed over his head. In a hazy reverie, Buell felt himself floating between the present and a long-ago summer when his father had laid out beehives in the garden back home. Cub used to lie under a pear tree and try to read a book as the heat of the day and the hum of the bees would lull him into a light, dreamy slumber, just as now.

Stretching south from where Cub Buell dozed ran Cemetery Ridge. Along most of the ridge a low stone wall seamed the ground like an ancient scar tissue. The stone wall started at the stand of trees called Ziegler's Grove. It led south several hundred feet, then made a right angle and ran west in the direction of the Rebel lines for 230 feet before it bent southward again and finally petered out in a few scattered stones. The wall had been slowly gathered by three generations of Gettysburg farmers to divide one field from another. It was still too low to restrain a cow, so a wooden rail fence had been raised above it. The Union men had quickly dismantled this wood planking and laid it on top of the wall to provide a few more inches of protection.

At the southernmost end of the line where the wall dwindled to nothing, the men scratched the stony earth with bayonets, boards, and sticks. They piled up earth a foot high, stacked up rocks and fence rails, and filled knapsacks with dirt to thicken their meager barricade.

In one unprotected section the men did nothing. They had heard their commander tell another officer, "There's no Reb fool enough to charge up here."

*　　*　　*

The face was deceiving. Lieutenant Alonzo Cushing had the features of a girl, a brown-skinned Indian maid, perhaps. His hair was dark and straight, his eyes an unexpected blue. The delicacy of his features was offset by the rest of his physique. Cushing was not tall or large, perhaps five feet nine inches and no more than 150 pounds. But his shoulders were powerful, and there was an unapologetic assurance in his movements and bearing.

Cushing, a twenty-two-year-old West Pointer, commanded Battery A, 4th U.S. Artillery, a unit of six guns. If anyone in his battery had misgivings over the unwarlike face of the commander, it had passed long ago. Cushing was fierce in battle and had unveiled an unbreakable will at Antietam and Chancellorsville. His men would follow Cushing into hell, and he was disposed to grant them every opportunity to do so.

Cushing's six guns were positioned between the clump of trees and the angle in the stone wall.

Dr. Joseph Holt, Assistant Surgeon, 2nd Mississippi Infantry, cupped his hand over his eyes and peered east into the Union lines. He knew what he wanted in an aid station, knew from dearly purchased experience. He must find a place balancing closeness and cover: too close to the front, then not enough safe cover; too far behind the lines, then time would be lost, time that could mean the difference between a treated wound or a mortal wound. Holt turned around and walked up the gentle rise of Seminary Ridge to a place he had scouted earlier. Behind the Emmitsburg Road, and running roughly parallel to it, was a slightly elevated dirt road. It would do. The two-and-one-half-foot height of the roadbed would provide just enough cover to shield the wounded. He gave final instructions to his litter bearers and orderlies and wandered back down Seminary Ridge to chat with the artillerymen.

A sergeant major came forward. "Anybody here got a watch keeps decent time?"

"I do," Dr. Holt answered, pulling out a pocket watch. "It's two minutes past one. Why?"

The sergeant major waved his arm toward the artillery spiking Seminary Ridge. "My captain says at half past one a signal gun on the right is going to cut loose every single damn gun on our side."

The artillery fired principally four different missiles, each with its assets and liabilities. For long distance and accuracy, solid shot served best, a cone-shaped or spherical hunk of solid iron which could crack a cannon barrel, demolish breastworks, smash wagon wheels, or wreak havoc among bunched troops. Against a strung-out line of men, however, solid shot was no better than a single musket ball, and a miss as good as a mile.

Providing wider destructive power but less accuracy were hollow projectiles. The hollow inside was filled with explosive powder to be detonated by a time fuse. The exploding powder shattered the hollow casing and spewed the deadly fragments over a wide area. Performance of the time fuse was critical, since these projectiles frequently exploded at the wrong time or not at all.

Even more deadly, but less accurate still, was spherical case, or shrapnel, a shell crammed with seventy-eight musket balls exploded by a fuse.

Finally, canister, the fourth major artillery missile, was nothing more than a tin can jammed with dozens of iron balls packed in sawdust. Canister contained no powder charge. The tin can was torn asunder on ejection from the barrel, and the iron balls sprayed over a wide arc. Canister was used against a charging enemy at close range, usually under five hundred yards. A cannon loaded with canister was essentially a giant shotgun.

Grapeshot was composed of three layers of three large iron balls. The three layers were separated by wooden or metal discs, with discs also at each end. The whole device was held together by a metal post running through the center of the discs. On expulsion from the gun, the missile flew apart, sending, in effect, nine small cannon balls in different directions.

Napier Bartlett of the Washington Artillery felt a spring-tight tension squeeze his brow. The elite New Orleans cannoneers had a task of honor this day. On receipt of the order, Number One gun was to fire, followed immediately by Number Two. The second shot would signal every one of the Confederate guns to open fire. The barrage was to pulverize the Union line and clear the path for the infantry to destroy the enemy. Nap Bartlett glanced at the men assigned to jerk the lanyards on One and Two. The man on Two constantly and anxiously rubbed his pant leg with his sweating palm.

Across the way, on Cemetery Ridge, their foe, the artillerymen of Cushing's battery, grabbed greedily at the rations of hardtack that had been wheeled up to them. The gunners of Brown's battery, positioned next to Cushing, griped loudly at the commissary soldiers. "Where's ours, you old women? You get some of that sheet rock over here or we'll turn these God damn guns around right on your rear-echelon asses."

"Where'd you learn your table manners, boys, in a pig sty?" a commissary man said, dumping an opened case of hardtack onto the ground.

Assistant Surgeon Joseph Holt glanced impatiently from his watch to the spine of Confederate cannon curving along Seminary Ridge. As the minute hand reached half past one, the doctor snapped his watch case shut and ran toward the gun batteries. "Time's up! Time's up!" he shouted. The gunners, tense, locked in ready positions, ignored him.

Farther down the ridge, a courier delivered a message from General Longstreet to Colonel Walton of the Washington Artillery. Walton read: "Let the batteries open. Order great care and precision in firing . . ."

Walton signaled Captain Buck Miller, who gave the order. "Fire One!" The gunner jerked the lanyard on Number One. Flame and white smoke burst from the barrel. "Fire Two," Miller ordered. The gunner with the sweating palms yanked the lanyard. Nothing. "Jee-ee-sus!" the man cried. "Fire Three," an annoyed Miller bellowed. Three fired clean. Its discharge unleashed the most deafening thunder ever heard on the North American continent. To Cub Buell watching from Cemetery Hill, the successive firing of the 176 Rebel guns reminded him of the powder snakes he used to set off as a boy on the Fourth of July.

On Cemetery Ridge, the cry of "Down! Down!" echoed along the line as the heat-dazed Yankees leaped to life, dove for cover, and hugged the earth. Soon the ridge seemed as deserted as a city street in a rainstorm. The driver who had just arrived with rations for Brown's battery spun his wagon about and dashed for the rear. Men dozing under blankets suspended from their rifle butts were jolted awake by a shower of splinters as solid shot smashed the butts to pieces.

A shell exploded in the cemetery on Cemetery Hill and flung twenty-seven bodies in all directions, left men hanging grotesquely on burial monuments and pitched them into open graves. A solid shot burrowed into the ground directly in front of a Union soldier. He sank safely into the excavation. A near-identical hit burrowed under another man, the force flinging his body into the air and spinning it about helplessly. He fell dead to the ground without a mark on him. An exploding shell drove forty-eight splinters into a twenty-year-old Maine man, stripping away his uniform and tearing off an arm.

A shot exploded over one of Major Cushing's ammunition chests and set off a chain explosion that shook the earth. Boxes, wagons, horses, and men were blown to bits. Solid shot shattered the stout oak spokes of the cannon mounts like matches, bent the iron wheel rims, and sank the gun barrels to earth.

On Little Round Top, General Hunt, the Union artillery chief, observed the Rebels' barrage with detached admiration. It was an undeniably grand spectacle. The chief of the Union artillery was all too aware that the Confederate cannonade would precede an infantry attack. Therefore, he would not exhaust his ammunition in a futile artillery duel; he wanted to amass as much firepower as he could when the inevitable gray tide came rolling in. Hunt ordered most of his battery commanders to hold their fire. Only thirty-five of over one hundred Federal guns returned the fire of 176 Confederate guns.

In the midst of this hellish din, General Hancock, on a glistening black horse, erect and oblivious to peril, rode along the shell-torn ridge. His staff followed him, and his battle flags flew above them. His cuffs and shirt gleamed as always. Hancock's horse became terrified and threatened to throw its rider. As thousands of men watched, Hancock dismounted imperturbably and swung himself onto another officer's horse. He was doing merely what officers in this age were expected to do, give heart to their men by courageous example.

But, underneath the unrippled calm, Hancock was anxious. He understood tactically the wisdom of Hunt's decision to withhold his artillery. But, as he rode along the ridge, he saw the frightened Union troops crouched behind the stone wall taking punishment, unresisting. Hancock began to fear that the unchallenged Rebel bombardment would demoralize his troops. The lashing back of the Federal guns would stiffen their spirits. Hunt's orders would have to be superseded. Hancock ordered all batteries in the center of the line to open fire. The seemingly unsurpassable din of the Confederate batteries was now almost doubled.

Now Gettysburg was a vast, shoreless sea of sound. No one detonation could be singled out. Each firing of the guns, every exploding shell paralleled and overlapped a hundred others, producing one pulsating roar. A hellish shriek overlay this constant, rumbling thunder as each conical, spherical, and hexagonal chunk of propelled iron cut and churned through the air, the jagged flanges and surfaces, each singing its own song, a hiss or howl, whine or whistle, all grating together in a harsh, dissonant symphony.

In front of Seminary Ridge, bare-chested Rebel gunners, soaking in their sweat, mechanically swabbed, loaded, rammed, fired, and swabbed again in a heat raised to an overpowering intensity by the sun's rays and the friction of the guns. Each gun crew was lost in a sulphurous fog of its own making, hiding from the men the results of their work.

Behind the stone wall, the Union infantrymen lay in two ranks, body to body, nearly head to toe. The searing sun beat down on their backs. Sweat dripped off their necks and chins and settled into small muddy puddles beneath their heads. The temperature was eighty-seven degrees. Men in the rear rank pulled their legs under them in a fetal curl.

As the bombardment continued, the men's eyes and ears soon became trained to the degrees of danger. Rounds from the slower smooth-bore cannon seemed to hover overhead and had the unnerving appearance of always coming right at the men. Missiles from the rifled cannon were too swift to be seen, but rent the air with a demoniac howl. If a shell exploded directly overhead, or past the men, no harm was to be feared. But if the shell exploded in front, shrapnel rained down on them.

In Ziegler's Grove, shells exploded in the treetops and sent a murderous sheet of splinters into the troops gathered below. Men began streaming to the rear, some with superficial wounds, some with limbs rudely torn off or dangling. Some were carried by comrades. Others dragged themselves along the ground.

Cemetery Hill was dotted with dead men and mangled horses. One corpse had been flung on its back before a tombstone with the hands falling across the chest.

Yet, for all the destructiveness of the Confederate barrage, the infantrymen lying behind the stone wall were taking relatively light casualties. The Rebel artillerymen had logically assumed that most of the Union forces would be taking shelter on the reverse side of the slope. They cut their fuses for this range. But most of the Union infantry were crouched behind the stone wall on the forward slope of the ridge, toward the enemy. Thus, the Rebel cannonade largely overshot its target. The bombardment rained its greatest fury on those least expecting danger, the rear-echelon troops.

Lieutenant Jack Adams began to believe that some vindictive force was set on his death. He had survived twenty-four hours without medical treatment of wounds that had been judged fatal at the outset. The friends who had visited him, Shackley and Younger, assumed that he had died.

During the night, the surgeons had decided that the hospital had to be moved to a safer place. Jack Adams had been laid on a board and hauled roughly toward the new site, a trip which broke open his barely congealed wounds. He had been left, again without care, on the side of the Taneytown Road.

In his loneliness and growing terror, the face of his dead brother haunted him. Was some rough justice at work? In his fevered imagination, Adams condemned himself for having abandoned his brother at Antietam. Cal had been missing for two days. Jack had questioned every man in Cal's company, hounded every field station, had retraced the swaying lines of battle until, finally, he had found Cal and knew instantly there was no hope. The bullet had pierced Cal's neck and had severed his spinal cord. He could not move. He could barely speak. Jack had wanted to stay with Cal to the end. His brother had lingered on, speaking in heaving gasps of the joyous reunion they would have when they got back home.

But Jack Adams had been a newly commissioned company commander. Whatever he wanted for himself, there was a higher claim on him now. As the hours passed, he was sure that Cal no longer recognized him. The wounded man's arms lay limp at his side, his mouth hung open, his eyes saw nothing. Adams had asked an old woman to promise to stay with Cal, and in the end Jack had, indeed, left his dying brother. Now, he too was abandoned and dying.

Where he lay behind the Union line, Confederate shells fell in an iron rain. Cooks, musicians, and stragglers suddenly found themselves in the hottest part of the field. If he was not killed by the shells ploughing the earth around him, Adams was sure he would be crushed by the wagons rushing madly past him. One wagon, clanging with mess equipment and propelled by a wildly shouting black, veered within inches of Adams' body. A runaway horse reared and plunged so close that clods of dirt pelted his head. Adams screamed to two stragglers hiding behind a gate to pull him to safety. They cowered with each shell blast and ignored his pleas. An officer on horseback saw Adams' plight and flashed his sword at the terrified shirkers and ordered them to drag Adams to a nearby ambulance. The two stragglers, cursing and trembling, ran out, grabbed the pain-racked Adams by his arms and legs, and flung him into the ambulance. The driver sped away from the deadly hail. As the ambulance whipped along the Taneytown Road, a shell burst blew a leg off one of the horses. The animal kept on running.

The humble house that General Meade had selected for his headquarters, Mrs. Leister's place on the Taneytown Road, was now the virtual point on which one hundred Rebel guns converged. A shell blew away the steps of the house, another swept away the porch supports. Solid shot and exploding shells tore through the roof and sent a cascade of splinters into the rooms below. General Meade and his staff were driven outside, where they found the ground littered with butchered horses. Frantic rear-echelon troops fled in every direction. "We will have to move the headquarters," Meade shouted to his aides through the din. They scouted a house on Power's Hill, about a mile behind the Leister house, where Meade would spend most of the battle.

Along the stone wall, the men still hugged the ground, yet their fears eased as the Rebels' awful miscalculation became evident. Lieutenant Frank Haskell strolled casually along the wall. "What do you think of this, men?"

"Kinder nice once you get used to it."

"Like it fine, Lieutenant."

"Glad I didn't hit for the rear this time," an old soldier cackled.

The monotonous, hypnotic, unceasing rumble of artillery actually lulled soldiers to sleep along the stone wall. Even the cries of the wounded could not keep them awake. They became indifferent to danger. A young lieutenant playfully put out his foot to stop a cannonball bounding lazily along the slope. It tore off his foot and he soon bled to death.

Union cannon avenged the Rebels shell for shell. Death rained down on Confederate troops hugging the ground in open fields and on the edge of the woods along Seminary Ridge. Shells plowed through the ranks, hurling bodies in all directions. The rounds fell so thickly that the cries of the wounded had to be ignored for now by the ambulance corps. An exploding shell struck a hospital and set it afire. The agonizing screams of men burning to death inside made hardened veterans cringe.

General Lee rode down from the point-of-the-woods and passed in front of Pickett's division, oblivious of the bombardment. The men cheered him hoarsely, and he waved his hat in courtly response.

General Lew Armistead paraded unconcerned before his troops. An infantry sergeant stood up and bellowed with authority, "You get down, General, y'hear!"

"You get down, Sergeant," Armistead laughed. "Don't you worry about me. It's the men with guns in their hands that will count today."

Ten yards ahead of his men, General Harrow strolled coolly with hands folded behind him, ignoring the geysers of dirt erupting around him.

"Look there," a lieutenant shouted to the officer next to him, "that's how you inspire men."

"Yep," the other man drawled; "if he don't get killed, in which case it might discourage them."

The solid shot smashed into Number Three gun with a ringing clangor. The right wheel flew off in a halo of sparks and splinters as the gun barrel sagged to the ground. The crew fled panic-stricken toward the rear. Lieutenant Cushing drew his revolver. "Get back to your posts!" Cushing's pretty-girl's face hardened cruelly. "The next man who leaves his gun, I'll blow his brains out." Sheathing his revolver, he grabbed a trembling soldier and flung him toward a parked caisson. "There's a spare wheel on the caisson. Now get it on the gun and be quick about it."

A Rebel shell landed in the middle of Brown's neighboring battery, struck the muzzle, and exploded. A fragment tore off the head of a gunner as he stood poised with his rammer. The same burst took off another man's arm at the shoulder. The man lay on the ground, writhing, an absurd grin on his face, moaning, "Glory to God but I'm happy. Tell my wife I die happy." Another shot struck the gun, quieting the grinning man and putting the rest of the crew out of commission.

Captain Rorty's battery had too few men left to serve the guns. Rorty rushed to the nearest infantry regiment, the 19th Massachusetts, and pleaded for volunteers. The regimental commander, Captain Mahoney, said, "You, Dougherty, McGivern, and you, Corrigan, step out and volunteer to work Rorty's guns. Any more of you want to go?" One man shouted, "We might as well get killed there as here," and led fifteen more men to the silenced guns. With a few minutes of instruction, Rorty's remaining cannon, however inexpertly, were firing again.

Many of the guns remained silent, their crews and dead horses sprawled about them. Cushing's six guns were down to three and Rorty's down to two when General Hunt, the artillery chief, rode up.

The University Greys, the college-boy company from the University of Mississippi, lay at the edge of the woods absorbing the Union punishment. They had spent the previous day in reserve, beside a stream, washing shirts and socks, mending the patches on their uniforms. The tailored frock coats and matching pants with the bold red trim were now worn, frayed, faded beyond recognition. During the middle of the night, the Greys had been rousted out and placed in the center of the line just below the crest of Seminary Ridge.

Their original company commander, the gallant Billy Lowry, no longer led the Greys. At twenty-one, Lowry was now a lieutenant colonel, lifted well above command of a single company. He had paid a price. His extraordinary good looks had been hideously marred by facial wounds suffered at Seven Pines. Today, the Greys were under the less certain command of Lieutenant John V. Moore.

As the Federal shelling continued, the earth around the Greys became the playground of an unseen, fitful giant who scooped up deep handfuls of earth and hurled them skyward. The Greys tried to merge their bodies with the ground, all but Jere Gage, who sat calmly gazing out over the Union lines. He had limped onto this field, still suffering from a hip wound received over a year ago. It eased the pain for Gage to sit. His messmate shouted through the shell bursts, "Jere, get your damn ass down. Are you crazy?" Jere smiled but did not move.

Only the officers were still standing, pacing before their men, preaching calmness in the face of the killing Union barrage. A 24-pound shell exploded before them. The earth shuddered. Pulverized dirt and the jagged chunks of iron streamed over the University Greys. Jere Gage toppled over.

"Where in the hell is my flag?" Colonel Coulter of the 16th Maine bellowed, and spurred his horse along Cemetery Hill. "Where do you suppose that cowardly son of a bitch color bearer's gone to? Find that pisspot, Major, and drag him right up to the front.

"Jesus! There's the coward," Coulter roared, and jumped from his horse. Huddled behind a tree, the regimental flag wadded under his body, the color bearer cowered from the artillery storm. Coulter snatched the banner, shook the folds from it. He jerked the man upright by the nape of his neck and thrust the flagstaff into the man's trembling hands. As Coulter double-timed the panic-stricken soldier toward the front, a shell exploded directly in front of them, killing a horse and gouging a crater into the ground. Coulter seized the flag from the man, who was now trembling uncontrollably. The officer jammed the flagstaff into the ground in the center of the crater.

"Now, you sniveling son of a bitch, you stand right there and hold it. If I can't get you killed in ten minutes, by God, I'll post you right among the batteries."

As he remounted his horse, Coulter winked to his adjutant. "The poor devil couldn't be safer. Two shells don't often hit in the same place. If he obeys, he'll be all right. And at least I'll know where the hell my headquarters is."

Surgeon Holt raced back to his aid station behind the road embankment. His practiced eye swept over the position: surgical tools in place, medicines ready, stretcher bearers poised. He squatted down and awaited the inevitable business.

The wait was brief. Soon after the Federal guns had begun to retaliate, a pair of stretcher bearers, backs hunched against the Union barrage, came stumbling over the embankment with their first burden, Jere Gage. He was pale and in shock. The doctor ripped away Gage's blood-drenched sleeve and exposed a shrapnel wound that had practically torn the arm off. Jere Gage raised his eyes, questioning the doctor. "It's no scratch, son," Holt said, "but you're going to be all right."

Gage smiled weakly. "Oh, no, doctor. That's nothing. Here is where I'm really hurt." He turned back the blanket covering him. The shell fragment had plowed across his abdomen, exposing his intestines and gouging out his pelvis with such searing ferocity that the wound had not even hemorrhaged.

Jere looked expectantly. Holt said nothing.

"Doctor, how long have I got to live?" Jere said evenly, without emotion.

The doctor stared down at the young man. The body was hard, muscular. A ruddy sunburn persisted through the wounded man's pallor. A shock of yellow hair fell across his forehead like a golden mane. He peered out from pale blue eyes. Even dying, Gage was a man of striking presence.

"You have a few hours."

"Doctor," he moaned, "I'm in agony. Let me die easy."

The doctor nodded. "You shall die easy. Rowell," he snapped to his knapsack bearer. "The anesthetic."

The man handed Holt a dosage of laudanum.

"No, that's not strong enough. Give me the black drop." It was concentrated opium. The doctor poured a spoonful of the drug into a cup with water. He pressed it into Gage's hand, then suddenly drew the cup back.

"Soldier, do you have any message to leave?"

Gage looked startled. "Oh my God. My mother! My darling mother. How could I have forgotten? Quick doctor, I want to write. Please help me sit up."

Holt sat beside Gage. He put his arm around the wounded man's shoulder and propped him against the embankment. An orderly smoothed a sheet of paper on the flat back of the knapsack and put the knapsack on Gage's lap. He put a pencil between the wounded man's fingers. Dr. Holt cupped his hand under Jere Gage's elbow to help guide his arm as he wrote.

Something compelling in this handsome, doomed man drew the
orderlies and other wounded around him. Tears streaked their faces as
Jere's hand raced with unexpected grace across the page: "On the
battlefield, July 3, 1863: My dear mother, This is the last you may
ever hear from me. I have time to tell you that I died like a man.
Bear my loss as best you can. . . ." He finished the letter and read
the last line aloud: "I dip this letter in my dying blood." He pulled
his blanket back and pressed the back of the page into the wound. He
handed the letter to the doctor and gave him instructions for mailing it.

"Come around, boys." Jere waved weakly. "Let's have a toast. You
can't drink to me. But I am going to drink to you—to the Confederacy—and to victory." He emptied the cup and soon slipped into
merciful sleep.

The Confederate charge would begin when the artillery had done its
job, when the enemy artillery had been driven off Cemetery Ridge
and the Union infantry broken. Longstreet sent a message to his
artillery chief, Colonel E. P. Alexander: "If the artillery fire does not
have the effect to drive off the enemy or greatly demoralize him, so as
to make our effort pretty certain, I would prefer that you should not
advise General Pickett to make the charge. I shall rely a great deal
upon your good judgment to determine the matter, and I shall expect
you to let General Pickett know when the moment offers."

Alexander shuddered. An angry helplessness swept over him. The
decision was being thrust on him! Why? Longstreet was his superior,
the commander in charge of this assault. Why should a twenty-six-
year-old colonel of artillery have to make the most fateful decision on
this field? Longstreet could see just as well as he, Alexander bitterly
thought, whether or not the artillery bombardment was effective. He
shook his head in despair and passed the message to General Wright
standing nearby.

"What do you think?"

Wright frowned. "He's handed it to you. I suggest you hand it
back."

Alexander called an aide and began drafting a reply to his superior:
"I will only be able to judge the effect of our fire on the enemy by his
return fire, as his infantry is but little exposed to view and the smoke
will obscure the field. If, as I infer from your note, there is any
alternative to this attack, it should be carefully considered before

opening our fire, for it will take all the artillery ammunition we have left to test this one thoroughly, and if the result is unfavorable, we will have none left for another assault, and even if this is entirely successful, it can only be so at a very bloody cost." Alexander felt deep relief as he watched his courier thread his way among the Confederate troops toward Longstreet.

The 8th Ohio, posted across the Emmitsburg Road on skirmishing duty near the corn field, had readied their cartridges and percussion caps as soon as the barrage began. There was little to do now but wait. They lay on their backs along a dismantled rail fence and watched the Federal artillerymen, jackets off, sleeves rolled up, working the guns across the way on Cemetery Ridge. Looking straight up, they could see a sky laced with the fiery traces of artillery shells. The unbroken fire reached such a heavy, rumbling monotone that many of the Ohioans fell asleep.

"From General Longstreet, sir."

Colonel Alexander took the message and looked ruefully to General Wright. The two men read it together. "The intention is to advance the infantry if the artillery has the desired effect of driving the enemy off, or having other effect such as to warrant us in making the attack. When that moment arrives advise General Pickett, and, of course, advance such artillery as you can use in aiding the attack."

Alexander cursed softly. "He's handed it back."

It made no sense, Alexander thought. I am an artilleryman. I am not commanding this assault. He looked out skeptically over the open expanse between him and the Federal guns. "General Wright, is it as hard to get up there as it looks?"

"Trouble isn't getting there. I took my brigade up there yesterday. The trouble is staying there after you get there! The whole Yankee army is there in a bunch."

"I am going to have to talk to Pickett," Alexander said.

General Pickett was preening before his adoring troops. He felt a sublime exhilaration. Destiny had promised him this day a soldier's purest glory. He would lead these men up that slope and they could not fail. The brave, romantic peacock, with perfumed gold ringlets hanging to his shoulders, greeted the artilleryman with a serene smile.

"Hello, Alexander, glorious day, isn't it." Pickett sniffed the air and breezily returned Alexander's salute.

Alexander told him of his uncertainty. Perhaps his guns could not silence the Union cannon. They might not drive off the enemy infantry. His ammunition was low.

Pickett answered cheerily, "I have no reservations about the attack. I consider myself in luck to have the chance to lead it." He tossed off another easy salute and resumed his confident amble among his men.

Buoyed slightly by Pickett's unalloyed confidence, Alexander returned to his guns and penned one more careful reply to Longstreet: "When our artillery fire is at its best, I will advise General Pickett to advance." There, that should do it, he thought with relief.

General Hunt had fretted uneasily ever since Hancock had superseded his order and commanded the Union artillery to conduct a full-scale barrage. The ammunition could not be permitted to run out. Inevitably, inescapably, Lee was going to fling his army against them. Why exhaust every round before the assault even began?

Hunt pressed his case vigorously to his superiors. "Let us cease fire for a time. The Confederates will conclude that we have been driven from the hill. So much the better. When they approach, we will destroy them."

Hunt's view finally prevailed, and he sped along the ridge ordering his batteries to stop shooting. At Brown's battery he found a grim sight. The ground was damp with the blood of cannoneers. Gun barrels were splashed red, and parts of human bodies had caught in the carriage and wheel spokes. Every officer in the battery was dead or wounded. General Hunt called gruffly to a sergeant who stood dazed but erect next to his gun. "Limber up, Sergeant, and take your battery to the rear."

Pickett had already asked Colonel Alexander twice if he should launch the assault. Alexander had felt his anger toward Longstreet mount. Along Cemetery Ridge, the Union guns still blazed like a volcano. It was madness, he thought, to send a column of men across open ground into that inferno. Why should he have to make that awesome decision? Yet, Pickett kept pressing him.

Ammunition was running low. Alexander finally sent a message to Pickett: "If you are to advance at all, you must come at once, or we will not be able to support you as we ought. But, the enemy's fire has not slackened materially and there are still 18 guns firing from Cemetery Ridge." Alexander felt crushed by the dilemma. Was he sending men prematurely into the mouth of death? Yet, if he waited longer and the ammunition was exhausted, the men must then make a charge unsupported by artillery. Sheer suicide.

Suddenly Alexander's heart leaped. The Union guns were falling silent all along Cemetery Ridge. He snatched at his field glasses. Through the clouds of gunsmoke, he detected something that made his pulse race. He saw a Federal gun being withdrawn! The bombardment had succeeded! He quickly scribbled another message to Pickett: "The 18 guns have been driven off. For God's sake come quick, or we cannot support you. Ammunition nearly out."

General Pickett rode over to Longstreet, proud, erect, swaggering even on horseback. He found his superior like a lion at bay, brooding, unapproachable. Longstreet failed to return Pickett's salute. He stared unseeing at his luxuriously coiffed subordinate. When at last he spoke, his voice was agonized, broken, drained of its customary blunt authority.

"Pickett, I am being crucified at the thought of the sacrifice of life this attack will cost." Pickett felt confused; his soaring self-assurance wavered. He had never seen Longstreet so morose.

"I had to instruct Alexander to watch the effect of our fire on the enemy," Longstreet said. "When it begins to tell, he'll have to take the responsibility and give you your orders. I just can't do it." Longstreet shook his head.

Pickett searched Longstreet's face, puzzled. Hadn't he been assured of adequate support? Hadn't Longstreet always led them to triumph? Why this alarming despondency now? As they stood silently examining each other, an aide came up and handed Pickett Colonel Alexander's last note. He read it and gave it to Longstreet.

"Shall I obey, Pete?"

Longstreet opened his mouth, but no words came. He turned his gaze downward. Pickett waited. Longstreet put his hand out to Pickett and bowed his head slightly.

"Then, General," Pickett said, resuming his confident bearing, "I shall lead my division on."

He had ridden off only a few paces when he stopped and drew a letter from his breast pocket. Against the firmness of his saddle he scribbled in a corner of the envelope, "If Old Peter's nod means death, Good-bye and God bless you little one." He rode back to Longstreet and held out the letter for La Salle Corbett. "You'll take care of this, Pete, should need be."

Longstreet took the letter without looking up. Down that hard, handsome face, Pickett saw tears shining.

Pickett's return sent a shiver of anxiety through the division. It must be soon now, they knew. Their throats were tight and coated, as much from anxiety as lack of water. They had lain here under the unclouded sun for hours, unable to move, unable to fill their canteens, wanting yet fearing the inevitable order. Here, where tens of thousands of men were gathered, it was now eerily still.

Pickett conferred with his three brigade commanders, Garnett, Kemper, and Armistead. Garnett, forty-four, like Pickett had been a strong Union man and had made speeches against secession. Kemper, thirty-nine, was a politician-turned-general with ten years in the Virginia State Legislature behind him. Armistead was all soldier.

The prostrate infantrymen watched the three generals nodding gravely as Pickett gestured and spoke. In an assault across these open fields an officer on horseback would be doomed. Officers would lead on foot today, Pickett instructed them. General Garnett balked. He had been kicked by a horse and was suffering great pain in his leg. Pickett reluctantly agreed to let him ride.

He gave the generals the order to have the men fall in for the assault. The word passed from the brigade commanders to the regimental commanders. The regimental commanders passed the word to their company commanders. The company commanders explained the mission to the men.

Armistead eavesdropped proudly on one of his captains, whose scarred and leathered face belied the softness of his voice. "Some of you boys been in this sort of thing before. Some of you haven't. The general tells me the position we're marching on is no stronger than us in numbers and certainly inferior in fighting qualities."

The men of the company drank in his every encouraging word.

"We will march on the enemy position which is about three quarters of a mile from here. Our batteries appear to have driven off the enemy artillery. So it's probably only some enemy infantry we'll be facing."

As he spoke, the Confederate batteries before them directed a sporadic fire at the Yankees. The Union line still remained silent. The full-scale barrage by both sides had ended after one hour and forty-five minutes.

"Now, anybody got an idea this is an impossible task, let me say this. General Pickett says yesterday General Wright had his troops right up where we're going. So it has been done, and it will be done again today.

"There's a few principles to such an assault as this. If you keep them in mind, it isn't half so bad.

"Don't be terrified if there is artillery. The bark is always worse than the bite. It's never as deadly as it sounds. And the quicker we move forward, the less time it has to hurt us.

"Now, mark my word. Stop for nothing. Don't stop to plunder the dead or to pick up spoils. Battles have been lost by such foolishness. And the file closers have orders to shoot dead any man foolish enough to try.

"Don't stop for any man who's hit and asks for your help. We have details assigned to care for the wounded. The best thing you can do for a wounded comrade is to drive the enemy from the field.

"When we get the word to move forward, I expect every man will do his duty. Now, everybody on your feet and form by line."

John Dooley lay on the ground with his company, waiting in the brittle stillness for the impending charge to begin. His breath came in short, quick gasps. He fought back nausea. His hands felt damp and boneless. He gripped hard at the handle of his pistol, seeking the reassuring press of flesh against iron. He raised his head just enough to search out among the men the familiar form of Willie Mitchell. He could not find him. He knew, though, that he should see Willie well enough when they started to move. Young Mitchell was now a regimental color bearer.

If Mitchell should drop that flag during the assault, someone else would surely pick it up. Many men might die keeping it on high, but the flag would keep flying. This preoccupation with the colors was no romantic fancy. The flag was the soldier's rallying point, his guide, no matter the confusion of battle. If the flag went forward, the men were to go forward. If the flag stopped, the men stopped. If the flag went to the rear, the men could go to the rear with honor.

To the right and well behind John Dooley, Willie Mitchell hugged the ground. His right hand gripped the regimental banner lying alongside him. In his left hand he twirled a stem of the wild chicory that burst in majestic blue profusion amidst the greenness of the fields. Willie studied the blossoms intently. The splendor of the sunshine splashing off the richly hued petals eclipsed all thoughts of battle for him. He mentally composed the descriptive note he would add to his record of wild flowers, as soon as he had a chance to write. The chicory was the most beautiful blue he had ever seen.

John Dooley had found no such distraction. He looked out over the smoke-shrouded field and wondered, what does a brave man think about on the brink of death? Avenging the insults to our country? Honoring our families? Defending our homes? I am thinking only, please, God, let me get through this safely.

The order came down the line for the men to form into line of battle. John Dooley sprang to his feet. Some men refused to get up. A man in a neighboring company had wound himself into a tight coil. He was trembling, whimpering, "Oh my God! Oh my God! Captain, please let me stay here." How lucky the man is, Dooley thought, he can't get up. And I couldn't stay down.

The Confederate troops before Seminary Ridge extended for nearly a mile in rows as precise as human beings could form. The ragged, motley uniforms fused into a solid yellow-gray mass. A sprinkling of skirmishers stood out in front of the main body. In the ranks, men were lined up practically elbow to elbow. Two paces behind them stood an identical row. Immediately behind this solid phalanx came the file closers, lieutenants and sergeants with an elemental task: to see that the line ahead closed up when men fell and to shoot any man who straggled. Since a file closer stood behind a double line, two men would have to be shot down before he was exposed. It was a prized position.

This same structure of skirmishers, two rows of infantrymen, and file closers was repeated again in two progressively shorter formations, each about one hundred yards behind the other. Thus, fully arrayed, Longstreet's assault consisted of three double lines of infantry, lined up one behind the other, altogether over ten thousand men.

Earlier, a sergeant named Kimble had crawled far forward for a closer look at the enemy ridge they were to storm. He came back white and shaken.

"Hey, Kim, how's it look?"

Kimble's voice quavered. "Boys, if we have to go, it won't be for us to decide. We'll just have to do our best." He tightened his trembling hand on his musket barrel.

A pleasant voice broke the ominous silence in the ranks, singing, "Backward, roll backward, O time in thy flight. Make me a child again, just for this fight." Yes, thought Kimble, and a girl child at that.

General Lew Armistead stopped pacing, locked his arms behind him, and cleared his throat to address his brigade.

"Remember, men, what you are fighting for." The words were rapped out brusquely. "Remember your homes and your firesides. Remember your mothers and sisters, your wives and your sweethearts. Now, come to attention."

Beneath the tension, the men were amused. Old Lew always made the same speech, always uncomfortably.

Scattered on the ground among the even-dressed ranks were some three hundred men who had been hit during the Union bombardment.

Armistead marched over to Sergeant Blackburn, the color guard, and pointed toward a clump of trees. "Sergeant, see the enemy's works yonder? You are going to plant those colors right up there."

"General, if mortal man can do it, I will."

Armistead turned toward the brigade. "Did you hear the sergeant, men?"

General George Pickett now strode to the head of the entire division. Most of the men were too far away to hear more than a few words of his speech, ". . . and charge the enemy. Remember Virginia." A band off at one end of the line struck up a ragged chorus of "Dixie," which sent shivers through the men. Pickett sang out the order, echoed by his officers down the line to the last rank, the last man. "Forward! March!"

As they moved forward, men spoke to friends in neighboring ranks and companies. "Good-bye, Calvin." "So long, Henry." "Bye, Willie."

Two soldiers shook hands. "Same deal like always, Lem?"

"Yep," the man answered. "When it's over, I'll look for you, and you look for me."

"I got everything in the haversack. Send it back to Mary Lee."

Their cartridge boxes and pockets bulged with sixty rounds of ammunition each. They passed through the powder-smeared, sweating artillerymen. Friendly nods were exchanged. A few gunners placed encouraging hands on the shoulders of the passing infantrymen. Some shook hands quickly. "Good luck, boys." "God bless you." The men who would stay behind looked uncomfortably into the eyes of men steeled for death and took off their hats in tribute.

"Why, just look at my line," Armistead shouted to Kemper, "it never looked better on dress parade." Armistead took off his black felt hat, impaled it on the tip of his drawn sword, and strutted out ahead of his men. "Forward at the quick step," he ordered.

Fifteen minutes had passed since the bombardment ended. The Union troops watched the lazily curling clouds of leftover smoke rise heavenward as they waited in a crackling, tense silence. At 3:15 they saw what they awaited. Blue-tipped flags poked over a gentle green rise less than a mile off, the banners of Pickett's division. Farther north, red-tipped flags appeared, the colors of Hill's division. A dull gray mass of men followed, filling the horizon and flowing toward them.

From vistas on Cemetery Ridge, the Round Tops, and Cemetery Hill, the Union men stared spellbound. Every man sensed that the symmetry and power of the spectacle before him was something he would never see again, no matter how long or how briefly he might live. They watched paralyzed in awe before the resistless tide whose sole purpose was their destruction.

On Cemetery Hill, artilleryman Cub Buell listened intently to his battery commander. "They mean business," Major Stewart said. "Notice how few of their officers are mounted. They are going to try to break our center. I think it will be their last effort."

The yellow-gray ranks edged forward at route step, a hundred yards every minute on a journey of 1760 yards.

Lieutenant Tom Galwey of the 8th Ohio stood far forward of the main Union line, rooted in wonder. What a grand sight, he thought, the grandest ever. While the men farther back on Cemetery Ridge watched the Rebels roll toward them from a distance, the Ohioans stood just yards north of the advancing enemy's path, near the outpost they had clung to so tenaciously during the night. To an untrained eye, the advancing gray lines might have a monolithic cast. But Galwey detected a flaw. The block farther south, Pickett's men, moved forward with a hard-surfaced invincibility. Closer to the 8th

Ohio marched the brigades drawn from Hill's corps. They lacked the awesome inevitability of Pickett's men. Their ranks were less perfectly drawn, less intimidating. Pickett's division had come fresh to the field, unbloodied so far at Gettysburg. The men of Hill's corps had been mauled savagely the first day, had taken forty percent casualties, enough ordinarily for a unit to be dispatched to the rear, not sent into a charge. The deeply depleted ranks had been replenished with cooks, clerks, extra-duty men, and the lightly wounded. The lines were dotted with bandaged heads and hobbling legs. Green young captains had been propelled by attrition to the command of whole regiments and brigades.

The Union soldiers watched with unabashed admiration as Pickett's men executed a perfect left oblique, a forty-five-degree turn that smartly closed the gap between the two blocks of advancing infantry. In front of Pickett's division they saw an officer, his sword held high, a strutting god of war, moving unhesitatingly toward the mouths of the Union cannon. The 8th Ohioans spontaneously waved their colors in tribute to a brave adversary.

When Colonel Alexander saw General Longstreet approaching him, the anger again welled within him for having had the fatal decision to launch the charge thrust upon him. Yet, the anguish in Longstreet's face told Alexander that the general shared his agony.

"Can you support them properly, Colonel?"

Alexander cupped his hands over his mouth and shouted over the hammering of the guns, "I don't really believe so, sir. My ammunition is running too low."

"Then we have got to stop Pickett where he is and replenish your ammunition." Longstreet's eyes blazed with fresh hope at the prospect of postponing the assault.

Alexander was startled. "We can't do that, sir. The wagon train has but little ammunition left. If would take an hour just to distribute it. In the meantime, the Yankees will only strengthen their position."

Gloom engulfed Longstreet's face. He leaned into Alexander's ear and confessed, "I didn't want to make this charge. I don't see how it can succeed. I would not make it now. But General Lee ordered it and expects it." He turned and walked, with hunched shoulders, back toward Seminary Ridge.

*   *   *

The thin shell of Yankee skirmishers, two hundred yards ahead of the main defense at the stone wall, watched uneasily as the gray phalanx moved closer to them. No stone barrier separated them from the enemy. They took what shelter they could in patches of wheat; behind the dead of the day before; in modest indentations in the earth. The skirmishers' mission was to alert the main Union force of the enemy's moves, though this day there was not a man in the Union line unaware of the Rebels' intent.

As the approaching Rebel skirmishers began firing at them, there suddenly appeared among the Union men the magnificent, mounted figure of General Winfield Scott Hancock. A Rebel major shouted, "Don't shoot him! Don't shoot, he's a gallant officer." The chivalry of the time called for sparing a conspicuously brave foe. They let Hancock ride off.

By now, the Union skirmishers had served their purpose. They unloaded a round or two at the approaching enemy and bolted for the rear, leaping over the low stone wall, gratefully melting into the stouter defenses of their comrades. Jake Cole of General Zook's regiment, wounded the day before, lay in the wheat field directly in the line of fire of a Confederate gun. "Get him out of the way," an officer barked. "We might drop a short fall on him." Two Confederate soldiers dragged Cole by his arms to the height of a small knoll. Cole clenched his teeth as his wounded leg bumped painfully along the ground. A Rebel soldier standing near him pointed proudly at Pickett's neat, square-cornered blocks of Southern manhood stretching as far north as Cole could see.

"Well, Yank, you're probably headed for the boneyard," the Southerner chuckled, "but I expect I'll be celebrating this Fourth of July in Philadelphia."

The Union guns remained silent, as General Hunt had ordered. General Webb came up to Lieutenant Cushing, commanding Battery A. "Lieutenant, the enemy attack is imminent."

"I know, sir," Cushing nodded. "I'd like to take my guns right up to the stone wall." The general gave his permission.

Cushing's men had collapsed exhausted on the ground during the artillery lull. The young lieutenant quickly had them on their feet, clearing away the debris and using the horses still living to haul away the remains of the dead horses and those in their death throes. The men put their shoulders to the gun mounts and rolled them up to the wall.

"Get the canister ready. That's what we'll be serving today," Cushing smiled.

The gun crews piled the heavy, metal-filled cans alongside each piece.

Cushing's and the other batteries in the center of the line had been heavily battered, and few of their guns were still in action. But beyond them, at each end of the line, on Cemetery Hill and on Little Round Top, the Union batteries remained virtually unscathed.

Lining the upper end of the Emmitsburg Road, directly in the path of the Confederate charge, was a stout post-and-plank fence. At the lower end of the road, a flimsier fence had already been easily swept away. But the men jammed rifle butts in vain against the sturdy upper barrier. The assaulting legions came upon this fence like waves crashing on a reef, and the carefully structured line had to be broken as the men clambered over to the other side. They moved into a slight depression in the road beyond the fence. The officers took advantage of this meager shelter to halt the men and redress their lines. Eight minutes had passed from the time they had started. They had covered roughly half the distance.

General Pickett rode with four aides about twenty yards behind his men, a good position for maintaining a perspective on the charge and for dispatching orders to his commanders. He moved back and forth behind his lines on a coal-black steed. When his last rank had cleared the Codori farmhouse, Pickett halted in the Codori orchard and chose this spot as his vantage point.

Well behind him, the commander of the Army of Northern Virginia watched the army flow out like a gray glacier toward the Federal defenses. General Lee had spread an oil cloth over an oak stump, and he sat there wordlessly with one hand holding the reins of his faithful horse, Traveler, and the other cupping his chin.

General Hunt held the poised spring of a great trap in his hand. He watched the flawless Rebel ranks come closer, closer, closer, then finally enter ideal artillery range. The signal went out. From Cemetery Hill, from batteries at the lower end of Cemetery Ridge, from Little Round Top, the Union guns spoke. Long-range ammunition first; solid shot and exploding shells flew out to greet the Confederate tide. The gunners could see the result of their work as green spaces of grass appeared in the gray ranks. Pickett's men still rolled forward, oblivious of losses, their momentum unchecked.

The Yankee shells exploded amidst Hill's ragged phalanx to greater effect. As the great puffs of smoke erupted among them, the men faltered, the forward motion slowed, even halted. Officers brandished revolvers, and file closers pricked their bayonets into the backs of the hesitant.

The stoic beast rolled on. Ears rang with the explosions and eyes burned from the smoke. Officers bellowed. Farm boys from the Piedmont, bookkeepers from Richmond, fishermen from the Tidewater, roughnecks and gentlemen moved steadily ahead, absorbing the blows, unstopping. The newer men marched with their heads bent down as if warding off a heavy rain, a blunder since this placed the most vulnerable part of their bodies in the most exposed position. A colonel was thrown, unharmed, into the air by the concussive force of a shell, but landed fatally on his sword point. Among Pickett's Virginians, an officer marched behind a regiment that included his son. He saw the boy crumple to earth, bent to kiss his lifeless face, and continued on.

A whole line cringed at the nearness of a shell blast. It struck only one man. He momentarily disappeared. Where he had been, an indiscriminate mass of limbs quivered on the ground, then went still. "Close up ranks. Dress on the center, men," an officer ordered. The men obeyed.

The cannoneers on Little Round Top cheered wildly with every round fired. This was easier than the practice range. They fired from the far left of the Union line. As the Rebels moved forward, every step put them more surely into an artilleryman's paradise. The charging soldiers were drawing almost parallel to the Union guns. A well-placed shot could tear through a dozen men. Hardly a round fired failed to score.

The greenest troops in the Union ranks were those now closest to the enemy. They were Vermonters, under the command of General George Stannard, men who had enlisted for nine months. Eight of those months had passed in training and guard duty in Washington. They had arrived on the field at Gettysburg with only a month, some with only three days, before their enlistments would expire. They had never before heard an enemy shot fired.

The untested Vermonters had been positioned one hundred yards ahead of the main body, at the far left of the Union line. They fidgeted behind scant heaps of dirt and piles of fence rails.

An officer purred reassurances: "Steady, boys, steady . . . hold your positions . . . don't fire till you get the word . . . stay calm . . . keep down . . ."

The Rebels came so close it seemed the Vermonters could reach out and touch them. Again the officer, the voice tight, straining: "Make ready . . . aim low . . . on your feet . . . Fire!"

The Southern line sagged with the force of the blow and began drifting toward the left, away from the punishing fire of the Vermonters. The Rebels had been taking artillery. Now, the first rifle fire had been leveled at them. The Vermonters had tasted their first blood.

The Union men behind the stone wall on Cemetery Ridge had emptied their cartridge boxes and lined the bullets along the top of the wall for quick loading. They waited the agonizing minutes, heard the Vermonters to their left unleash their first volleys, saw the terrifying slaughter when a cannon-burst scored. Yet, the gray tide swept on, threatening to engulf them. 350 yards. Silence reigned in the Union line. 300 yards. Jaws tightened, knees ached, legs trembled with tension. 275 yards. Fingers curled impatiently around triggers. 250 yards. Up they rose. "Fire!" the command rang out. A solid sheet of flame leaped at the enemy. Half the Rebel battle flags dropped to the ground at once. The parade-ground smartness of the Rebel ranks came undone. The stone wall and the blue coats had disappeared behind a cloud of gunsmoke. Then a thousand harsh red bursts burned through the smoke screen, a hot hailstorm interspersed by the great deafening bellow of canister. The clover field was beginning to run bright red.

Private William Monte of the 9th Virginia drew a watch from his pocket. "We have been just nineteen minutes coming. What a sublime sight," he said. Then a chunk of canister struck him dead.

* * *

Lieutenant Galwey, 8th Ohio, felt the blood pounding against his temples. He purged every charitable impulse from his being and longed only to inflict death on the enemy. Though close to the Rebels, the regiment was relatively safe. They watched from just beyond the northernmost edge of the Confederate charge. The Rebels, intent on that clump of trees, viewed the scattering of Ohioans to their left as no more than pesky insects as they moved toward their objective.

The 8th Ohio commander, Lieutenant Colonel Franklin Sawyer, bridled at this passive role. He strung out his remaining troops in a single line to make it look more numerous and sent them charging against the Rebel flank. A party of New York troops hustled down the Emmitsburg Road and joined this brazen initiative.

The end of the Rebel line began to crumble. The Ohioans moved among the demoralized enemy, grabbing off clusters of prisoners. Yet, the main body rolled mechanically toward its objective.

General Hays, the senior Yankee officer at the far north of the line, saw what was happening and smelled rare opportunity. The Southerners moving toward the clump of trees would pass well below his troops. They could stay where they were and watch the show in virtual security. Or—and this was the chance Hays seized—he could bend his line around so that it would face directly on the flank of the oncoming Rebel attackers.

The Vermonters were becoming adept at warfare by minutes and seconds. Uncertainly but unhesitatingly they followed their officers' orders, and executed a wheeling motion which swung them around so that they no longer faced the enemy frontally but sideways. They advanced, firing, until they were delivering a telling fire from only fifty yards as the Confederates paraded past them. Almost every shot found its way into a target.

With the Vermonters pouring fire into them from the south, with Hays' men firing into them from the north, with muskets and cannon blasting from the stone wall in front of them, the Rebels now took brutal punishment from three sides.

"Load canister, fire!" Lieutenant Cushing shouted from his emplacement at the stone wall. The muzzles flamed and the guns lurched. Hundreds of iron balls fanned out in an arc of death. The men in the silent Rebel ranks spun, staggered, and fell as they waded through hellfire.

Young men who scant years before were fussed over by doting mothers, who had had skinned knees tenderly kissed, who were warned, "Don't you go catching cold," were now told to walk where flying pieces of iron tore into them, maimed them, smashed their skulls, and plunged through their chests. When boys they grew up with, brothers, cousins, and neighbors, fell before the Federal guns, the only words of solace heard were, "Close up men, keep steady, keep moving, a little faster, don't fire yet."

Captain Harrison was down. Lieutenant John Dooley automatically assumed command of C Company. "Steady . . . dress to the right . . . give way to the left . . . don't jam the center . . . not too fast . . . keep in line."

A shell shook the earth, and Dooley felt someone's blood spatter against his cheek.

"Close it up!" he shouted to the men flanking the fresh hole in his line.

"Captain Norton," he called out to the officer of the next company, "can you give way a bit to the left? Your men are driving me out of place."

"Sorry, Dooley." Norton shouted a command to his men. Before they could carry it out, he was heaved into the air by a shell blast.

Dooley did not see the color bearer marching behind him sink to his knees. Willie Mitchell uttered a childlike cry of disbelief, handed the flagstaff to a passing infantryman, and fell to the ground. He opened his eyes briefly to see wild chicory blossoms flooding his vision with their blue brilliance. His hand reached out for them haltingly, and then fell lifeless, crushing the small, vivid flowers.

Up ahead, John Dooley could now make out the individual enemy riflemen behind the wall. He could see a forest of barrels sighting on his men. Only thirty yards to go. The Southerners began their frenzied battle cry, began to return fire and dogtrot up the slope.

It was a perfect training-manual shot. The round struck John Dooley through both thighs. He sank to the ground. Through the legs of the men marching past him, he glimpsed another dimension of the battle—the ground level of wounded, dead, and dying littering the field all around him. Blood gushed from his wounds. Dooley put his hand before him and stared hard at the fingernails of his left hand. If they began to turn white and purple, he would be bleeding to death. The nails were still a pale pink. I cannot bleed to death! he swore.

Lieutenant Cushing absently put his hand to his shoulder and drew away bloodstained fingers. He barely glanced at them. Sergeant Fuger had seen the shoulder strap fly off the lieutenant's jacket, saw the wound, but knew better than to say anything to his commanding officer. "Load canister!" Cushing shouted.

A shell burst directly in front of the gun. Cushing let out a long, grotesque sigh. This time, Fuger did not hesitate. He caught Cushing as the man slid along the barrel of Number Three cannon. Cushing's hand clutched at his genitals. Blood ran from between his fingers and darkened his light-blue trousers in a fast-spreading stain. Cushing looped his arm around the gun barrel and refused to fall.

"Fuger . . . Fuger"—his words came in short gasps—"you stand by here . . . relay my orders to the battery."

"Please, Lieutenant, you're hit bad." Fuger shouted into the man's ear to overcome the screams and explosions that filled the air. "You've got to go to the rear."

"I'll stay here and fight it out or die in the attempt." Cushing lifted his head and searched out the fast approaching enemy. "At one hundred yards, give 'em triple canister."

Driven in from left and right, the long, lean rows that had stretched out a mile at the beginning of the charge were now crammed into a two-hundred-yard front. What had begun as six clean lines of infantry were now being pressed into a shapeless mob. Only a few men in the front ranks could fire without hitting their own comrades. Bunched before the blazing Yankee rifles and roaring cannon, the Confederates took fierce punishment. Still, they edged forward, a great beast, bleeding and clawing its way to within twenty yards of the angle in the wall. Then they sagged back and hung there, absorbing the Union hammer blows.

"Bright! Captain Bright!" The jauntiness had drained from Pickett's voice. The young aide rode to his commander and saluted. Pickett gazed out at the torn and bloodied blanket of men that his division had laid over the green fields. "Now listen carefully. You get back to General Longstreet. You tell him I can carry the Union front, but I must have reinforcements. I cannot do it without reinforcements!"

Speeding to the rear, Bright was appalled to find knots of un-wounded men streaming in the same direction. He wheeled his horse sideways to block a group of stragglers. "What are you men running away for?"

"Why, Captain," one of the men sneered, "ain't you running away yourself?"

It is a military axiom. A column—that is, men piled deep behind each other—can break a line of men stretched out in a narrow row. It is the principle of the battering ram. The pressures from north and south on the charging Confederates had compressed their line into a thick column. General Armistead saw the opportunity shaping up and seized the moment. He pushed his sagging black hat once again to his sword point and began elbowing his way through the troops to the head of the stalled force.

"Come on, boys!" he shouted, emerging in front of the Rebel troops. "Give 'em the cold steel. Who'll follow me?" Two hundred men sprang forward, so close to the stone wall now that they could feel the heat of the cannon's blast against their cheeks.

Behind the wall, Lieutenant Alonzo Cushing, in unbearable agony, ignored the pleas of his crew to go to the rear. With one hand clutching the wound in his groin, he gasped, "I'll give 'em one more shot!" At Cushing's command, the guns sprayed canister into the rushing Confederates, point-blank. When the smoke cleared, a Rebel, still standing, dropped to one knee and took careful aim. The bullet went through Cushing's mouth and smashed into the base of his brain. He fell to the ground trying to say "Good-bye" as the blood strangled his words. Cushing was the third artillery battery commander to die behind the stone wall since the barrage had begun.

The charging Rebels, Armistead in the lead, surged toward the angle in the stone wall. Their savage cry pierced the roar of the guns and sent a shiver through the Union troops. The Union defenders in the angle broke and began fleeing to the rear. Lieutenant Frank Haskell, galloping past, was horrified to find the line giving way. He placed his horse athwart the fleeing men. Haskell drew his sword and began beating them with the flat side. "Stop! Turn around! Resume your fire!"

General Webb rushed up to help Haskell repair this potentially fatal rupture in the line. As the Rebels began to scale the wall, Webb ordered a group of reserve troops standing on the crest of Cemetery Ridge to repel them. "Charge!" The Union line stood rooted in place. "Charge, you damn fools!" he screeched at the top of his lungs. They continued to fire but would not go forward. Webb grabbed at a regimental flag. The color bearer would not give it up. Haskell maneuvered the hindquarters of his horse into the backs of the men to drive them forward. Still they would not move, but fell instead in precise rows before the fire of the charging enemy.

Armistead, his hat held high on the sword tip, was now over the stone wall through the gap into the Federal defenses. His men were among Cushing's silenced cannon. At this point, the two armies became a milling, sprawling, bloody mob. No room to load, aim, and fire. The Union defenders gripped their gun barrels and brought the stocks smashing into the faces of the intruders. An artilleryman snapped an enemy neck with one swing of his handspike. Frightened, angered, insane men drowned out the sharp crack of gunfire with their screaming.

General Garnett was shot down in front of the wall, killed attacking the Union that he still believed in. His aide reached down and took his watch. General Kemper fell wounded. Only Armistead remained of Pickett's three brigade commanders.

If the outcome of this struggle could be pinpointed to a single instant, it was now. The fate of the charge hinged on the next seconds. The fate of the battle hinged on the charge. The fate of the Confederacy hinged on the outcome of this battle.

Armistead, well into the Yankee line, reached his arm out to lay claim to one of Cushing's guns. An astonished look froze in his face, his eyes rolled upward, and he fell to the ground, shot through the body and leg, a few feet from Cushing.

The now leaderless Rebels who had pierced the Union defenses saw before them seemingly endless rows of blue uniforms, silhouetted along the crest of Cemetery Ridge. The long blue line was edged with the flashing flames of their guns. The Confederates could press forward no further; they began to drift toward the shelter of the clump of trees, anxiously peering over their shoulders. But instead of the expected surge of comrades following their lead, they saw only chaos among the main Confederate body. Backs were turning against the murderous fire. The forward motion was spent.

Only to the south, on the other side of the grove of trees, was there any fight left. Here, another break in the Union line had tempted the Confederates. The spot in the line was defended by a single battery of five cannon. A Rebel major crouched with his men behind the scant protection of some rough ground. They waited for the Union artillery crew to have to reload their guns. The major seized the chance. He dashed forward yelling, "Take the gun, take the gun!" His men loyally followed.

"Load double canister," Captain Cowan, the commander of the battery, shouted.

"Captain, it's our last round."

"I know, Jake. Load!"

The private barely had time to get the charge into the muzzle before he went down with three bullets in the head. Another private leaped between the gun barrel and the advancing Rebels and finished ramming the charge home before bullets tore through both his legs. Gunner MacKenzie threw his hands to his bloodstained face and fell over the trail of the gun.

When the chargers were ten yards off, Cowan ordered, "Fire!" The five guns of Cowan's battery lurched in unison. The battery disappeared in flame and smoke as ninety-six balls of hot iron belched from each muzzle. When the smoke cleared away, the charging Rebel line had vanished. Five yards in front of the first gun lay the mangled remnants of the Confederate major. For a brief time, it was quiet along Cemetery Ridge.

To the south and well out front of Cemetery Ridge, General Stannard swelled with pride at his Vermonters. His one-day veterans were outflanking Pickett's southernmost troops with cool professionalism. Beside him, on his horse, sat the impeccable Hancock, who said nothing, but whose satisfaction was nonetheless evident.

An odd slapping noise sounded against General Hancock's saddle. Stannard saw the handsome face wince. "Grab him," Stannard shouted to his aides. They caught Hancock as he slid wordlessly from the horse. He was bleeding profusely from a deep wound in the gut. The ball had driven a saddle nail and splinters of wood into the wound. Hancock's life was rapidly ebbing from him.

At the northern end of the Rebel line, the 11th Mississippi advanced with its shrunken company of University Greys against the Union troops just above the clump of trees. They were no longer a line, but scattered clusters of men, halting, firing, advancing amidst the screams of the wounded. Thirty-two Union cannon leveled their fire directly into the advancing Mississippians. As each blast tore into the ranks of the Greys, Captain Moore would turn around and march backward a few paces, shouting to his men to close the gaps in a nonexistent line.

The Greys advanced unwavering to within musket range of the stone wall. They could hear a distant Yankee command shouted. Four ranks of Union riflemen suddenly rose from beyond the wall and fired as one. The random blasts of the artillery were now joined by a solid blade of bullets which cut through the 11th Mississippi.

The withering fire in their front was matched in deadly effect by the fire from the other Federal troops, who had swung around and were firing into the Rebel lines from the side. As the Confederates filed past, the Union soldiers fired into them at will, a well-placed shot ripping through two, three, even four Rebels before the bullet was spent.

Lieutenant Baker, second in command of the University Greys, shouted above the roaring inferno to Captain Moore, "For God sakes, John, give the order to charge!"

"I can't take that responsibility," Moore shouted back.

"Then, by God, I will," Baker yelled. "Come on, men!" He waved his pistol overhead, and the surviving Greys raced for the stone wall. Ten feet from it Lieutenant Baker went down. Private De Gaffenreid leaped the wall, but was quickly shot.

Young Tom McKie, numb with fear, mindlessly propelled himself forward. He had survived ten more actions since his mother had written to President Davis begging his release. The man in the war office had read the request and said, "But who will fight the war if all the children go home?"

The shot caught Tom McKie full in the chest, and he slumped to the ground. As the boy lay dying, the contribution of the University Greys to the Confederate cause had become total. Three-quarters of a mile behind young McKie, Jere Gage, lying under a blanket at Dr.

Holt's field station, passed from sleep into death. The Greys, with fourteen dead and seventeen wounded, had been annihilated at Gettysburg.

Like a wave running to the shore, the Confederate attack had rolled to a high point and now hung briefly suspended, moving neither forward nor back. On the Rebels' right flank, the nine hundred Vermont troops now extended almost to the Emmitsburg Road, advancing and pouring on deadly enfilading fire. On the left, the Yankees, with increasing brashness, closed in on bewildered clots of Pettigrew's survivors, felling them with muskets and two death-spewing Napoleons. Only along the stone wall was the pressure not yet fully applied. The aggressive Lieutenant Haskell ached to drive the men on Cemetery Ridge against the stalled Rebel front. A neat row of fallen men marked the line where the Union soldiers stood on Cemetery Ridge, a line from which they kept firing, but from which they refused to advance. Behind a Massachusetts regiment, file closers joined hands, forming a human chain to prevent the troops from running away when they dropped back to reload.

"Major," Haskell shouted to an officer commanding troops just behind the ridge. "Lead your men over the crest. They'll follow!"

"According to tactics, I understand my place is in the rear of the men," the major shouted back.

"Begging your pardon," Haskell scoffed. "I thought you were fit to lead. Obviously, your place *is* in the rear of your men."

He turned hopefully to another officer. "Come on, Sapler. Come out with your men."

"Ah yes, but let me stop our fire from the rear first or we'll be hit by our own men."

"Damn you!" Haskell sputtered.

He rushed to a sergeant holding the stars and stripes on a shattered stump, the sixth man to have picked up that fallen banner this day.

Haskell put his face close to the man, who stared straight ahead, face flushed, hands trembling. "Sergeant, I want you to march forward with your color." He grabbed the man's shoulders and shook him. "Let them see it close to their eyes once more before they die." Haskell gave him a shove. The man started ahead haltingly.

"Will you let your color storm the wall alone?" Haskell shouted to the men still on the ridge. No one followed. As he neared the wall, the color bearer crumpled in a rain of musket fire.

As the flag struck the ground, some inexplicable force moved the Union troops. Without an order, they swarmed down the ridge, a deep Yankee cheer pouring from their throats. Rifles were fired so close that men's clothes were scorched by the flash. Bayonets laid open heads and bellies. Rocks flew. Disarmed men wrestled and beat their enemies' heads against the stone wall. The blue wave kept rolling down the slope, over the wall.

All along the Rebel front, handkerchiefs and bits of white cloth fluttered from eager hands. "Don't shoot, don't shoot!"

"Drop your arms and come over the wall. We won't hurt you." The clatter of falling muskets sounded all along the line as hundreds of Southerners gratefully chose Yankee captivity over death. Less than forty minutes after the Confederates had stepped smartly from Seminary Ridge, the charge had been crushed.

The extended outpost of the 8th Ohio, well ahead of the Union line, proved fortuitously placed as the Rebel charge was broken. The fleeing Confederates came streaming toward the Ohioans, liberating themselves of anything detachable—muskets, cartridge belts, haversacks, anything that might slow their retreat. The 8th Ohio dashed among them, taking unresisting prisoners in droves.

Lieutenant Colonel Arthur Fremantle had been maneuvering all day for a good view of the fight, unsuccessfully, it turned out, since he always seemed to lag a step behind the action. Early in the afternoon, he had headed for town to take up a position in the cupola near Ewell's headquarters. No sooner had he passed through the toll gate into town than the Confederate bombardment began. When the Federal guns replied, Fremantle found himself in a hot cross fire, with shells bursting uncomfortably near. He then headed out the Chambersburg Pike, still littered with battle debris and lined with the rotting Union dead of two days before. He turned and rode south through the woods toward the center of the line. If he could only find Longstreet, he knew he would have a good seat for the battle. As he rode through the trees he heard the heavy rumble of the artillery barrage finally trail off. After a long silence, punctuated by an occasional cannon, he heard the sharp staccato of musket fire, then, later, the unmistakable shrieking war cry of his Confederate hosts. As he began to emerge from the woods, a few wounded passed him from the opposite direction. The closer he moved toward the fighting, the greater the number of injured and stragglers who passed him. Soon he found himself running against an engulfing tide of retreating men. He finally found Longstreet sitting on a fence at the edge of the wood. "Good afternoon, sir," he said, and swung down from the horse and sat on the fence, peering out toward the Union front. He smiled his toothy smile. "Magnificent. I wouldn't have missed this for anything."

Longstreet measured him cynically from the corner of his eye. "The devil you wouldn't," he laughed bitterly. "I would like to have missed it very much."

The Englishman looked puzzled.

Longstreet pointed ahead. "Look there. We've attacked and been repulsed. The charge is over."

Turning to a young captain who waited impatiently on horseback, Longstreet said, "Colonel Fremantle, this is Captain Bright, Pickett's staff. George sent him back to me for reinforcements."

"Pleasure," the Englishman said, smiling and saluting casually. Bright remained grim-faced.

"Captain Bright," Longstreet said, "you go back to General Pickett and tell him what you just heard me say to Colonel Fremantle."

As the officer began to leave, Longstreet shouted after him, "And tell him Wilcox's brigade is in that peach orchard. He can order Wilcox to assist him, if he wants to."

He turned to the Englishman. "Colonel, what do you have to drink?"

Fremantle fished an elegant silver flask from his brown frock coat and handed it to Longstreet.

The general took a long draft of the rum within.

"I'd be honored, sir, if you would keep the flask in remembrance of our friendship."

"Much obliged," Longstreet said, his eyes fixed on his broken, retreating legion. He capped the flask and shoved it into his pocket.

The general may be discouraged now, Fremantle thought. But this English officer had seen the mettle of these Southerners, and when he returned to England soon, he intended to tell his friends that there could be no doubt as to the final victor in this war.

*   *   *

General Cadmus Wilcox was confused and angered. Pickett had sent three separate messengers to make sure he got the word to join in the attack. Did the man think his two brigades could make the difference? It was plain to anyone on the field that the assault had failed.

Wilcox knew he had been ordered to make a useless sacrifice. His own frustration was communicated to his men, and they marched sullenly, grudgingly toward the Federal guns. They had been ordered forward as support troops. But there was no assault to support. They were separated from the very troops they were to reinforce by a line of Vermonters who were still laying their deadly fire into Pickett's flank.

Wilcox's men had now come within artillery range of the Federal batteries. The pointless waste began as the canister tore through them. It was swiftly elevated by an unexpected maneuver of the Vermonters. In a smart about-face, they turned away from Pickett's battered force toward Wilcox's regiments. Wilcox watched with sickening despair as men threw their muskets into the air and fell to the ground. His men would die no longer for nothing. He ordered them back. The last Rebel troops who would ever march at Gettysburg were now in retreat. Wilcox's brief advance had cost 214 men in their futile moment on the field.

Private Kimble felt that no human had ever run faster as he raced back from the hell of Cemetery Ridge. He was in the fortunate minority, those who had survived the charge. Seven thousand of those who began it were now dead, wounded, or missing. Kimble leaped uncaring over wounded men on the ground who held out pleading hands. He slipped on the gore of bodies that had been blasted beyond human form, righted himself, and plunged on. Coming alongside him was a man moving even more swiftly. The man stiffened and plunged headlong to the ground. Kimble saw a fresh wound oozing from his back. He glanced over his shoulder and saw an unmistakable figure on horseback bearing down on him. General Pickett. Kimble felt deep shame. But Pickett made no attempt to stanch the retreat of his men. His eyes stared ahead. His face was wet with tears as he moved past Private Kimble.

"General Pickett, sir, General Pickett." A Confederate artillery major, W. T. Poague, tried vainly to win Pickett's attention. "General, my orders are that as soon as our troops get the hill, I am to move as rapidly as possible to their support. But I don't like the looks of things up there."

Pickett looked at the man with sad, pained eyes.

"Our men appear to be leaving the hill. What do you think I ought to do under the circumstances?" the major asked.

Pickett spurred his horse forward and said, "I think you had better save your guns."

As he approached the point from which his men had originally set out, little more than a half hour before, he found a sergeant haplessly trying to regroup the retreating troops. "What are you doing?" Pickett shouted in cold anger.

"General, we got orders to form the men behind Seminary Ridge, so's they'll be ready for a Yankee counterattack."

Pickett glared down at the man. "Don't you dare stop any of my men. Tell them we will gather behind the woods at the camp they occupied last night."

Their firing this day had made Cub Buell, the young artilleryman, sick. On the first two days, when the issue had been his life or that of his enemy, he had found it natural to hate, easy to work himself into a killing rage. Today, on Cemetery Hill, he knew no danger. He and his crew simply blew men to pieces, men whose faces he could not see, men who posed no threat to him, men no more than toy soldiers arrayed on a distant carpet.

As the Rebels on the northern flank faltered, he hoped secretly for the order to cease firing. Instead, their guns pursued the retreating Southerners, inflicting as much death on them in retreat as when they had charged.

Major Stewart, the battery commander, sudddenly raised his fist and shouted, "By God, boys, we've got 'em now! They've broke all to hell!"

"Are they whipped now, sir?" Cub asked.

Stewart smiled at the earnest young face. "Yes, son. They are whipped now for good. They can't recover from this. It's the last of them."

Sergeant Fuger knelt between his dead commander, Alonzo Cushing, and the wounded Confederate officer. The Rebel general searched Fuger's face carefully. "I thought it was you. Yes, I knew it."

Fuger smiled slightly and nodded his head. "Yes sir, General, the old Sixth Infantry, out West."

General Lew Armistead whispered hoarsely, "If I had known you were in that battery, I never would have led the charge against you."

"You were as brave a man as I have ever seen," the sergeant answered.

Armistead reached a hand feebly toward Fuger. "Tell me, Sergeant, my dear friend General Hancock, is he here?"

"I hear tell General Hancock is wounded—bad, too."

"Oh, no." It was a soulful moan from deep within the wounded man.

Surgeon Henry Bingham soon came and knelt before the Confederate. The doctor examined Armistead's wounds. The man's strength was slipping rapidly.

"Fear nothing, doctor," the grizzled fighter said. "I am an old soldier. You can speak plainly to me."

"General, you are dying."

"I knew so, doctor. Will you take my watch, my spurs, and some letters I have written? Perhaps you can see that they get to General Hancock. I'd like him one day to get them to my wife."

"Of course I shall, General."

"And doctor, say to General Hancock for me that I have done him and you all a grievous injury which I shall always regret."

A stretcher team gently lifted Armistead onto a cot and bore him to the field hospital where he would live out his last hours.

General Meade, with his son George serving as his aide, had left his latest headquarters near Power's Hill and headed toward the front. As he rode past his old headquarters at the Leister house, he became alarmed. Streaming down the side of Cemetery Ridge were hundreds of Confederate soldiers. "They're unarmed, Father," George calmed him.

"Yes, yes, of course," the older man muttered. He spurred his horse quickly through the surrendering enemy to the crest where he found Lieutenant Haskell.

"Lieutenant"—the voice was anxious—"how is it going here?"

"General, I believe the enemy attack has been repulsed."

"Repulsed? What? Already?" The huge eyes stared disbelieving.

"It is, sir."

Meade shook his head in wonder at the continuing stream of prisoners and clusters of battle flags channeled to the rear.

Deeply, gutturally, he whispered, "Thank God." Then, raising his hat, Meade shouted a loud "Hurrah." The men nearby picked up the cry. "Hurrah! Hurrah! Hurrah!" The manly cheer undulated from end to end of the Union line. The men flung their caps in the air, jumped on the stone wall, and screamed aloud in the pure exhilaration of survival.

Union troops roved the fields beyond the stone wall, rounding up prisoners, fighting for a fallen Rebel flag, a knife, a cap, a belt, any memento of their triumph. A Union sharpshooter spied a general's insignia on a Confederate corpse. He took out his knife and deftly cut the emblem from the fabric of General Garnett's coat.

Behind the lines, Yankees eagerly demonstrated generosity to their captives. Whatever bread, hardtack, salt pork they had was pressed on the Southerners.

"You done real well, Yank," a half-starved Rebel said between voracious bites at a loaf of bread. "Doggone if we's any match for you all today."

"Well, you know," a grinning Union sergeant said, clapping the prisoner on the back, "every rooster fights best on his own hill."

Two captured sharpshooters revealed wounds common to their craft. Both had been wounded in the jaws and face. They were trying, in uncomplaining agony, to chew hard oatmeal bread. A private of the 155th Pennsylvania watched their painful efforts. He dug from his haversack a fresh-baked loaf of soft bread. He wandered over. "You fellers want to trade?"

They looked up guardedly. They handed him their hard bread. He broke his loaf in two and gave each half.

Among the horde of Confederate prisoners was a wounded man, a powerfully built, brooding misfit named Lewis Powell. Powell's captivity would be short-lived. Two years after escaping from his Yankee captors, Powell, alias Lewis Paine, would go to the gallows for his part in the assassination of the Union President.

The wound in General Winfield Scott Hancock's abdomen was excruciatingly painful, likely fatal. Only the leaden paleness of Hancock's face and the tightness of his eyes suggested his agony. Still, no one had dared suggest that he leave the field.

An aide knelt at his side reporting the repulse of Pickett's assault. Hancock fired staccato, economical questions at the man. Level of remaining enemy artillery fire? Number of prisoners taken? Union batteries still in action? Ammunition reserves? Likelihood of a renewed assault?

"Then, Captain, you're absolutely convinced. The issue is no longer in doubt?"

"I am, sir."

"Very good. Then get me into an ambulance."

As the wagon bounded down the Taneytown Road, Hancock shouted, "Halt! Stop this contraption."

"I'm sorry, sir, I'm going as easy as I can," the driver said. "The road's terrible."

"Never mind the road. I must get a message off to General Meade immediately, before we leave the field."

Hancock's adjutant, riding with him, quickly poised a pad and pencil on his knee. Hancock dictated swiftly, the pain of his wound interrupting but never breaking the thread of his reasoning.

"And add this: 'I did not leave the field until the victory was entirely secured. The enemy must be short of ammunition as I was shot with a ten-penny nail. If the 5th and 6th Corps have pressed up, the enemy will be destroyed.' "

The message dispatched, Hancock, the most aggressive Union general on the field, finally left Gettysburg, and with him probably the best hope of a Union counterattack which could produce a decisive defeat of the Confederacy, not just a single defeat of Lee.

A strangely sublime peace shone from the face of Robert E. Lee as he picked his way among the survivors of the attack. His expression exuded understanding, kindness, forbearance for all. He approached an officer with the remnant of his regiment milling around him.

"Colonel," he said gently, taking the man by the hand, "rally your men and protect the artillery. The fault is mine. But it will be all right in the end."

Lee spied the wounded General Pettigrew, a brilliant thirty-five-year-old lawyer, a former Greek and Hebrew scholar. "General, I am sorry to see you wounded. You must go to the rear at once."

A bony mountaineer with crazed eyes stopped Lee in his path.

"Please, General, please, let us go it again," his voice sobbed. "We can make it." Lee smiled sadly and sidestepped the hysterical man.

General Pickett rode up, his eyes baleful, faintly accusing. He had been so cocksure of victory. His division had held the honored place in the charge. But Pickett had believed that every brigade under Lee's command would be thrown into the assault. They were not. His proud Virginians had been slaughtered. Of the three generals commanding his men, one was dead, another dying, a third gravely wounded. Twelve of his fifteen regimental commanders were killed, and the field was littered with sixty percent of his division, 2800 men, not including the thousands from Hill's corps who had fallen. Pickett's lips trembled as he attempted to speak to Lee. No words came.

The beneficence faded for the briefest moment from Lee's face. A trace of annoyance tinged his voice. "General, place your division in the rear of this hill. Be ready to repel the advance of the enemy should they follow up their advantage."

Pickett bowed his head. "General Lee, I have no division now. Armistead is down. Garnett is down. Kemper is mortally wounded."

"Come, General Pickett. This has been my fight. The blame rests on my shoulders. The men and officers of your command have written the name of Virginia as high today as it has ever been written before."

Lee turned from Pickett and resumed his passage among the men. He came upon the stretcher bearers carrying Pickett's subordinate, General Kemper, to the rear.

"General, I hope you are not seriously wounded?"

"They tell me it's mortal," Kemper said stoically.

"I hope it will not prove to be as bad as that," Lee said. And then to no one in particular, he added so softly that few heard him, "It's all my fault. I thought my men were invincible."

The fevered absorption in battle had ended. Tom Galwey and the men of the 8th Ohio could now count the cost of holding a corn field for twenty-four hours. They moved slowly down the slope toward the Emmitsburg Road. The ditch was filled with wounded. The grass along the road bank was stained brown-red. Pools of blood glistened in the ditch. Galwey spied two of his closest friends, Sergeants Fairchild and Kelly. Fairchild sat staring at his left leg. Only a scrap of flesh connected the knee to the rest of the leg. Ironically, Kelly had a virtually identical wound. Galwey could not hold back the tears. His tightened throat choked the words of encouragement he wanted to say.

When they mustered, Galwey found that the already thinned 8th Ohio, which had reached Gettysburg with only 216 men, had suffered 103 dead and severely wounded. He also learned that his appointment as second lieutenant had been officially confirmed. The next day he would be seventeen.

Jimmy Finnegan waited until the last shot had died away, until the battle was surely ended. Then curiosity, not courage, drew Finnegan onto the field. His rightful place, he knew, was behind the lines, amusing the troops with his untutored wit and picking up a dollar here and there barbering, or tailoring, or washing clothes. Finnegan was a wiry imp with twinkling eyes and an ineradicable grin. The war had provided Jimmy Finnegan with escape from a shrewish wife and the noisome brood they had spawned. He had known no greater happiness in life than to be jester to Company D, 155th Pennsylvania. No amount of drill, no inspection, no punishment had ever succeeded in making a soldier of him.

As Finnegan inched his way among the rocks of the Devil's Den studying the dead and wounded, he was stopped short by a drawling voice from behind a huge rock. "Hey, Yank, you unarmed?"

"Naked as a babe," Finnegan answered nervously.

A musket flew from behind the rock and clattered to the ground near Finnegan's trembling legs, quickly followed by three more guns.

"Well," the voice said, "now, so are we."

"What is it you're after?" Finnegan asked.

"We want to surrender."

The scrawny Union soldier's eyes shone. "Surrender? Unconditional?"

"Yep, unconditional."

Some minutes later, the men of the 155th Pennsylvania roared with laughter. Headed toward them were four Rebel toughs stepping lively to the absurd orders of Private James Finnegan, who marched behind them with his hands in his pockets. He paraded his captives past his comrades stretched to his full five-foot-two-inch height and halted them before the regimental adjutant, Major Montooth.

Montooth stared in amazement. "Finnegan, did you capture these men?"

"I did that, Major," he answered smugly.

"How, man, how did you do it?"

"I surrounded 'em."

Along the stone wall the curious spectacle of celebration amidst slaughter went on. General Meade rode along the front, his hat held high, awkwardly yet avidly drinking in the unaccustomed adulation. The wounded were being quickly removed to the rear. But on the other side of the stone wall one could have walked on Rebel dead from one end to the other without touching the ground. Near the angle, fifteen bodies were heaped within fifteen square feet. Inside the angle, forty-two Confederate bodies were flung about in disarray. Many of the dead, the victims of point-blank cannon fire, were grotesquely mutilated. The slaughter from the entire assault was contained in a verdant plot ten acres square.

The screams and wailing from the field were muffled by a band's spirited salute to the victorious Union commander. "Hail to the Chief," they chose.

A war correspondent smiled playfully at Meade. "General, do you know you are in very great danger of becoming President of the United States?"

"Nonsense," Meade snorted shyly.

From a small tent behind Power's Hill at Gettysburg, a single telegraph wire ran along a turnpike to Hanover. From Hanover to Hanover Junction, transmissions were carried on a railroad wire to Washington and into the telegraph office of the War Department.

Messages from Gettysburg had been sporadic ever since the fight began. Communications with the capital had broken off entirely during the time that Meade was moving his headquarters. As the fighting raged over the three days, President Lincoln hounded the telegraph office. Now the easy banter with the operators was missing. The President was grave, distant, and unapproachable most of the time. His occasional jests died half formed and he was quickly lost in thought.

By the third day of battle, the President had become unbearably tense and impatient. Whenever the operator said, "Gettysburg,"

Lincoln would spring from his chair and stare, as the message was transcribed, with an intensity that made the operator's hand tremble.

On the afternoon of July 3, the chief cipher operator in Gettysburg had tapped out the news that a vast Confederate attack had been unleashed. As they impatiently awaited the outcome of the assault, Lincoln's fevered anxiety infected the entire telegraph office.

"Here it is, here it is," the operator at last exclaimed. All leaped to their feet and crowded around the man, Lincoln towering above them. The tap-tap-tap of the receiver spelled it out. The Confederate charge had been repulsed. "Thank God!" the cheer went up. Lincoln was jubilant. The anxious mask slipped from his face and was instantly replaced with twinkling eyes and a broad, creviced smile. The potential of the situation flashed through his mind in an instant. Within Meade's grasp at this moment, if he would unleash a counterattack, was not simply triumph in this battle, but victory in this war.

John Dooley had now lain on the field of Pickett's shattered charge for eight hours. A steady rain pelted him. The merciful numbness had long since worn off and his legs throbbed with excruciating pain. His thirst was searing. His teeth chattered uncontrollably. He endlessly repeated prayers of hope and acts of contrition for his sins. Dooley was not alone. Of the 155 men in his outfit who paraded up Cemetery Ridge, 120 had fallen, most of them within a few dozen yards of where he lay. Finally, the prayers ceased. Dooley slipped into an exhausted sleep.

One minute Warren Goss had seen his constant companion, red-haired Wad Rider, at his post. Then the Rebels had charged over the wall behind a cloud of smoke, and Wad was gone. Now, with the fighting over, Warren and Old Joe picked their way among the casualties searching for their young friend.

As soon as the Confederates had stormed the wall, Wad Rider had felt a rude shove against his chest. He had lost the world in a swirling blackness. When Was later regained consciousness, he found himself on the ground, soaked in a warm wetness. The wetness, he discovered, was his blood.

Alongside Rider lay a hulking Southerner who had ripped off half his clothes in a desperate search for his wound. Now the man was motionless, his skin an unhealthy wax. Only his eyes moved, darting suspiciously over his surroundings.

Wad Rider forced a wry smile through his pain. "Well, Reb, how do you like the North so far?"

The wounded Confederate struggled to raise himself. "Why, you little piss ant." The man suddenly produced a large knife and thrust it at Wad Rider. Rider instinctively jammed his bayonet against the knife and easily forced the weakened man's arm to the ground. "Christ," Wad panted with exhaustion, "haven't you had enough fight for one day?"

The effort drained the last trace of strength from the Rebel. His arms fell to his side, the knife dropped from his hand, and he breathed heavily in a wheezing, rattling exhalation.

Wad Rider groped for his canteen, pulled the stopper, and gulped down the water. The Confederate eyed him pitifully.

"All right! Dammit!" Wad cussed. "Don't look so miserable." He passed the canteen to the man.

The Rebel took a long draft and smacked his lips. "Mighty kind of you, Yank."

"Oh, there's nothing small about me except my feet," Wad chuckled.

"You know, I have had me a bellyful of fighting," the Rebel conceded, his voice slow, hollow, rasping.

"Why don't you start acting it?" Wad said.

The enemy soldier gave a small, painful laugh. "I guess you're right. You ain't such a bad sort, Yank. If I ever met up with you down in Virginny, I might buy you a shot of red-eye."

"I been in Virginia," Wad said, "and the only shot I ever got was lead."

"Don't make me laugh, Yank." The man was coughing and gasping. "It hurts something fierce."

As the two wounded men lay laughing, Warren Goss and Old Joe came upon them. Warren looked out over the field of wailing, moaning, and motionless figures and then down to the two soldiers at his feet. "Wad, you got a sense of humor that won't quit."

Rider looked up, surprised, beaming. "Hey, I sure am glad to see you fellows."

"You are, eh?" Old Joe said sourly, "Looks to me like you're having a gay old time out here with the Rebs."

Warren Goss knelt down to check Wad Rider's wound. "Shut up, Joe," he said, "maybe if we'd had a few more men out here laughing, there wouldn't be so many out there dying."

They heeded Wad's plea to take both him and his Rebel acquaintance back to the field hospital together. As they headed back toward the hospital, Warren Goss tried to wring some grand meaning from the savagery around him. The best he could manage was that he and his comrades had survived to fight another day.

The lamentations of the wounded, the prayers of the dying, the screams of the deranged were muted by a drizzling, then heavy rainfall. The waters drenched the earth and washed the blood from the grass as though nature were cleansing herself of men's folly. Well behind the stone wall, the four unscathed men of Cushing's original seventy-five cannoneers had laid out the broken and powder-burned bodies of the dead. They covered them over as best they could and sat quietly by the mounds of earth as the downpour beat against their sodden blankets. A bell tower somewhere sounded midnight. It was now July 4, 1863.

6 | THE RESTING PLACE

LEUTENANT JOHN DOOLEY AWOKE in the morning to the footsteps and cursing of Yankee litter bearers. A swift kick was their favored test to distinguish the Rebel wounded from the dead. A bearer saw Dooley struggle to sit up. "We'll be with you in no time, sonny." Dooley glared but said nothing. Within a half hour they returned. Dooley choked back a scream as one of them grabbed him roughly by his bullet-torn legs.

"Put me on that litter by the shoulders, you fool!" he ordered through tightly clenched teeth.

"Oh, begging your pardon, cap'n." The Yankee soldier laughed.

Dooley was hustled over the stone wall and into an ambulance, where they set him alongside a coarse, huge-bellied Union soldier. The man was wounded in several places, and, as the wagon bumped along, made scant effort to mask his agony.

"Bee Jesus, Lord. Stop it! Aaah. God have mercy. Jesus Christ and all the saints. You're trying to kill me. Oh me ass is breaking. Lord! Lord! Deliver me from these murdering sons o' bitches."

Dooley eyed the man with cold loathing. Southern soldiers cursed mightily in camp, he thought, but they bore their wounds like men.

They put John Dooley down on the ground outside a field hospital. The Union wounded were placed inside the hospital tent. Dooley saw a Confederate soldier standing nearby, wringing the rain from his blanket. Dooley recognized him as a man from his company.

"Scammel, is that you? Are you all right?"

The soldier turned slowly, stiffly. "Oh no, Lieutenant. Look." Scammel opened his shirt. A shell fragment protruded from his chest.

Dooley shouted to a passing Union surgeon. "Lord, will you look at that man? Do something for him."

"Of course," the surgeon said, without stopping, "just as soon as I can have my coffee."

Dooley's wounds tortured him, but his head remained unmercifully clear. He had been denied the sedative of delirium that shielded so many wounded from the pain and horror around them. One Rebel soldier walked blissfully among the litters saying nothing, heeding no one. He had a great cleft in his skull large enough to fit a man's hand. Another man near Dooley was dying of hunger and thirst. He had a badly fractured jaw. His throat was deeply lacerated, and no one knew how to feed him or give him water. He made an odd whistling sound as he breathed.

Near Dooley was a boy with a wound similar to his own, shot through both thighs, except that in the boy's case the ball broke both thigh bones. His shrieking never ceased the entire day. "Why don't he die, God damn him. Why don't he die!" a maddened Rebel cried.

Later in the day Dooley learned that Scammel from his company had died, untreated, with the jagged metal still jutting from his chest.

Amid the screams, the groans, the muttered and shrieked inanities and obscenities, one voice said slowly and calmly, "I am proud to belong to the First Virginia." Dooley looked in the direction of the firm, manly voice. The man repeated it, louder this time: "I am proud to belong to the First Virginia." He said it again, then again, each time raising his voice until finally he was screaming, his face livid, the veins standing purple on his neck, "I am proud to belong to the First Virginia!" He collapsed in exhaustion, but soon resumed his chant, again calmly.

Union orderlies came through dispensing water. Dooley glanced into the bucket. It was fetid and had something swirling in it. Blood, Dooley thought. "No, thank you," he said, "I'd rather die of an honest wound."

"Well, then, Johnny Reb, suit yourself."

The man's rolling speech caught Dooley's attention. "Irish, aren't you?"

"Faith and I am," the man answered.

John Dooley's notes.

"Then," Dooley said, "I imagine you'll have heard of a true Irish patriot, John Mitchell?"

"I'll have ye know I was with Mitchell in '48!"

"God, man, you tell me you fought with John Mitchell and here you are, for a few dollars trying to crush a brave people who are striving, just like the Irish, to have their own freedom?"

"What have you Rebs got to do with John Mitchell?"

"Do you know," Dooley said, "that John Mitchell has three sons fighting for the Confederacy?"

"No, no, sir, you jest?"

"I do not jest, one of them was somewhere on that field with me yesterday. God knows where Willie Mitchell is now. And you, my friend, standing there in that cursed blue uniform, what do you think John Mitchell would think of the likes of you fighting for a foul tyranny?"

"I . . . why, I don't know, sir. They got me to enlist . . . forced me, really . . ." He backed away awkwardly, then ran off. Within minutes the man was back. He placed a dry blanket, some bread, and a tin of clear, clean water alongside John Dooley and slipped wordlessly away.

For the briefest instant, John Dooley was not aware of his wounds, his pain. He would survive this battle.

All across the Union camp the scene was repeated that Saturday morning. Major Stewart, commanding Battery B, 4th U.S. Artillery, turned to the sergeant. "Sergeant, call the roll." The sergeant's usually impassive face betrayed a reluctance for the task. Time for the butcher's bill, Cub Buell thought.

The men broke off their morning routine and mustered on the side of Cemetery Hill.

"Ackerman?" The sergeant called out.

"Wounded," someone answered.

"Buell?"

"Here."

"Cook?"

"Here, Sarge."

"Knight?"

"Missing."

"Maffitt? . . . Maffitt?"

"Dead," someone said.

Major Stewart turned away.

"Price?"

"Here."

"Packard?"

"Here."

"Sheehan?"

"Dead."

"Sprague?"

"Dead."

The sergeant droned his way to the end of the roster and then took a count of the horses. As usual in battle, the battery had suffered roughly the same losses of men and animals, forty men dead and wounded and thirty-six horses lost.

Major Stewart returned as the sergeant completed the muster. He had one more duty this morning. He ordered the battery to attention. The men stood in a parade-ground precision that salvaged a certain dignity from their dishevelment.

Stewart stood before a quaking private. "Step forward," the officer shouted.

The small, narrow-shouldered private who had dismounted without permission during the first day's fighting stepped out. Large, exposed front teeth gave his face a chronic expression of inane surprise. His shoulders trembled.

Stewart stood a foot from the soldier. He spoke in a voice that carried to every man in the battery. "Private, this is a company of men. Your kind has no place in it. You are not worth the least part of any man we left on this field. There is no artilleryman in you. I am sending you back to the regiment. And I'm asking them to send us a man."

The soldier's mouth went slack, exposing even more tooth and gum. He searched the major's face dully.

"Get out of here now. Do you hear me?"

The private trotted off, looking back over his shoulder with a foolish, uncomprehending grin.

The surgeon had fainted over the operating table. Twelve hours through the night, cutting, sawing, and stitching in an airless, odor-choked room had felled him. He was carried out of the improvised field hospital and set down next to another resting surgeon wearing a blood-stiffened apron, who puffed serenely on a pipe. Smelling salts brought the unconscious doctor around. The morning air quickly revived him.

"Have a smoke, doc." The seated man held out a tobacco pouch to his groggy colleague. The doctor shook his head hard and blinked his eyes rapidly, throwing off webs of confusion.

"I don't know what happened. I must have been on the hundredth man or so. All of a sudden everything just went black."

"I cut about the same number," the second doctor nodded.

Orderlies carried two dead patients from the hospital and set them down in a fast-growing row under a nearby tree.

"I can take off arms and legs all day long with no more thought than dressing a chicken," the pipe-puffing doctor said. He pointed his pipe toward the three dead bodies. "But when they say to you, 'Will you please write to my wife and tell her how I died, and tell her to kiss little Mary for me' "—the man shook his head—"that I cannot take."

The telegraph operator at the War Office in Washington copied down the last words of the message which General Meade had addressed to his victorious troops at Gettysburg. The operator rushed the copy to an impatient Lincoln.

The President's eyes roved quickly over the brief text. "The Commanding General . . . thanks the Army . . . glorious result . . . an enemy superior in numbers . . . flushed with the pride of a successful invasion . . . utterly baffled and defeated."

Lincoln's eyes fixed on one sentence. He reread it aloud in a voice shrill with disbelief. " 'The Commanding General looks to the Army for greater efforts to drive from our soil every vestige of the presence of the invader.' "

Lincoln's arms fell wearily to his sides. "Drive the invader from our soil? Is that all?"

Yes, Meade had heard plainly the arguments of his corps commanders counseling counterattack. Lee, they reminded him, had exhausted his men in the charge, had exhausted his ammunition in the cannonade, had exhausted his supplies, and was far from his base. On the other hand, they, the Union forces, still had large reserves of barely used troops to unleash in a countercharge.

Meade had just concluded three days of successful defensive fighting. He could not easily reverse the mental habits of these days, indeed of a lifetime of cautious movement. He heard them out and said quietly, "We have done well enough."

The two artillerymen Cub Buell and Pat Packard took advantage of early dismissal to retrace the action of the first day's battle. Their route covered terrain that had been in Rebel hands for nearly three days, as the bodies scattered about testified. The Confederates had removed their wounded and buried their dead. Nearly all the corpses left on the field were Union men. A nauseating stench rose from them and clung to the green, undulating fields. The sun had baked and swollen the bodies nearly black and to nearly twice normal size. The wheels of departing Confederate wagon trains had worn paths through some bodies. Cub felt ashamed that he could feel nothing but disgust toward these grotesque shapes. He could not relate mangled, bloated carcasses, with swollen tongues and burst intestines, to comrades he had loved and mourned. This was offal, not men. They came across a Union soldier's body on the far side of Willoughby Creek. "Got to be Iron Brigade," Cub said. "They got about as far west as anybody." They could not be sure. The man had been stripped naked.

"The sons of bitches left something," Packard observed. Weighted down under a rock next to the body was a letter.

"Yep, you're right, Cub. This letter's addressed to C. A. Warren, Company E, 7th Wisconsin. That's Iron Brigade." Packard opened the envelope and started to read. The tough old artilleryman's eyes blinked. He handed the letter to Cub. "Poor family, they don't know the worst yet." The letter informed C. A. Warren that a relative had been killed in the siege of Vicksburg.

All over the field they passed burial details. If the burial party could identify the body, they wrote the man's name on a slip of paper and pinned it somewhere on his breast. They laid the bodies side by side, in rows of fifty to one hundred. In front of each row the burial detail dug a trench about seven feet wide and two feet deep. They laid the men in the trench and covered the faces with a hat, if one could be found. Along the edge of the trench, they hammered in wooden headboards with names and regiments penciled on them. The unknown were buried separately.

Cub Buell and Pat Packard stood for a time watching the detail shovel dirt over the misshapen bundles of dead. The gravediggers had tied cloths over their noses and mouths. Still, a man would drop out from time to time to vomit.

A short, bow-legged man with a gap-toothed grin came up to the trench. "How many stiffs in this one?" he asked.

"Seventy-three," one of the diggers answered.

"Make it seventy-three and a foot." He laughed and threw a booted leg into the grave.

The two artillerymen left for the Chambersburg Pike and headed back into town. The road was paved with the detritus of battle, broken muskets, haversacks, canteens, belts, smashed cannon, dead men, and dead horses. One horse was not yet dead. Both of the animal's forelegs had been shot off at the knee. The horse had lain in this spot for three days. Its dim eyes brightened faintly at the approach of the two men. The animal made a feeble attempt to get up and sank back with an almost human cry of despair. Cub Buell called to a nearby officer. The officer came over, unsheathed his revolver, and ended the animal's agony.

As the officer was leaving, Cub put a finger to his lips signaling Pat to be quiet. A devilish grin lighted his face. Packard looked at Buell quizzically. When the lieutenant was gone, Cub casually squatted down and reached underneath a rail fence. He drew out a shining canteen. He eagerly pulled the stopper off and sniffed the contents. He smiled contentedly and took a long draft. He wiped his mouth and gave the canteen to Pat. Packard's Adam's apple bobbed as the fluid gurgled down his throat.

"What do you think?" Cub grinned.

"Well, it ain't commissary rot gut. Damned if I don't think it's fine old Monongahela rye."

They continued trading generous drafts from the canteen until it was emptied. They walked back to town, past the refuse of war, feeling much better.

Mrs. Wade, in tearless grief, told the Union captain of the burden in her cellar. He sent four men to help her. A coffin would be a problem. One of the men had an idea. They went to an empty lot where the Confederate dead had been laid out. Some of the Rebel officers were in coffins. They pried one open and removed a shrunken, clay-colored figure. "Sorry, Colonel, it's back to the ranks with you." They set the body in a row of shapeless gray forms and took the wooden box back to the little brick house on Baltimore Street.

Jennie Wade was initially buried in the garden behind the house. Her soft white hands were folded across her breast. Faint traces of flour and dough still clung to her fingers. In her pocket the soldiers had found a picture of her fiancé, Jack Skelly, terribly boyish looking even at nineteen, with a sparse effort at a mustache. Jennie Wade was the only private citizen of Gettysburg killed in the battle. Skelly, gravely wounded at Winchester, Virginia, would outlive his childhood sweetheart by ten days.

Near Jennie Wade's home, the burial detail encountered a scene which briefly penetrated their hardened detachment. The man lay in an enclosed yard with his head propped against the fence. Through sightless eyes he gazed on the daguerreotype held in his hands. A gravedigger gently tugged the picture from the dead man's grip. From it three neatly dressed, solemn-faced children looked out, the oldest perhaps five. No identification could be found on the body. A number was assigned to it. Later, somebody had the idea of circulating the photograph of the children through the newspapers to find out who this man was.

*   *   *

The soldiers found them amusing, these civilians who combed the field after the battle. Many were medical men and clergymen, who gained entry by posing as volunteers to help the wounded. They moved among the bodies and speculated on the circumstances that may have led the poor creatures to die in this or that ridiculous posture, or to have their limbs distributed on the ground in a certain pattern, or why those bodies had become so implausibly intertwined. They held white linens to their nostrils to screen out the stench as they grabbed greedily at souvenirs. Cannonballs and muskets were the favorites, but a haversack, cartridge box, even an abandoned Bible would do.

A young, smirking soldier watched a frock-coated gentleman poking with a cane in a bloodied patch of grass. "Here's somethin' for you, cap'n." The soldier grinned and tossed the man an unexploded percussion cap. The man happily stuffed it in his satchel. Another soldier walked over and talked the man out of his prize. He set the explosive gently on the ground.

Another civilian rummaged through a heap of twisted and charred ammunition boxes. A young soldier of the Pioneer Corps tossed something on the heap. "Got one of these yet, mister?" The man recoiled. It was a hand.

Samuel Wilkeson, correspondent of *The New York Times*, had filed his account of the battle. Now he searched for one of the participants, his nineteen-year-old son, a lieutenant with the Union artillery. He located young Bayard's grave on the northeast side of town where he had been buried two days before, near the point where, astride his white horse, he had inspired his cannoneers, stalled the entire Confederate advance, and bought the retreating Union armies minutes of precious time, paid for with his life.

Their greatest problem was to find ice. Captain Favill had instructed General Zook's orderly to scour Gettysburg. But ice in a sweltering town that had lately become a charnel house was in precious short supply. They found just enough to pack the general. He had been wounded in the abdomen. Medical treatment was pointless. The general had passed a spasmodic night, animated and effusive one minute, depressed and silent the next. Then he died.

They loaded him, with dozens of other rough coffins, onto a

freight car headed for Baltimore. Captain Favill and another staff officer named Broom sat on top of the general's coffin watching the Pennsylvania and Maryland countryside slip past the freight-car door.

Josiah Favill pondered the tragic magnificence of it all, the unimaginable spectacle, the epic scale, the enormous blood sacrifice, the joy of rising triumphant from a noble, cataclysmic crusade. It was even more powerful, more soul-stirring, than in his boyhood imaginings. His eyes ran awestruck over the tragic burden of the freight car and rested on the exhausted and rumpled form of Lieutenant Broom.

"They sure do stink, don't they?" Broom said.

As the Rebels prepared to leave Gettysburg, Charley Wesley edged as near to the Union line as he dared in his search for his master, Wayland Dunaway. The slave had heard the instruction so many times: If the master falls, bring him home. If he cannot be found, bring the horse back. He rolled dead and wounded men over and studied their faces. He would not find Dunaway on this field. His master had been taken prisoner.

The Army of Northern Virginia was beginning its retreat back across the Potomac, and Charley Wesley could not delay longer.

"Boy where you going with that fine animal?" Covetous eyes followed the uneasy black man.

"This here's Captain Dunaway's horse, 40th Virginia," Wesley answered warily. "I'm taking it back to his brother, Thomas, in Kilmarnack, captain's orders." He broke away from the main body at the first chance and took lonely side roads, which would make it less likely that he would fail in obeying Master Wayland's last order to him.

The evening the nation's capital learned of the Union success at Gettysburg, a spontaneous crowd gathered at the White House and musicians appeared to serenade Abe Lincoln. It was Independence Day and also the moment of triumph for a victory-starved Union. The President felt obliged to make a small, impromptu speech.

"How long ago was it? Eighty-odd years since on the Fourth of July for the first time in the history of the world, a nation, by its representatives assembled, declared as a self-evident truth that all men are created equal . . ."

*   *   *

The reporter for the London *Morning Advertiser* caught Sir Benjamin Disraeli, the Conservative leader, outside Parliament soon after word of Gettysburg had reached England.

"Sir Benjamin, in light of the news from America, is there anything further likely on the matter of recognition of the Confederacy?"

Tipping his hat and smiling to a passerby, Disraeli whispered from the corner of his mouth, "Almost put our foot in it, didn't we?"

The telegraph lines out of Gettysburg fed an unending stream of messages to Waterville, Maine, and hundreds of other northern towns. A husband, a son, a father had been wounded in the battle. The family might wish to come. Thus his wife had learned that Captain Charles Billings, 20th Maine, lay gravely wounded at Gettysburg.

Charles' brother accompanied the woman on the arduous journey from Maine to Pennsylvania. By the time they reached the last leg from Hanover to Gettysburg, practically the entire train was crowded with wives, mothers, fathers, children making the same anxious pilgrimage. The brother crowded evil portents from his own mind during the trip by constantly buoying the woman's hopes with manufactured optimism.

On their arrival in Gettysburg that evening, the brother, with great difficulty, found a place in the hopelessly crowded town where his sister-in-law could pass the night while he went to find Charles. He glanced back. She smiled through a tear-swollen face and waved like a trusting child.

Weaving his way through tents, barns, and homes housing the wounded, he at last found the Reverend Robert Parvin of the Sanitary Commission, still tending the 20th Maine's wounded.

"You haven't brought Captain Billings' wife out here tonight, I hope?"

The minister's words sent a chill through the man. "Why, no, I left her in town."

"That is just as well. I regret to have to tell you, your brother's body has been sent to the embalmers."

The man sat down on a small stool, held his head in his hands and sobbed softly. He dried his eyes and looked up at the minister. "I cannot tell her. I cannot trust myself to tell her. I brought her all this way for this?"

"You have done what you had to."

"No, no, Reverend, you must . . . you must tell her."

Gettysburg had produced the greatest bloodletting to that point on the North American continent.

On this field, 5664 men had died in three days. Over 27,200 men were wounded, thousands of whom would die of their wounds. Over 10,400 were missing or prisoners. Ten generals were killed, four Union and six Confederate. At least one out of every four of the 170,000 men on the field became a casualty.

The total loss for 72 hours, for both sides, dead, wounded, missing, was over 43,000. Some 6000 horses died at Gettysburg, unwitting conscripts to the violence of men.

The guns had been still for over four months. Rains had long since washed away the chloride of lime that had been spread over Gettysburg's streets to kill the smell of death. Leander Warren, with fifteen thousand others lining the streets, craned his neck trying to catch perhaps the only glimpse of a President that he might ever have.

Leander felt a part of this day. Since last October, he had done a man's work. The resettlement of the Union dead in the new national cemetery had been parceled out on a contract basis. Basil Biggs had the contract to dig up the soldiers from the shallow graves on the battlefield and to put them into white-pine coffins. Frank Biesecker had the contract to dig the graves in the new cemetery and to bury the men permanently. Sam Weaver's contract was to take the bodies from their original sites up to the new cemetery. Young Leander Warren had obtained the use of his father's wagon and had subcontracted a good share of the hauling from Sam. Another fellow had a two-horse team which could haul nine coffins at a time. Leander's one-horse rig could haul only six at once. But it worked out about the same because Leander could move faster. Of the 3512 Union bodies moved, he had taken hundreds up to Cemetery Hill and had earned himself a nice piece of change for a lad of fourteen.

At last the eager crowd saw the President approach. He rode a horse which Lincoln's lank frame seemed to envelop. He wore a black suit, white gloves, and high silk hat. At the beginning of the march to the cemetery, Lincoln looked unaccustomedly resplendent. But, as the procession moved down Baltimore Street, then to the Emmitsburg

Road, his arms had gone limp at his sides, his head hung down. He was oblivious of the crowd.

The brilliant sunshine of this lovely fall morning failed to penetrate the blackness that gripped him. Lincoln's thoughts had wandered back to the old woman who had come to him in the White House a few months before. She had pleaded that, with three sons and a husband serving the Union, she could not survive. Lincoln had written out a discharge for one of her boys on the spot. The old woman had traced her son here to Gettysburg, where she found him dying in a hospital. She had returned after the boy's death, more broken than before, and begged the President to give her back another of her sons.

On the train to Gettysburg, a father had approached Lincoln and had started to explain how proud he was to have given his son in the defense of Little Round Top. But the man had broken down before he could finish and had to be led away, sobbing softly. Will this leaden cross ever be lifted from me? Lincoln wondered.

From the Taneytown Road, the procession entered the newly sown Union cemetery located near the angle where the Louisiana Tigers had been repulsed. The plot covered seventeen acres secured with a two-hundred-dollar-an-acre option.

The guest speaker had not yet appeared. The President and other dignitaries sat on the platform for forty-five minutes listening to the United States Marine Band, waiting for Edward Everett. Everett, his life heaped with honors, President of Harvard, Governor of Massachusetts, United States Senator, Minister to England, and Secretary of State, was the foremost orator in America. He arrived at noon.

Everett did not fail his reputation. His resonant voice rolled out over the crowd and engrossed every thoughtful listener as he traced the roots of the war and refought the battle with his finely honed phrases, flawless in every detail, powerful in every poetic illusion, faultlessly memorized to the last syllable.

"Overlooking these broad fields now reposing from the waning years, the mighty Alleghenies dimly towering before us, the graves of our brethren beneath our feet, it is with hesitation that I raise my poor voice to break the eloquent silence of God and nature.

"As my eye ranges over the fields where sods were so lately moistened by the blood of gallant and loyal . . .

"The whole earth is the sepulcher of illustrious men," Everett intoned.

Lincoln lifted his head. Everett appeared to be nearing the end.

"Down to the last period of recorded time, in the glorious annals of our common country, there will be no brighter page . . ."

The ovation was thunderous. Everett had spoken for one hour and fifty-seven minutes.

The Baltimore Glee Club began an ode composed especially for the occasion. Lincoln put on a pair of steel-bowed glasses, drew two sheets of paper from his coat pocket, and glanced over them.

The choir finished. A member of Lincoln's entourage got up and announced simply, "The President of the United States."

Lincoln rose slowly, interminably, to his full height. He adjusted his spectacles and began to speak in a high-pitched voice, with, to these Easterners, a peculiar Kentucky twang. Within two minutes, the President made the "few appropriate remarks" allotted to him in the program, and sat down to brief scattered applause.

Beneath the ground on which the crowd stood there stretched the rows of man-boys who had left home and come forever to this final resting place. They lay there for reasons they could not have expressed even if granted speech again. They lay there for something having to do with marching bands, waving flags, and the words the towering, gaunt figure had just spoken above their eternal stillness.

BIBLIOGRAPHY

My Enemy, My Brother is a re-creation of the Battle of Gettysburg based on documentary evidence. The people described in the book existed. What they say and do is drawn from the historical sources listed here.

I have employed certain devices, literary license, if you will, to reconstruct the battle as eyewitness experience. These literary devices provide a means of filling out bare spots, of surmising with the facts at hand what men likely said and did when we cannot know with absolute certainty.

The total of such novelistic connective tissue is not great, no more than ten percent of the whole book, which is otherwise conventionally documentable history. The excerpts from diaries, letters, and note-books have been quoted verbatim. Yet the dramatic devices, however lightly employed, are important, indeed indispensable to achieve the author's purpose of allowing the reader to experience the Battle of Gettysburg unfolding before him.

One literary device employed in the book is to take situations described in narrative terms in the original research and adapt them to dialogue form. This approach was used, for example, in relating the call of the roll after the battle in Cub Buell's artillery battery. Similarly, a narrative description of the arrival of the 20th Maine on the battlefield has been rendered as a first-person reminiscence.

Also, I have taken material presented in general terms in the historic sources and reworked it in specific terms. For instance, the account of the amputation of a young soldier's leg is drawn from several accounts of Civil War surgery.

The final problem was how to handle conflicting versions of the same event. Here, I weighed differing accounts of the same event and chose the version which the evidence seemed reasonably to support.

The fallibility of memory, the trick mirror of bias, the passage of time all make perfect reconstruction of the past impossible. History is essentially beyond total recovery. The most scrupulous scholar is haunted by the knowledge that his sources, however respectable, contain an unknowable quotient of fiction. In each case where imaginative leaps were made, I asked whether the spirit of the battle was violated or better illuminated by the reconstructive device employed. My object throughout has been to present the participants and their experiences as close to the truth as possible and with maximum confidence that this is the way it was.

Adams, George W., *Doctors in Blue,* Henry Schuman, New York, 1952.

Adams, John G. B., *Reminiscences of the 19th Regiment,* Boston, 1899.

Alleman, Mrs. Tillie Pierce, *At Gettysburg, or What a Girl Saw and Heard of the Battle,* W. Lake Borland, New York, 1889.

Andrews, A. J., *A Sketch of the Boyhood Days of Andrew Jackson Andrews,* Hermitage Press, Richmond, Virginia, 1905.

Bakeless, John, *Spies of the Confederacy,* J. B. Lippincott Co., Philadelphia and New York, 1970.

Bardeen, Charles W., *A Little Fifer's War Diary,* C. W. Bordeen Publisher, Syracuse, New York, 1910.

Bartlett, Napier, *A Soldier's Story of the War,* Louisiana State University Press, Baton Rouge, 1964.

Barton, William E., *The Life of Abraham Lincoln,* Bobbs-Merrill Co., Boston and New York, 1925.

Bassler, J. H., *Reminiscences of the First Day's Fight of Gettysburg,* Albright College Institute, Reading, 1895.

Bates, David Homer, *Lincoln in the Telegraph Office,* The Century Company, New York, 1907.

Bates, Samuel P., *History of Pennsylvania Volunteers,* Vol. IV, Harrisburg State Printer, 1870.

Bellah, James Warner, *Soldier's Battle: Gettysburg,* David McKay Company, New York, 1962.

Benedict, G. G., *Vermont in the Civil War*, Vol. II, The Free Press Association, Burlington, 1888.

Bennet, Edwin C., *Musket and Sword*, Coburn Publishing Co., Boston, 1900.

Benton, Charles E., *As Seen from the Ranks*, G. P. Putnam's Sons, New York, 1902.

Billings, John D., *Hardtack and Coffee*, R. R. Donnelley & Sons Company, Chicago, reissued 1960.

Brooks, Noah, *Washington in Lincoln's Time*, The Century Company, New York, 1895.

Brown, Maud Morrow, *The University Greys, 1861–1865* Garret & Massic Inc., Richmond, 1940.

Buell, Augustus, *The Cannoneer*, The National Tribune, Washington, 1897.

Casler, John O., *Four Years in the Stonewall Brigade*, State Capital Printing Company, Guthrie, Oklahoma, 1893.

Catton, Bruce, *Gettysburg: The Final Fury*, Doubleday & Co., Garden City, New York, 1974.

Catton, Bruce, *Glory Road*, Doubleday & Co., Garden City, New York, 1952.

Clark, Robert Denning, "How to Load a Civil War Musket," *Civil War Times Illustrated*, December 1963.

Cleaves, Freeman, *Meade of Gettysburg*, University of Oklahoma Press, Norman, 1960.

Cole, Jacob H., *Under Five Commanders*, News Printing Co., Paterson, New Jersey, 1906.

Corby, William, *Memoirs of Chaplain Life*, Scholastic Press, Notre Dame, 1893.

Crotty, D. G., *Four Years Campaigning in the Army of the Potomac*, Dygert Brothers, Grand Rapids, 1874.

Culp, Karen Marie, *Historical Background of the Culp Family*, Gettysburg (local genealogical study, n.d.).

Davis, Burke, *Our Incredible Civil War*, Holt, Rinehart & Winston, New York, 1960.

Davis, Washington, *Campfire Chats of the Civil War*, B. B. Russell, Boston, 1887.

Dracha, Richard M., *History of the Culp Farm* (local genealogical study, n.d.).

Dunaway, The Rev. Wayland Fuller, *Reminiscences of a Rebel*, The Neale Publishing Co., New York, 1913.

Durkin, Joseph T., S.J., *John Dooley, Confederate Soldier: His War Journal*, Georgetown University Press, Washington, 1945.

Eisenschimal, Otto, "Medicine in the War," *Civil War Times Illustrated*, Vol. 1, No. 2, May 1962.

Farmer, John S., *Americanisms Old and New*, Thomas Poulter & Son, London, 1889.

Favill, Josiah M., *The Diary of a Young Officer*, R. R. Donnelley and Sons Company, Chicago, 1909.

Frassanito, William A., *Gettysburg, A Journey in Time*, Charles Scribner's Sons, New York, 1975.

Gerrish, Rev. Theodore, *Army Life, A Private's Reminiscences of the Civil War*, Hoyt, Fogg & Donham, Portland, Maine, 1882.

Gilbert, J. Warren, *The Blue and the Gray*, Curt Teich and Company, Chicago, 1922.

Gordon, Gen. John B., *Reminiscences of the Civil War*, Charles Scribner & Sons, New York, 1903.

Goss, Warren Lee, *Recollections of a Private*, Thomas Y. Crowell Co., New York, 1890.

Haight, Theron Wilber, *Three Wisconsin Cushings*, Wisconsin History Commission, April 1910.

Hancock, Almira, *Reminiscences of Winfield Scott Hancock*, C. L. Webster Company, New York, 1887.

Haskell, Frank A., *The Battle of Gettysburg*, Houghton Mifflin Company, Boston, 1969.

Hoke, Jacob, *The Great Invasion*, Thomas Yoseloff, New York, 1959.

Inman, Arthur Crew, editor, *Soldier of the South, General Pickett's War Letters to His Wife*, Houghton Mifflin Company, Boston, 1928.

Johnson, Rossiter, *Campfire and Battlefield*, Bryan Taylor and Son, New York, 1894.

Jones, Gordon W., "Wartime Surgery," *Civil War Times Illustrated*, Vol. 2, No. 2, May 1963.

Jones, Walter B., "William Calvin Oates," *Alabama Historical Quarterly*, Fall 1945, Montgomery.

La Brie, Ben, editor, *Campfires of the Confederacy*, The Courier–Journal Job Printing Co., Louisville, 1898.

Livermore, Thomas L., *Days and Events 1860–1866*, Houghton Mifflin Company, Boston, 1920.

Lokey, J. W., "Wounded at Gettysburg," *Confederate Veteran,* Vol. XXII, September 1914, Nashville.

Long, E. B., *The Civil War Day by Day,* Doubleday & Co., Garden City, New York, 1971.

Lord, Walter, editor and commentary, *The Fremantle Diary, Being the Journal of Lt. Col. Arthur James Lyon Fremantle, Coldstream Guards, on his three months in the Southern states,* Little, Brown & Co., Boston, 1954.

McCrea, Tully, *Dear Belle, Letters from a Cadet and Officer to his Sweetheart 1858–1865,* edited by Catherine S. Crary, Wesleyan University Press, Middletown, Conn., 1965.

Major Haverty's Illustrated Catholic Almanac, (cited in) Official Program, Reunion of the Army of the Potomac and the Army of Northern Virginia at Gettysburg, The American Graphic Co., New York, 1888.

Malone, Bartlett Yancey, *The Diary of Bartlett Yancey Malone,* The James Sprunt Historical Publications, Vol. VI, No. 2, University of North Carolina, Chapel Hill, 1919.

Medical and Surgical History of the War of the Rebellion, U.S. Surgeon General's Office, General Printing Office, 3 volumes, 1870–1888.

Mencken, H. L., *The American Language, Supplement I,* Alfred A. Knopf, New York, 1945.

Miller, Francis Trevelyan, editor, *The Photographic History of the Civil War,* 10 Vols., Thomas Yoseloff, New York and London, 1957.

Montgomery, James Stewart, *The Shaping of a Battle: Gettysburg,* Chilton Co., Philadelphia and New York, 1959.

Moore, Frank, editor, *The Civil War in Song and Story,* P. F. Collier, New York, 1889.

Murdock, Eugene Converse, *Patriotism Limited 1862–1865, The War Draft and the Bounty System,* Kent State University, Kent, Ohio, 1967.

Nash, Captain Eugene, *A History of the 44th New York Volunteer Infantry,* R. R. Donnelley & Sons, Chicago, 1911.

Nolan, Alan T., *The Iron Brigade,* Macmillan, New York, 1961.

One Hundred Fifty-fifth Regimental Association, Under the Maltese Cross: Campaigns 155th Pennsylvania, narrated by the Rank and File, Pittsburgh, 1910.

Partridge, Eric, *Slang Today and Yesterday,* London, 1920.

Pinchon, Edgcumb, *Dan Sickles, Hero of Gettysburg and "Yankee King of Spain,"* Doubleday & Co., Garden City, 1945.

Poindexter, James E., "General Lewis Addison Armistead," *Confederate Veteran*, Vol. XXII, November 1941, Nashville.

Price, William H., *Civil War Handbook*, Prince Lithograph Co., Fairfax, Virginia, 1961.

Pullen, John J., *The Twentieth Maine*, J. B. Lippincott Co., Philadelphia and New York, 1957.

Rice, Allen Thorndike, editor, *Reminiscences of Lincoln*, Wm. Blackwood and Sons, Inc., Northan Publishing Co., New York, 1886.

Ross, Fitzgerald, *Cities and Camps of the Confederate States*, edited by Richard Barksdale Harwell, University of Illinois Press, Urbana, 1958.

Ross, Ishbel, *Angel of the Battlefield*, Harper & Row, New York, 1956.

Sandburg, Carl, *Abraham Lincoln, The Prairie Years*, Dell Publishing Co., New York, 1959.

Sandburg, Carl, *Abraham Lincoln, The War Years*, Harcourt, Brace & Co., New York, 1939.

Schenck, Martin, *Up Came Hill*, The Stackpole Co., Harrisburg, 1958.

Small, Harold Adams, editor, *The Road to Richmond, Civil War Memoirs of Major Abner R. Small*, University of California Press, Berkeley, 1939.

Souder, Mrs. Edmund, *Leaves from the Battlefield of Gettysburg*, Caxton Press, Philadelphia, 1864.

Stackpole, Edward J., *They Met at Gettysburg*, Bonanza Books, New York, 1956.

Stevens, Captain C. A., *Berdan's United States Sharpshooters*, Press of Morningside, St. Paul, 1892.

Stewart, George, *Pickett's Charge, A Microhistory of the Final Attack at Gettysburg, July 3, 1863*, Houghton Mifflin Company, Boston, 1959.

Stiles, Robert, *Four Years Under Marse Robert*, The Neale Publishing Co., New York and Washington, 1904.

Swanberg, William Andrew, *Sickles the Incredible*, Charles Scribner's Sons, New York, 1956.

Taylor, Walter H., *Four Years with General Lee*, Bonanza Books, New York, 1962.

Tucker, Glenn, *Lee and Longstreet at Gettysburg*, Bobbs-Merrill Co., Indianapolis, Kansas City, and New York, 1968.

Vautier, John D., *History of the 88th Pennsylvania Volunteers in the War for the Union,* J. P. Lippincott Co., Philadelphia, 1894.

Warren, Leander H., *My Recollections of What I Saw Before, During and After the Battle of Gettysburg,* Gettysburg, Webb Printing and Stationery, n.d.

Whitman, Walt, "Slang in America," *North American Review,* 1885.

Whittemore, Rev. Edwin Carey, editor, *The Centennial History of Waterville, Kennebec County, Maine,* published by the Executive Committee of the Centennial Celebration, Waterville, 1902.

Wiley, Bell Irvin, *The Life of Billy Yank,* Doubleday & Co., Garden City, New York, 1971.

Wiley, Bell Irvin, *The Life of Johnny Reb,* Doubleday & Co., Garden City, New York, 1971.

Wiley, Bell Irvin, *They Who Fought Here,* Bonanza Books, New York, 1959.

Wilkeson, Frank, *Recollections of a Private Soldier in the Army of the Potomac,* G. P. Putnam & Sons, New York, 1887.

Williams, E. Harry, *Lincoln and His Generals,* Vintage Books, Random House, New York, 1967.

Wolfe, Hazel C., editor, *Campaigning with the First Minnesota, Diary of Isaac Taylor,* Minnesota History, Vol. XXV, 1944, The Minnesota Historical Society, St. Paul.

Other titles of interest

**THE ANNALS OF THE
CIVIL WAR**
**Written by Leading Participants
North and South**
New introd. by Gary W. Gallagher
808 pp., 56 illus.
80606-1 $19.95

**BATTLE-PIECES AND
ASPECTS OF THE WAR**
Herman Melville
New introd. by Lee Rust Brown
282 pp.
80655-X $13.95

A BRAVE BLACK REGIMENT
**The History of the 54th
Massachusetts, 1863-1865**
Captain Luis F. Emilio
New introduction by
Gregory J. W. Urwin
532 pp., 89 photos, 9 maps
80623-1 $15.95

**CHANCELLORSVILLE AND
GETTYSBURG**
General Abner Doubleday
New introduction by
Gary W. Gallagher
269 pp., 13 maps
80549-5 $12.95

**FROM MANASSAS TO
APPOMATTOX**
General James Longstreet
New introd. by Jeffry D. Wert
760 pp., 30 illus., 16 maps
80464-6 $17.95

MY STORY OF THE WAR
**The Civil War Memoirs of the
Famous Nurse, Relief Organizer,
and Suffragette**
Mary A. Livermore
New introd. by Nina Silber
710 pp., 20 illus.   80658-4 $19.95

**THE WARTIME PAPERS OF
ROBERT E. LEE**
Edited by Clifford Dowdey and
Louis H. Manarin
1,012 pp.
80282-1 $19.95

THE STORY OF THE CONFEDERACY
Robert Selph Henry
526 pp.   80370-4 $14.95

**DESTRUCTION AND
RECONSTRUCTION**
Personal Experiences of the Civil War
General Richard Taylor
New introd. by T. Michael Parrish
288 pp.
80624-X $14.95

TRAGIC YEARS 1860-1865
**A Documentary History of the
American Civil War**
Paul M. Angle and
Earl Schenck Miers
1108 pp.   80462-X $23.95

Available at your bookstore

OR ORDER DIRECTLY FROM 1-800-386-5656

VISIT OUR WEBSITE AT WWW.PERSEUSBOOKSGROUP.COM